Technology and Emergency Management

Technology and Emergency Management

Second Edition

John C. Pine, Ed.D.

Research Professor
Department of Geography and Planning
Appalachian State University, Boone, NC, USA

Registered Office
John Wiley & Sons, Inc., 111 River Street, Hoboken, NJ 07030, USA

Editorial Office
111 River Street, Hoboken, NJ 07030, USA

For details of our global editorial offices, customer services, and more information about Wiley products visit us at www.wiley.com.

Wiley also publishes its books in a variety of electronic formats and by print-on-demand. Some content that appears in standard print versions of this book may not be available in other formats.

Library of Congress Cataloging-in-Publication Data

Names: Pine, John C., 1946– author.
Title: Technology and emergency management / John C. Pine, Dr. John C. Pine, Professor,
    Department of Geography and Planning, Appalachian State University in Boone,
    North Carolina.
Other titles: Technology in emergency management.
Description: Second Edition. | Hoboken : Wiley, 2018. | Revised edition of the author's Technology in
    emergency management, c2007. | Includes bibliographical references and index. |
Identifiers: LCCN 2017018770 (print) | LCCN 2017034826 (ebook) | ISBN 9781119234227 (pdf) |
    ISBN 9781119235521 (epub) | ISBN 9781119234081 (paperback)
Subjects: LCSH: Emergency management–Technological innovations. | Emergency management–Data
    processing. | Information storage and retrieval systems–Emergency management. |
    Emergency communication systems.
Classification: LCC HV551.2 (ebook) | LCC HV551.2 .P56 2017 (print) | DDC 363.34028/4–dc23
LC record available at https://lccn.loc.gov/2017018770

Cover Design: Wiley
Cover Image: © BlackJack3D/Gettyimages

Set in 11/13pt Berkeley by SPi Global, Pondicherry, India

V10011691_062619

CONTENTS

CONCEPT

The Emergency Management Institute within the Federal Emergency Management Agency initiated the development of this publication in support of disaster science and emergency management academic programs in higher education institutions. Individuals working in disaster and emergency agencies wanted a better understanding of technology tools and their application to emergency management. Universities and colleges had developed a broad curriculum that was intended to prepare individuals for a career in emergency management in public, private, and nonprofit organizations. The scope of this book was developed in collaboration with representatives from disaster planning, response and recovery agencies, and the staff of the Emergency Management Institute.

The first edition of *Technology in Emergency Management* in 2007 provided an introduction to a rapidly developing set of resources for disaster preparedness, mitigation, response, and recovery. Much has changed since that time and this second edition provides a solid base for the many technologies that have become a critical part of emergency management within many organizations. This second edition not only clarifies the current state of the use of technology in emergency management but also provides a foundation for understanding the many emerging technologies that will be used by agencies in the future.

Book Organization

The book is organized to introduce the role of technology in emergency management and provide a context for addressing specific technologies and their use by agencies in emergency preparedness, mitigation, response, and recovery. The tools and resources examined in this book have been applied throughout the world as public, private, and nonprofit organizations attempt to deal with ever changing hazards and disaster impacts. It is hoped that by clarifying what technologies are being applied to the threats and impacts of disasters we can ensure that our citizens, businesses, and infrastructure are protected.

Technical Information

Technology and Emergency Management includes 11 chapters and is approximately 300 pages in length. The book includes many photographs and graphics and data tables. Each of the chapters clarifies the learning outcomes and intended outcomes along with goals and outcomes for the reader. Case studies are used throughout each chapter to demonstrate how various technologies were used in dealing with hazards and disasters. Terms are clearly defined and questions are posed throughout the book to focus on the application of technology in various situations. Today, there has been extensive research on the nature and use of technologies in disasters. An extensive reference list is included with each chapter to clarify the source for many of the concepts introduced in the text and to support further reading.

ABOUT THE AUTHOR

John C. Pine was Director of the Research Institute for Environment, Energy & Economics (RIEEE) and is Research Professor, Department of Geography and Planning, Appalachian State University, Boone, NC. He joined the Appalachian faculty in 2009 after serving 30 years at Louisiana State University in Baton Rouge where he directed a graduate and undergraduate Disaster Science and Management Program. He also served as a Professor in the Department of Geography and Anthropology and the Department of Environmental Sciences conducting research on disasters and emergency management. His research and publications focus on emergency preparedness and operations, risk assessment, and disaster recovery. He has worked with many federal, state, and local entities to identify tools and strategies to enhance community preparedness and ensure the resilience of communities impacted by disasters. His recent publications include *Hazards Analysis: Reducing the Impact of Disasters* from Taylor Francis Publishers in 2014, which utilizes many of the technologies addressed in this text. He serves on the board of directors for the New River Conservancy, a multistate conservation agency. His publications have been included in *The Journal of Disaster Studies, Policy and Management, Disasters, Journal of Race and Society, International Journal of Mass Emergencies and Disasters, Oceanography, Journal of Emergency Management, Natural Disaster Review, Journal of Environmental Health,* and *the Journal of Hazardous Materials.* He received his Doctorate in Higher Education Administration and Public Administration from the University of Georgia, Athens, in 1979.

Office Address: 124 North Forrest Ave. Lookout Mountain, TN 37350, USA
E-Mail: pinejc@appstate.edu, Phone: (828) 262–2764 (Office)
Web Site: http://www.rieee.appstate.edu

LIST OF CONTRIBUTORS

Dr. Andrew Curtis
Department of Geography, Kent State University, Kent, OH, USA

Dr. Jacqueline W. Curtis
Department of Geography, Kent State University, Kent, OH, USA

Josh Kastrinsky
Coastal Resilience Center of Excellence, University of North Carolina at Chapel Hill, Chapel Hill, NC, USA

Dr. John J. Kiefer
Department of Political Science, University of New Orleans, New Orleans, LA, USA

Dr. Burke McDade
Department of Geography and Planning, Appalachian State University, Boone, NC, USA

Dr. Jessica Mitchell
Department of Geography and Planning, Appalachian State University, Boone, NC, USA

Dr. Cindy Norris
Department of Computer Science, Appalachian State University, Boone, NC, USA

Dr. John J. Walsh Jr.
Program in Disaster Research and Training, Vanderbilt University Medical Center, Nashville, TN, USA

ABOUT THE COMPANION WEBSITE

This book is accompanied by Instructor and Student companion websites:

www.wiley.com/go/pine/tech&emergmgmt_2e

The Instructor website contains:

- ▲ MCQ's
- ▲ Self checks,
- ▲ Review questions,
- ▲ Applying This Chapter
- ▲ You try it
- ▲ Solutions

The student website contains:

- ▲ MCQ's
- ▲ Self checks,
- ▲ Review questions,
- ▲ Applying This Chapter
- ▲ You try it

1

THE NEED FOR TECHNOLOGY IN EMERGENCY MANAGEMENT

Starting Point

Go to www.wiley.com/go/pine/tech&emergmgmt_2e to assess your knowledge of using technology.
Assess your knowledge of emergency management and technology. (Determine where you need to concentrate your effort.)

What You'll Learn in This Chapter

▲ The definitions of focusing events and windows of opportunity
▲ The types of technology as applied to the emergency management process
▲ How technology can assist in emergency preparedness, mitigation, response, and recovery

After Studying This Chapter, You'll Be Able To

▲ Examine what technology is used in emergency management.
▲ Examine what technology tools have been applied during disasters.
▲ How focusing events can be used to gain community support for greater emergency management resources.

Goals and Outcomes

▲ To be able to select technology that improves disaster preparedness, response, mitigation, and recovery
▲ To perform a comprehensive technology needs assessment for emergency management
▲ To understand the value of encouraging a community to commit greater resources toward emergency management by using focusing events and the needs assessment

Technology and Emergency Management, Second Edition. John C. Pine.
© 2018 John Wiley & Sons, Inc. Published 2018 by John Wiley & Sons, Inc.
Companion website: www.wiley.com/go/pine/tech&emergmgmt_2e

INTRODUCTION

We live in a highly connected global community where we have the potential to observe the nature and extent of disasters firsthand. We can receive and transmit information within seconds and can communicate from anywhere, at any time, and anyplace. **Technology** allows those engaged in emergency management to utilize resources from local, regional, and national organizations reflecting public, private, and nonprofit entities (Hodgkinson and Stewart, 1991). Technology may be used by those involved in emergency management in decision making, communication, hazard situational awareness, operational functioning, and public safety. Technologies have been developing at a fast pace and have had a dramatic impact on emergency management in communities, at regional and national levels.

We can only imagine the new ways that technology will evolve and be used in the future. Technology has allowed us to use a broader range of information resources and enhance resource acquisition and allocation. We, thus, have been able to make use of new tools and technologies and become more efficient and allow the public, public safety, and healthcare personnel to anticipate ad meet community needs in disasters (Cutter et al., 2015). Technology has enabled us to better analyze complex issues, enhance our decision making, and communicate in times of crisis. The key is to recognize that technology is critical in all stages of disaster management and supporting rapid scientific assessment of usable knowledge to decision makers (Alcántara-Ayala et al., 2015).

1.1 Technology and Disaster Management

Emergencies and disasters are extreme events that cause significant disruption. Effective response efforts in a disaster require timely information and deliberate decision making. Effective action requires coordinated application of resources, facilities, and efforts beyond those regularly available to handle routine problems. Disasters arise from both natural and human-caused events. Fortunately, we now have more technology tools and systems available for our use than ever before so that communities, organizations, and individuals manage effectively in a disaster. Technology provides a means of applying scientific concepts, methods, and principles to achieve desired outcomes (NRENaissance Committee, 1994). Technology supports the emergency management process including the following:

▲ Organizational and personal communication;
▲ Timely observations of the nature and extent of events;
▲ Enhancement in capabilities to estimate and model potential outcomes of disaster events;
▲ Recording the changing nature of response and recovery events;

▲ Communicating with multiple organizations and individuals simultaneously;
▲ Analyzing events to understand how disasters evolve and change over time;
▲ Connecting individuals and organizations so as to enhance communication;
▲ Extending how public and private organizations may access information as disaster evolve;
▲ Using mapping and geo-positioning systems (GPSs) to support situational awareness; and
▲ Taking advantage of hazard modeling technology to enhance our understanding of both the threats associated with hazards and their potential impacts.

Technology enables individuals and organizations to contribute to the emergency management process in new ways and with productive impacts (Kara-Zaitri, 1996). For example, we can identify the location of those in need for timely and effective emergency response. We can communicate simultaneously with multiple partners to enhance our capacity to cope with evolving complex situations. We have the tools not only to communicate with an unlimited audience but also to engage this audience in community and organizational decision making. Technologies allow both individuals and organizations to communicate and share information and make informed decisions as a disaster unfolds (Fischer, 1998). We can incorporate new information with existing data and visualize our analysis results in different and useful forms (Steering Committee, 1996). Technologies thus allow us to expand our individual and organizational capacities to more effectively prepare, mitigate, respond, and recover from disasters. Science-driven applications of technology allow disaster risk management to help communities become more resilient and reduce the human and economic impacts of disasters (Alcántara-Ayala et al., 2015).

1.1.1 Focus on Current and Emerging Technology

Alcántara-Ayala et al. (2015) suggest that there is a lack of a comprehensive assessment of disasters limiting our understanding of disaster risk research, practice, and experience. This text is intended to examine the current state of technology and emergency management and clarify how technology may be used to support those engaged in all phases of disaster management.

Technologies are being used in innovative ways and are impacting our capacity to manage effectively in times of crisis (Cutter et al., 2015; Hodgkinson and Stewart, 1991). Becoming more aware of the application of technology in emergency management allows individual citizens and organizations to cope in times of crisis and minimize or avoid the adverse effects of disasters.

Research on the weather–climate nexus has also advanced our understanding of the global oceanic forcing of drought and flood conditions across continents. Public health surveillance systems and disease outbreak detection have been enhanced with the use of the Internet and social media such as Twitter, providing real or near-real time health surveillance (Brownstein et al., 2009; Chunara et al., 2013).

Despite our great success in understanding of the dynamics and processes behind hazards, there are still many challenges related to hazards science. Specifically, we need to reduce uncertainties in forecasting of hazard events, local resolution of models, and prediction of lead time, among others (Alcántara-Ayala et al., 2015). Technology provides us with many tools and resources to allow us to reduce uncertainties.

In this chapter, we will gain insights on how technology contributes to the emergency management process and how to prioritize what technology tools are needed, and understand what resources are required for the effective use of technology.

1.2 Technology as a Management Tool

We use technology to manage our personal time and our organization. We also use technology to manage disasters and hazards. **Hazards** are events or conditions that have the potential to create loss. Technology can be used to prepare for, respond to, recover from, and mitigate future disasters. We prepare for disasters before they happen, often without definite knowledge that they will happen. We respond to disasters when they happen and recover from disasters after they happen. During and after recovery and preparation, we try to mitigate disasters. To **mitigate** a disaster means that we try to lessen the effects of the disaster. For example, to mitigate a levee collapse, the Army Corps of Engineers would try to strengthen it with sandbags or use barges to prevent the water from flooding an area. To mitigate the effects of a hurricane, many home and business owners board up their property to prevent damage. Throughout the entire emergency management cycle, technology is a key contributor to building resilient communities. Technology helps us in many ways. We can be better prepared by recording weather data in remote locations. We can do this by using satellites. We can also process information in new ways. We can directly observe disaster events. In an emergency response, computer applications allow us to access detailed information, such as data about hazardous chemicals, in more assessable ways (Pine, 2014). In mitigation and recovery, we use technology to model disasters and devise an emergency response plan. Technology is especially important in conducting mitigation activities. Mitigation activities include boarding up homes before a hurricane, evacuating an area, and other actions that reduce losses.

Alcántara-Ayala et al. (2015) stress that scientific assessments of disaster risks can contribute to our enhancement of knowledge on risk at scales ranging from local to global. Bessis et al. (2011) stress that during an emergency response information management becomes crucial.

Technology gives us the ability to receive and send information quickly. Information is critical for all involved in the emergency management process. Weather, chemical, security, and transportation information are just a few types of essential data. Quick access to information is important not only to emergency managers, but also to citizens. The quicker emergency managers can give orders to evacuate or to shelter in-place, the more lives are saved. Technology ranges from individual sensors that record information to internal and external organization networks, including the Internet, to the Emergency Broadcast System. Communication devices are ever-changing, from vehicle-mounted applications to remote satellite systems and real-time video teleconferencing. The frequency of natural disasters has steadily increased from 405 per year in 1980 to 650 in the 1990s, 780 in 2000–2009, and 800 events in 2010s (Wirtz et al., 2014).

1.2.1 Response to Complex Disaster Events

Kapucu and Garayev (2013) note that the complex nature and great impacts of disasters proves to be a major factor for a single organization to tackle on their own and reveals the need for a collaborative approach to management. Organizations find themselves involved in a networked governance that involves shared goals and responsibilities as well as the need for a coordinated and unified action to produce desired community results. Networked governance is a combination of inter-organizational interactions spread across a timeline and greatly influenced by the structure of the network, the organizational relationships, and contextual factors (Birkland, 1997; NII 2000 Steering Committee, 1996).

Networks are dynamic structures comprising multiple organizations often located in geographically different sites. A **network** is a set of two or more devices, typically called **nodes**, which are connected in some way to allow communication between them (see Chapter 2). They are multisite groups of organizations with different informal preferences, norms, and values or mandated by legal or regulatory arrangements coming together for a common goal and relying mainly on common interfaces and communication (Isett et al., 2011). Networks are generally characterized by a flexible administrative structure but impacted by issues pertaining to leadership, trust, accountability, and performance measurement (Ward and Wamsley, 2007).

Kapucu and Garayev (2013) found that information communication technology, network relationships, and network complexity all contribute to the overall effectiveness of collaborative networks and impact the sustainability of the network. They note that "emergency management networks are effective to the extent that agency relationships are enhanced for more sustainable relationships" (p. 325).

Further, the exposure of people, assets, and infrastructure in hazard-prone areas affects vulnerability (UNISDR, 2013). Changing population patterns and human-induced environmental changes increase the adverse impacts of disasters (Pelling and Blackburn, 2013) so as to create the frequency of billion dollar events.

1.2.2 Ease of Use of Technology

Technology needs to be easy to use for anyone in the emergency management process. It should not be viewed as an "expert system" only available to a select few. Ongoing training for officials will be critical in the effective use of technology in crisis situations.

Singh et al. (2009) stress the importance of information sharing in response to catastrophic events. Given the interdependence of organizations in disaster response, organizations can benefit from sharing information quickly in a secure environment. They stress the need for information quality including timeliness, security, accessibility, completeness, accuracy, coherence, relevance, validity, and format.

We have seen improvements in hazard modeling and geo-referenced tools and spatial information (Birkland, 2014; Emrich and Cutter, 2011). We thus have great tools for evidence-based hazards analysis to base our emergency preparedness programs. Disaster risk data associated with vulnerability and exposure are a key research and policy issue. Data reflecting our assets and human capital is not widely available and must be developed beyond baseline effort to allow officials to make sound decisions (Gall et al., 2009; Kron et al., 2012; Wirtz et al., 2014).

Information technology is widely used extensively and effectively throughout the United States as explained by Reddick (2011). This national study of emergency managers identified a wide range of technologies used in emergency preparedness and response. All the technologies were viewed as very helpful but the lack of financial resources and support from public officials was a significantly limiting factor on state and local capabilities. Organizational performance was enhanced where public agencies utilized e-government technology and had robust information networks and capable support staff.

1.3 Using Technologies

Also, not every new technology will be applicable for every hazard nor will every new technology be applicable to every emergency management organization. For example, you may live in California and appreciate earthquake risks and be concerned about preparing for earthquakes. Another emergency manager may live in Texas and be concerned about the next hurricane. You may wish to understand how to utilize hazard modeling and remote sensing technologies that clarify possible hazards and provide current information for an emergency response. We thus need to use technology effectively within our own region to support emergency management activities. In a survey of state emergency management agencies, information technology was viewed as very helpful and effective in the emergency planning and response phases (Reddick, 2011). Communication technologies, database resources, mapping sciences, and hazard modeling were seen as very helpful in times of disaster. Figure 1-1 diagrams the role of technology in the emergency management process.

Information technologies have been widely adopted not only in networks and communication devices but also in interconnected objects that provide information from environmental sensing associated with buildings, transportation networks, community utilities, business transactions, and the analysis of information to provide information for situational awareness. The range and extensiveness of things that are now connected allows for the manipulation and control of our systems so that if there is a system failure, immediate action may be possible for immediate action (Gubbi et al., 2013). The Internet of things allows the technology to make critical infrastructure elements and services including administration, education, healthcare, public safety, real estate, transportation, and utilities more aware, interactive and efficient (Belissent, 2010). One ends up with a smart home or office environment, smart business transactions, an array of smart city utility services, smart agriculture, and

Figure 1-1

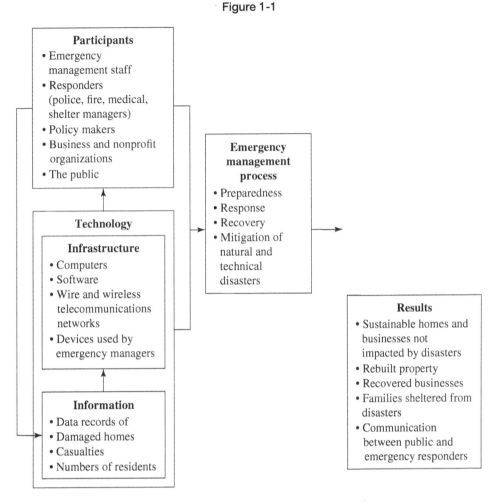

The role of technology in the emergency management process.

transportation. Information and communication technology reflecting business, information, and social processes and able to interact with the environment to exchange data and take action without direct human intervention. The system may be user-centric but also has the capacity to operate within a large network so as to store and analyze information on an ongoing basis (Zanella et al., 2014).

FOR EXAMPLE

When Technology Fails

In May 2006, a strong earthquake with a magnitude of 6.0 hit near Tonga, a group of 170 islands. The Pacific Tsunami Warning Center in Hawaii issued a tsunami alert. Tonga, however, failed to receive the warning due to power outages. Although a tsunami did not occur there, the inability to receive the warning was troubling and is forcing the Pacific Tsunami Warning Center to create additional methods for sending warnings.

1.3.1 Technology in a Changing Environment

Emergency management is an ever-changing process and is not static. We respond to emergencies in an effort to reduce losses which are defined as loss of property and loss of life. As we saw with Hurricane Katrina (2005) and later for Hurricane Sandy (2012), natural hazards can create great losses. As we saw with the terrorist attacks of 9/11, human-caused hazards can cause substantial direct and indirect losses as well. Emergency managers try to reduce any and all potential losses. To do this, we have to prepare for disasters, have a good response plan when there is a disaster, and reduce our vulnerability to hazards. Emergency management is based on a systems approach, which means that each organization has a unique role in reducing losses and contributing to an effective local response. In addition, public agencies at all levels have to all work together to successfully prepare for and respond to hazards.

To reduce losses, emergency managers and agencies have to achieve a high degree of performance. Any misstep could cost lives. Technology not only enhances emergency response capabilities in times of crisis, but also helps in a wide range of preparedness activities. Technology has also had major effects on all organizations, allowing emergency managers to clarify the nature and extent of a potential hazard. In addition, technology can help us understand risks from hazards locally, regionally, and nationally. Further, technology such as remote sensing can be used to clarify the nature of a hazard over time.

1.3.2 Examples of Technology

Chemical sensors help us detect harmful chemicals. After the devastating tsunami of 2005, the Pacific Rim countries have installed a tsunami warning system for a timely emergency response. There are several software programs that help model what would happen if an area were hit by a disaster. For example, before Hurricane Katrina, emergency managers simulated what a Category 5 storm would do to New Orleans. The software modeling program showed public officials that the city of New Orleans would flood. These modeling programs help responders know what the outcome of different hazards could be, and therefore know what planning should address. GPS software can help in effective response effort and track supplies, getting the supplies to their target destination very quickly. They can pinpoint where to direct emergency personnel for rescue operations or postdisaster cleanup of chemical containers, boats, or building debris.

1.3.3 Communicate Quickly

With cell phones, the Internet, e-mail, and satellite phones, we can now communicate in any type of disaster, regardless of the damage to the area's infrastructure. We can also quickly send large amounts of information instantaneously through e-mail. Plus, we can quickly warn people to evacuate through the use of information on Web sites and e-mails in addition to the traditional media of television, radio, and newsprint.

1.3.4 Develop a Better Understanding of Hazards

With our advanced equipment, we can better understand how hazards occur. For example, with the tsunami sensor system in place in the Pacific Rim, we can gain a better understanding of tsunamis and increase our ability to predict and warn residents of a tsunami.

1.3.5 Improve Response

With the enhanced ability to communicate quickly, we also know when response activities are not going well. For example, during Hurricane Katrina we all saw that there were problems getting supplies to New Orleans. Based on that information, public and nonprofit agencies were able to adapt their efforts to get supplies to the hurricane victims.

1.3.6 Increase Coordination

With increased communication and an increased ability to predict hazards, it is easier for emergency managers to work with first responders in their own community. It is also easier for emergency managers to work with state emergency management agencies and the Federal Emergency Management Agency.

1.3.7 Improve Efficiency

Computers and other forms of technology have made all organizations more efficient, which has led to a reduction in the number of people needed in each organization.

1.3.8 Training

Improve training and risk communication programs. With software programs, it is very easy to scan the results of surveys on training and risk communication programs and evaluate the results. This evaluation process leads to improvements in the programs.

The National Research Council noted in 2005 that many technology issues are human in nature and not just issues associated with the technology resources used by public agencies. They note that "better human organization, willingness to cooperate and a willingness of government at higher levels to listen to those at local levels are critical factors in making better use of information technology for disaster management" (p. 2).

1.4 Completing a Needs Assessment

FOR EXAMPLE

Training

For the use of technology to be effective, staff members must be trained. Research has indicated that many tools that are available to emergency managers and staff, such as software modeling programs, are not used because the staff is not properly trained on how to use it. FEMA and state emergency management agencies offer different types of training. Not only should staff members be trained initially on the technology, but refresher courses should also be held periodically.

1.4.1 Nature of a Needs Assessment

Participants in the emergency management system from public agencies, nonprofit and profit business organizations, and the general public all make use of technology. Each agency has its own perspective, role, needs, and capabilities, which enables the emergency management system to function. Understanding the players in the system is critical to effective use of technology. Not every emergency management organization has a budget for all the software and computers that they would like to have. Nonetheless, there are certain items that every organization should have:

▲ Satellite phones. During Hurricane Katrina, the New Orleans infrastructure was badly damaged. Mayor Ray Nagin was cut off from all communications and could not contact anyone at the state and federal level to update them on the situation. Mayor Nagin's staff ended up breaking into an office supply store and taking satellite phones so they could communicate their needs. This is just one example of why every emergency manager needs satellite phones.

▲ Web sites. Web sites are a great way to warn people of hazards, provide information on hazards, and outline mitigation strategies. For large jurisdictions, you can give specific neighborhood information. For example, some neighborhoods may be in the hazard's direct path and will be more affected than those neighborhoods outside the hazard's path. Web-based resources are being used today by public agencies, citizens, businesses, and nonprofit agencies in gathering information about disasters. The National Hurricane Center provides ongoing information about hurricanes for state and local emergency management agencies, businesses, and the general public to support decision making. The number of people who rely on Web sites for information is growing every day. At the very least, many people will use the Web as one of their sources for information.

▲ Digital cameras. You may need to take photos of hazard damage and transmit them quickly over the Internet to state or federal authorities. Digital cameras were an essential resource in documenting property damage following Hurricanes Katrina and Rita.

▲ Access to HAZUS-MH. HAZUS-MH stands for the software program Hazards US-Multi Hazard. You can use this program to estimate losses from earthquakes, floods, and hurricane winds. The program analyzes the impact of a disaster. The program also displays estimates of damages and losses. You can request this program through the FEMA Web site (www.fema.gov).

You may be the emergency manager of a small community. If so, you may need only the basic equipment. Or you may be the emergency manager of a large jurisdiction and need every advantage new technology offers. Before you can submit a budget request for new technology, you must determine what you truly need.

1.4.2 Steps to Complete a Needs Assessment

Step 1: Inventory your use of technology today. How are you using technology and contributing to the emergency management system? What do you need to know to identify other means of utilizing technology?

Step 2: Determine your community's vulnerability. For example, if you have several industrial facilities that work with hazmat, then you may need chemical sensors installed. If you live in a community that is on the transportation route for dangerous nuclear waste, you may need cameras installed along the route within your community in an effort to prevent a terrorist hijacking. If you have completed a Hazard Vulnerability Assessment (HVA), this will go a long way in determining what type of technology you need.

Step 3: Determine how to educate the community on mitigation strategies. For example, you may determine that one way to educate the public is to provide a comprehensive Web site. You may decide that you need to send e-mail messages to residents. Or you could decide to hold several news conferences. Your strategy will most likely consist of reaching people through several different media.

Step 4: Determine how the emergency management community can better coordinate efforts between agencies (including first responders). For example, you may need satellite phones, GPS devices, or a Web portal to streamline communication and provide assistance more efficiently.

Step 5: Determine how you could be more effective in predicting hazards. For example, you may need modeling software to determine what parts of the jurisdiction would be affected by a hurricane.

Step 6: Determine how you could be more effective in responding to hazards. For example, if all traditional lines of communication are knocked out, you may need satellite phones or some other means of communication.

Step 7: Assess the threat and your needs. What is the most likely threat? What hazard would cause the most damage? What equipment and software would help you the most?

1.4.3 Implementing the Needs Assessment

Once you determine your needs, you need to prioritize them based on the greatest need. You will want to submit budget requests for new equipment and software that can be useful for all hazards. You will also want to submit budget requests for equipment that will have a direct impact should you get hit with the hazard that your community is most vulnerable to. Public organizations have been facing critical financial limitation. Expenditures for technology must be viewed as cost-effective, especially in serving the community in nonemergency operations.

Outside the normal budget cycle, a good time to submit a request for new equipment is when there is a **focusing event**. A focusing event is a national disaster resulting in large losses that receives extensive media coverage. Hurricane Katrina is a focusing event. The tsunami in the Pacific Rim is a focusing event. These events give you a **window of opportunity** to advocate for better and newer equipment. A window of opportunity is the chance to argue that a focusing event could occur locally if certain precautions are not taken. During this window of opportunity, you will need to make the argument that such a disaster "could happen here." Because this window of opportunity will not be open for long, you must take advantage of it as soon as you can. Once decision makers are over the shock of the magnitude of the disaster, they will turn their attention to the annual necessities for the community. For example, decision makers know they have to fund the school bus system, as this is a definite need. Your job is to convince decision makers to prepare for a disaster that may or may not happen.

1.4.4 Impacts of Implementing Innovation

Technology innovations have resulted in more than just new devices; they have also resulted in changes in human interactions. The changes, especially those in communications, provide more information for decision making and provide key linkages between response agencies, the public, and local enterprises. This would be a positive impact if it were not for the possibility of inaccurate, incomplete, or misdirected information. So often our developments in technology suggest that there is a quick fix for whatever our problems are (Quarantelli, 1997). A focus on gadgetry leads us in the wrong direction; we need to view technology as simply a tool with strengths and limitations. Technology brings us unprecedented amounts of information that can clarify problems or confuse us. For example, a geographic information system on a personal computer can provide us with extensive information about a jurisdiction; however, the emergency manager may need simple directions from one location to another as provided by many Internet sites, such as MapQuest or Google Earth. The key is to find the fit between technology and our emergency management needs.

The Internet provides a great resource to the emergency management community by allowing agencies to communicate in real time and in a manner that fosters coordinated outcomes and accurate activities. Internet-based system can link and integrate federal, state, local, and nonprofit agencies and facilitate resource allocation and task tracking. Because it is digital, it maintains a historical memory (data files) for evaluating agency response and coordination.

The photo in Figure 1-2, from New Orleans after Hurricane Katrina, illustrates several applications of technology and emergency management. First, the Red

Cross, local government damage assessment teams, and insurance adjusters linked photos of residents, businesses, and critical infrastructure to datasets documenting property damage from disasters. Second, the high watermarks on the house were used by a survey team to document high water elevations in the city; the high water levels were used by digital surveying equipment. Finally, digital images such as this photo of a home are used by the media, public officials, and many other organizations to document in printed and online documents and presentations the social, economic, and environmental impacts of disasters.

FOR EXAMPLE

Focusing Event: 9/11

One of the many tragedies of 9/11 was the fact that so many firefighters had faulty communications equipment, and they did not hear the directive to vacate the World Trade Center. If they had heard these instructions, there is no doubt that more lives would have been saved. The 9/11 Commission issued their report months later and urged all municipalities to ensure their communications equipment is maintained and always works properly.

Figure 1-2

Digital images used in post Katrina needs assessment September 2005.

SUMMARY

In this lesson, you have defined focusing events and windows of opportunity. You have assessed different ways that technology can help you be more effective in all phases of emergency management. You have evaluated how to perform a needs assessment and how to ask your community for more resources. Technology provides tools to link local, regional, and national resources. A technology needs assessment is critical because agencies in the emergency management system have different technology needs and financial resources. Once you know your needs, you can ask for the tools that will help you mitigate and respond to hazards more effectively.

KEY TERMS

Focusing event	A disaster resulting in losses that receives extensive media coverage as well as public attention by citizens, agencies, and public and private officials.
Hazard	An event or physical condition that has the potential to create loss (economic, social, or environmental).
Mitigate	To take an action that may reduce vulnerability to a hazard.
Network	A set of two or more devices, typically called **nodes**, which are connected in some way to allow communication between them.
Technology	The application of scientific methods or objects to achieve a practical purpose.
Window of opportunity	A chance to compare areas that have been impacted by a disaster event with other similar areas allowing emergency managers the opportunity to explain that the "same situation could happen here" and to gain support to provide resources to enhance emergency preparedness, response, recovery, and mitigation at a local, regional, or national scale.

ASSESS YOUR UNDERSTANDING

Go to www.wiley.com/go/pine/tech&emergmgmt_2e to evaluate your knowledge of using technology. This website contains MCQ's, self checks, review questions, applying this chapter and you try it.

References

Alcántara-Ayala, I., Altan, O., Baker, D., Briceño, S., Cutter, S., Gupta, H., Holloway, A., Ismail-Zadeh, A., Díaz, V. J., Johnston, D., McBean, G., Ogawa, Y., Paton, D., Porio, E., Silbereisen, R., Takeuchi, K., Valsecchi, G., Vogel, C., Wu, G., & Zhai, P. (2015). *Disaster Risks Research and Assessment to Promote Risk Reduction and Management.* Paris, France: International Council for Science and the International Social Science Council. http://www.icsu.org/ (accessed May 10, 2017).

Belissent, J. (2010). *Getting Clever About Smart Cities: New Opportunities Require New Business Models.* Cambridge, MA: Forrester Research.

Bessis, N., Asimakopoulou, E., & Xhafa, F. (2011). A next generation emerging technologies roadmap for enabling collective computational intelligence in disaster management. *International Journal of Space-Based and Situated Computing,* 1(1), 76–85.

Birkland, T. A. (1997). *After Disaster: Agenda Setting, Public Policy, and Focusing Events.* Washington, DC: Georgetown University Press.

Birkland, T. A. (2014). *An introduction to the policy process: Theories, concepts and models of public policy making.* Abingdon: Routledge.

Brownstein, J. S., Freifeld, C. C., & Madoff, L. C. (2009). Digital disease detection—harnessing the Web for public health surveillance. *New England Journal of Medicine,* 360(21), 2153–2157.

Chunara, R., Aman, S., Smolinski, M., & Brownstein, J. S. (2013). Flu near you: An online self-reported influenza surveillance system in the USA. *Online Journal of Public Health Informatics,* 5(1), e53. http://nrs.harvard.edu/urn-3:HUL.InstRepos:11708633 (accessed May 5, 2017).

Cutter, S. L., Ismail-Zadeh, A., Alcántara-Ayala, I., Altan, O., Baker, D. N., Briceno, S., Gupta, H., Holloway, A., Johnston, D., McBean, G. A., Ogawa, Y., Paton, D., Porio, E., Silbereisen, R. K., Takeuchi, K., Valsechhi, G. B., Vogel, C., & Wu, G. (2015). Global risks: Pool knowledge to stem losses from disasters. *Nature,* 522, 277–279.

Emrich, C. T., & Cutter, S. L. (2011). Social vulnerability to climate-sensitive hazards in the southern United States. *Weather, Climate, and Society,* 3(3), 193–208.

Fischer, H. W. (1998). The role of the new information technologies in emergency mitigation, planning, response and recovery. *Disaster Prevention and Management: An International Journal,* 7(1), 28–37.

Gall, M., Borden, K., & Cutter, S. L. (2009). When do losses count? Six fallacies of natural hazards loss data. *Bulletin of the American Meteorological Society,* 90(6), 799–809.

Gubbi, J., Buyya, R., Marusic, S., & Palaniswami, M. (2013). Internet of Things (IoT): A vision, architectural elements, and future directions. *Future Generation Computer Systems,* 29(7), 1645–1660.

Hodgkinson, P. E., & Stewart, M. (1991). *Coping with Catastrophe: A Handbook of Disaster Management.* London: Taylor & Frances/Routledge.

Isett, K. R., Mergel, I. A., LeRoux, K., & Mischen, P. A. (2011). Networks in public administration scholarship: Understanding where we are and where we need to go. *Journal of Public Administration Research and Theory,* 21, 157–173.

Kapucu, N., & Garayev, V. (2013). Designing, managing, and sustaining functionally collaborative emergency management networks. *The American Review of Public Administration, 43*(3), 312–330.

Kara-Zaitri, C. (1996). Disaster prevention and limitation: State of the art tools and technologies. *Disaster Prevention and Management, 5*(1), 30–39.

Kron, W., Steuer, M., Löw, P., & Wirtz, A. (2012). How to deal properly with a natural catastrophe database—analysis of flood losses. *Natural Hazards and Earth System Sciences, 12*(3), 535–550.

NII 2000 Steering Committee. (1996). *The Unpredictable Certainty: Information Infrastructure Through 2000*. Washington, DC: National Academies Press.

NRENaissance Committee. (1994). *Realizing the Information Future: The Internet and Beyond*. Washington, DC: National Academies Press.

Pelling, M., & Blackburn, S. (Eds.). (2013). *Megacities and the Coast: Risk, Resilience and Transformation*. London: Earthscan.

Pine, J. C. (2014). *Hazards Analysis: Reducing the Impact of Disasters*. Boca Raton, FL: CRC Press/Taylor Francis Group.

Quarantelli, E. L. (1997). Problematical aspects of the information/communication revolution for disaster planning and research: Ten non-technical issues and questions. *Disaster Prevention and Management: An International Journal, 6*(2), 94–106.

Reddick, C. (2011). Information technology and emergency management: preparedness and planning in US states. *Disasters, 35*(1), 45–61.

Singh, P., Singh, P., Park, I., Lee, J., & Rao, H. R. (2009). Information sharing: A study of information attributes and their relative significance during catastrophic events. In K. J. Knapp (Ed.), *Cyber-Security and Global Information Assurance: Threat Analysis and Response Solutions*. Hershey, PA: IGI Publishers.

Steering Committee. (1996). *Computing and Communications in the Extreme: Research for Crisis Management and Other Applications*. Washington, DC: National Academies Press.

UNISDR. (2013). *The Global Assessment Report on Disaster Risk Reduction*. Geneva: UN Office for Disaster Risk Reduction (UNISDR). Available at: http://www. preventionweb.net/english/hyogo/gar/2013/en/home/GAR_2013/GAR_2013_2. html (retrieved on October 16, 2014; accessed April 24, 2017).

Ward, R., & Wamsley, G. (2007). From a painful past to un uncertain future. In C. B. Rubin (Ed.), *Emergency Management: The American Experience 1900–2005* (pp. 207–242). Fairfax, VA: Public Entity Risk Institute.

Wirtz, A., Kron, W., Löw, P., & Steuer, M. (2014). The need for data: natural disasters and the challenges of database management. *Natural Hazards, 70,* 135–157.

Zanella, A., Bui, N., Castellani, A., Vangelista, L., & Zorzi, M. (2014). Internet of things for smart cities. *Internet of Things Journal, IEEE, 1*(1), 22–32.

2

COMPUTER NETWORKS AND EMERGENCY MANAGEMENT

Cindy Norris

Department of Computer Science, Appalachian State University, Boone, NC, USA

Starting Point

Go to www.wiley.com/go/pine/tech&emergmgmt_2e to assess your knowledge of computer systems.
(Determine where you need to concentrate your effort.)

What You'll Learn in This Chapter

▲ Components of a network
▲ Categories of networks based upon the distance spanned
▲ What the Internet is and its protocols and implementation
▲ Wired communication technologies
▲ Wireless communication technologies
▲ Internet of Things concept and implementation
▲ How the Internet has changed emergency management
▲ What a Smart City is and what technologies support it

After Studying This Chapter, You'll Be Able To

▲ List the types of networks based upon the distance spanned.
▲ Explain the difference between an access network and a backbone network.
▲ Compare the various types of wired access networks.
▲ Compare the various types of wireless network technologies.
▲ Understand how network communications can fail during an emergency.
▲ Explain why some communication technologies are more robust than others.
▲ Explain how the Internet is different from the traditional telephone network.
▲ Examine what technologies can be applied during each phase of emergency management.
▲ Explain how IoT technologies can be useful for emergency management.

Technology and Emergency Management, Second Edition. John C. Pine.
© 2018 John Wiley & Sons, Inc. Published 2018 by John Wiley & Sons, Inc.
Companion website: www.wiley.com/go/pine/tech&emergmgmt_2e

Goals and Outcomes

▲ Use the Internet effectively in the emergency management process
▲ Come up with recovery solutions in the event of network failure
▲ Argue for Smart City initiatives that can support emergency management
▲ Select appropriate technologies that will facilitate emergency management

INTRODUCTION

The Internet and mobile communication devices allow residents and professional emergency responders to share information and coordinate activities in response to emergencies and major disasters. Many uses of the technology are planned and coordinated among federal and local organizations. For example, Presidential Alerts (warnings of national concern), Imminent Threat Alerts (alerts about weather events), and Amber Alerts (alerts about the disappearance of persons) are automatically sent to Wireless Emergency Alert–enabled cell phones (https://www.ready.gov/alerts). Another example is the Person Finder service provided by Google. This service has been used after major disasters including the Kyusyu Kumamoto Earthquake, Typhoon Yolanda, and the Boston Marathon bombing to find and report the finding of missing individuals. However, often the use of the Internet for communication during an emergency is unplanned and occurs spontaneously in response to an ongoing crisis. For example, during the peak of Hurricane Sandy, users made 20 million Twitter posts related to the storm in spite of the loss of cell phone service.

The Internet can play a particularly vital role in communication during an emergency as other forms of communication often fail. For example, during the Tohuku Earthquake and Tsunami in 2011, residents used the Internet to communicate after landlines and cell phones failed (EJC, 2012). A special hashtag, #j_j_helpme, was used on Twitter to identify people that were in need of assistance. Google engineers had Google Person Finder online within 2 hours after the earthquake and over 140 000 names were entered during the search and rescue period. In addition, Google maps helped rescuers navigate through the devastated area. In response to the failure of landlines and cell phones, Next Human Network (NHN) Corporation created the line application which allows users to exchange texts, images, video, and audio, and conduct free voice over IP (VoIP) conversations and video conferences. VoIP, or Internet telephony, allows interactive voice communication over the Internet.

The implementation of an increasingly popular concept known as the **Internet of Things (IoT)** can significantly improve the ability of emergency personnel to detect and respond to an emergency or potential emergency. The driving idea between IoT is that any device can be connected to the Internet. Consider the August 2007 collapse of the I-35W bridge over the Mississippi River in Minneapolis, Minnesota. When the bridge collapsed, dozens of cars plunged into the river resulting in the deaths of 13 people and the injury of 145. The cause of the collapse was undersized steel gusset plates that were inadequate to support the intended load of the bridge, a load that had increased over time as the bridge continued to be resurfaced. When the new I-35W bridge was built, it was instrumented with more than 300 sensors that monitor movement, strain, load distribution, vibrations, temperature, and potential for corrosion. The data from the sensors flows through wires to a nearby computer that is hooked up to optical fiber cables leading to the Department of Transportation and University of Minnesota networks. The use of the sensor network allows structural problems to be detected and shared, averting a potential emergency.

The ability to communicate to the public and professional emergency responders is vital in the fight to protect lives and property. This chapter covers the technologies that enable communication over the Internet, the technologies behind the IoT concept, and how emergency personnel use these technologies in all four phases of emergency management: mitigation, preparedness, response, and recovery. In addition, the chapter discusses how network technologies can fail and how to recover from those failures.

2.1 What Is a Network?

A **network** is a set of two or more devices, typically called nodes, which are connected in some way to allow communication between them. A device may be a host (or end system) such as a desktop, laptop, smartphone, tablet, gaming console, security system, or even an appliance such as an Internet-enabled toaster. These devices are called end systems because they are typically the source or destination of a communication. If not an end system, a device is a connecting device, such as a **router**, which connects networks to other networks, or a switch, which is used to connect devices. Devices are connected by communication links made from various materials including coaxial cable, copper wire, optical fiber, and radio spectrum. Connecting devices receive data from one incoming communication link and forward that data onto one or more outgoing communication links. The process of determining the outgoing communication link is called **switching**. Figure 2-1 displays a picture of a local area network connected to other networks, that is, a network of networks. Note that the switch connects the end systems to create a network and the router connects the network to other networks (not shown).

2.2 Types of Networks

A traditional method to categorize the types of networks is by the distance the network spans. This categorization yields the following types of networks: local area network (LAN), metropolitan area network (MAN), wide area network (WAN), and personal area network (PAN).

2.2.1 Local Area Network

A **local area network (LAN)** is one that connects end systems in a single geographic area such as an office, a building, or a campus. All of the devices on the network are owned by a single entity such as a university or business. A LAN could be as simple

Figure 2-1

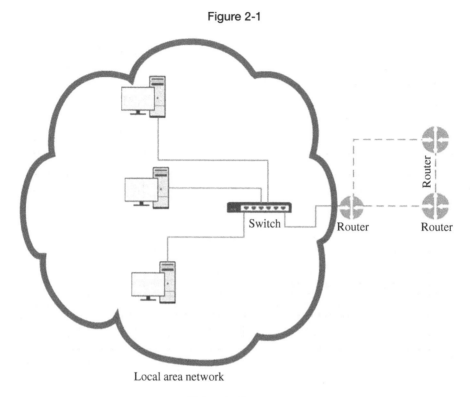

Local area network

Network diagram.

as two computers and a printer within a single office. Figure 2-1 shows a picture of a LAN consisting of an Ethernet switch connected to three desktop machines.

2.2.2 Metropolitan Area Network

A **metropolitan area network (MAN)** is one that spans a city or a town. A MAN connects multiple LANs via high-speed communication links such as optical fiber links. Unlike a LAN, the devices within a MAN are not necessarily owned by a single entity, but the entities that own the LANs want to be able to share resources over a high-speed connection. One of the most common ways for organizations to build this kind of network is to use microwave transmission technology. For example, TV news vans often use microwave antennae to transmit video and sound to the TV studio.

2.2.3 Wide Area Network

A **wide area network (WAN)** spans a much wider geographical region than either a LAN or a MAN, spanning a town, a state, a country, or even the world. Another significant difference is that is a LAN interconnects end systems and a WAN inter-connects connecting devices, such as routers. In this respect, a WAN is similar to a MAN. The main difference between a MAN and a WAN is that a WAN is not

Figure 2-2

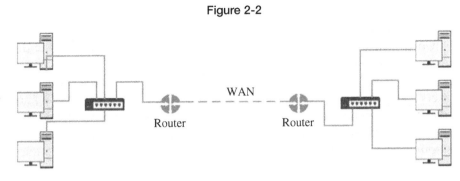

WAN connecting two LANs.

restricted to a particular geographic region. Figure 2-2 shows a picture of two LANS that are connected via a WAN. The routers in the picture direct the packets received from a host in one LAN to a destination host in the other LAN. The switches direct a packet to a destination within the same LAN as the source.

2.2.4 Personal Area Network

A **personal area network (PAN)** is an interconnection of devices within a short distance from each other, typically less than 10 m. In addition to allowing devices within the PAN to communicate, the PAN can support the transmission of data from the devices to the Internet by identifying one of the devices to be the master that plays the role of the Internet router. A PAN can be wired or wireless. A wired PAN is typically constructed using USB or FireWire connections. For example, you can form a wired PAN by connecting an iPhone to a Mac or Windows machine, gaining access to the Internet through the iPhone via the USB cable. Protocols for wireless PAN (WPAN) include Bluetooth and ZigBee. (Bluetooth and ZigBee are discussed later.)

2.3 The Internet

The **Internet** is a WAN that spans the entire world and interconnects hundreds of millions of computing devices. These devices include desktop machines, laptops, smartphones, high-performance computers known as servers that store and provide data, gaming consoles, and a myriad of other Internet-enabled devices.

The Internet is a **packet switched network**, which means that the data sent from a sender to a receiver is broken into chunks called packets that are transmitted independently and reassembled at the destination. These packets don't necessarily follow the same paths to the destination and therefore can arrive out of order. In addition, no resources are reserved in the path from the source to the destination thus a packet could get dropped at a router if there is no room to store the packet when it arrives. In contrast, in a **circuit switched network** a connection is established between the source and the destination and needed resources along the path are reserved before any data is transmitted. The resources along the path are dedicated to the communication until the connection is terminated. Circuit switching is used in the traditional telephone network.

Two principal protocols, the Transmission Control Protocol (TCP) and the Internet Protocol (IP), collectively known as TCP/IP, control the sending and receiving of data across the Internet. The IP protocol specifies the format of the packets that are transmitted and received by end systems. IP packets (also known as datagrams) contain an IP header that contains, among other things, the IP addresses of the source and destination end systems. Routers along the path from the source to the destination use the destination IP address to determine the outgoing communication link upon which the packet is transmitted. A router maintains a forwarding table that maps a range of IP addresses to each communication link. Thus, the IP address and the forwarding table are used for switching. Two types of IP addresses are widely used: IPv4 and IPv6. IPv4 addresses are 32 bits supporting a total of 2^{32} (over 4 billion) devices. With the growth of the Internet, especially with the growing interest in IoT, the number of IPv4 addresses is expected to run out. Thus, IPv6 is being employed to provide more IP addresses. IPv6 addresses are 128 bits supporting 2^{128} addresses, enough to assign every grain of sand an IP address! Because of the near impossibility of an immediate change from IPv4 to IPv6, IPv4 and IPv6 addresses will probably coexist for some time.

The body of the IP packet is called the payload. Typically, the payload is a TCP segment. (The payload could be some other type of packet, but we will only discuss TCP segments.) The TCP protocol defines the format of the TCP segment and provides error-free, in order delivery of the transmitted data. Among other things the TCP header contains a segment number that allows the transmitted data to be put in order at the destination. The TCP header also contains bits, called **checksum** bits, which can be used to determine whether an error was introduced to the segment (the TCP header and/or payload) during transmission. Bit errors are generated by noise on the network. For example, cables that are too close to a noise source, such as lights, can suffer from bit errors. A simple error detection approach is to store an extra parity bit for every 8 bits in the packet. The parity bit is 0 if the number of 1s in the group of 8 bits is even; otherwise, the parity bit is 1. This very simple scheme can successfully detect an odd number of bit errors. (Note: the actual TCP checksum implementation is more sophisticated than this simple scheme.)

As can be seen in Figure 2-3 the message that is sent by an application (e.g., a Web browser) is encapsulated first in a TCP header. This encapsulation is performed

Figure 2-3

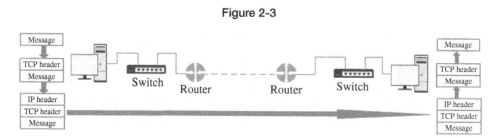

TCP/IP encapsulation/decapsulation.

by transport layer software running on the end system. In fact, for large messages, several TCP segments may be created to transport a single message. Network layer software then encapsulates the TCP segment with an IP header. Routers between the source and the destination examine each IP header in order to choose the appropriate outgoing links. The packet is decapsulated by software at the destination host. Transport layer software reassembles the TCP segments using segment numbers in the TCP headers and the message is delivered to the receiving application (e.g., a Web server).

The backbone of the Internet is a collection of large networks owned by communication companies such as Sprint, Verizon, AT&T, and NTT. These backbone networks are connected to each other at **Internet Exchange Points (IXPs)**, which is a physical infrastructure consisting of one or more network switches and routers to which the backbone networks are directly connected. The networks connected to these IXPs typically have a public peering relationship, meaning that they accept each other's traffic without charge. Provider networks are connected to the backbone networks and pay for the services of the backbone. Customer networks are connected to the provider networks; the customer networks are those that contain end systems that use the Internet. The backbone and provider networks are also known as **Internet Service Providers (ISPs)**. Figure 2-4 illustrates the organization described in this paragraph.

Often an organization desires its own private network (end systems, connecting devices, and links) to ensure that communication across the network remains confidential. However, creating the physical network to support this is very costly. Instead, an organization can create a **virtual private network (VPN)** over the Internet by encrypting data before it is transmitted over the public Internet and

Figure 2-4

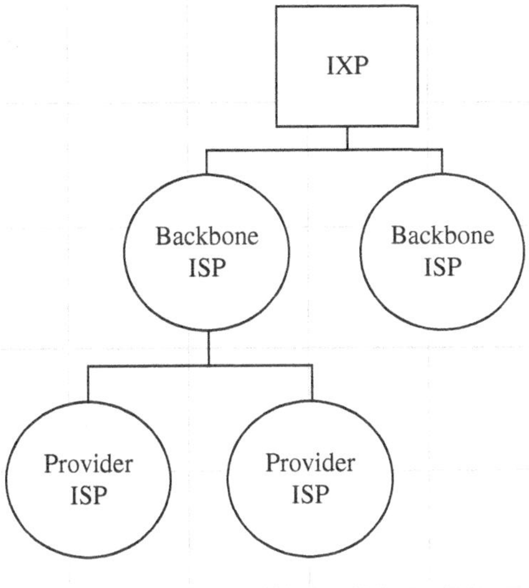

Internet backbone.

decrypting it at the destination. The protocol that provides this service is IPSec. IPSec can be used in two modes. In transport mode, IPSec protects the TCP segment by encrypting it and adding to it an IPSec header and trailer. The IP header added to that is not protected by IPSec; thus the source and destination addresses are visible. Only the source and destination hosts are aware that IPSec is being employed. In tunnel mode, IPSec encrypts the entire IP packet and adds a new IP header whose destination address is the router that connects the destination host to the Internet. The router then decrypts the IP packet and delivers it to the destination.

2.4 Communication Technologies

An **access network** physically connects a host or end system to the first router, called the edge router, on its path to another end system. For example, you probably have access to the Internet via your cell phone. How is it that your cell phone connects to a router that can send your request for a particular Web page to the appropriate destination? Beyond the connection to the first router, the **core network** or backbone network is the part of the network that connects the access networks. For example, in Figure 2-2 the two LANs are access networks; the WAN is the core network. This is a very simple example. In fact, the core network can consist of many connecting devices and communication links.

Access and core networks are either **wired** or **wireless**. If the network is wired, data is transmitted across a physical medium such as twisted-pair copper wire. Wireless enables the transmission of data over a distance without requiring wires, cables, or any other electrical conductors. The data is transmitted through the air by using electromagnetic waves like radio frequencies, infrared, and microwaves. The remainder of this section discusses different technologies for creating wired and wireless networks.

2.4.1 Wired Network Technologies

Dial-up

Before telephone companies and cable companies offered Internet access, access from the home was obtained via Dial-up over traditional twisted-pair copper wire. A computer generates digital signals and the telephone line requires audio; thus a modulator/demodulator (modem) was used to convert digital to audio and vice versa. Software on the computer would explicitly dial the ISP. Unfortunately, dial-up service is very slow and when the computer for the Internet connection is using the phone line, it cannot be used as a regular telephone. Figure 2-5 illustrates how dial-up works. Note that the user is directly dialing the ISP.

Most Internet users are now able to obtain access to the Internet via a **broadband** service. Broadband services provide a high rate of transmission over a wide range of frequencies. The wide range of frequencies allows a lot of data to be transmitted simultaneously, increasing the data rate (i.e., the number of bits transferred per second).

Figure 2-5

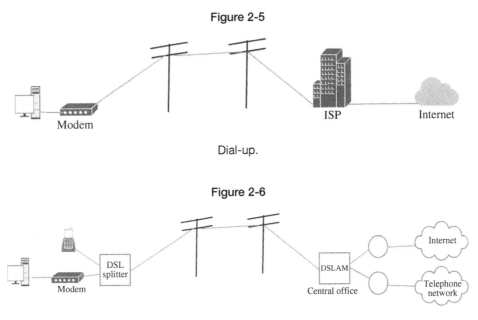

Dial-up.

Figure 2-6

Digital Subscriber Line.

Digital Subscriber Line

Telephone companies developed the Digital Subscriber Line (DSL) to provide higher-speed, broadband, Internet access. DSL allows the telephone line to be simultaneously used for both voice and data by sending the data at a higher frequency. A home's DLS modem takes digital data and translates it to high-frequency tones for transmission over the telephone lines. At the telephone company's central office, a digital subscriber line access multiplexer (DSLAM) converts the analog signals back to digital format and directs voice communication to the telephone network and the data communication to the Internet. At the customer end, a DSL splitter separates the analog signal into the high-frequency data and low-frequency voice and forwards the Internet data to the DSL modem. This process can be seen in Figure 2-6. Note the telephone lines connect to the telephone company's central office, which separates the voice and data.

Cable

Cable companies provide television signals over a coaxial cable, which is a type of wire that consists of a center wire surrounded by insulation and a grounded shield of braided wire. The shield minimizes electrical and radio frequency interference. Cable companies provide customers with Internet access by dividing the coaxial cable bandwidth into three bands: a video band that occupies frequencies from 54 to 550 MHz, a downstream data band (for downloading data from the Internet) that occupies frequencies from 550 to 750 MHz, and an upstream data band (for uploading data to the Internet) that occupies frequencies from 5 to 42 MHz. Similar to a DSL splitter, a cable modem is used at the customer's end that separates the

Figure 2-7

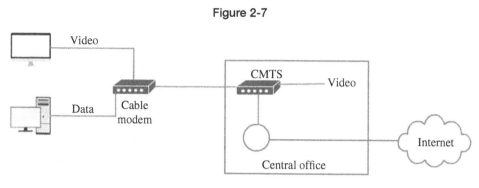

Cable Internet access.

Internet data from the television data. In addition, the cable modem converts the digital computer network data into analog signals for transmission. At the cable provider's end, a cable modem termination system (CMTS) converts the analog signal back to digital format. Figure 2-7 illustrates cable Internet.

Fiber to the X

Fiber to the X where X represents the destination of the fiber is an initiative to replace traditional copper wire used for telephone communications and CATV by optical fiber. Optical fiber is flexible, transparent fiber made from glass or plastic that is used to transmit data in the form of light at a much higher rate than metal wires. In the case of fiber to the home (FTTH), the fiber extends to a box outside of a customer's home. Fiber to the last amplifier (FTTLA), or more commonly called hybrid fiber coax (HFC), is a technique that is used by cable companies to replace coaxial cable by fiber all the way to a neighborhood. Coaxial cable then extends from there to the customer's home. Optical fiber can provide enormous improvements in the rate at which data can be provided to the consumer, potentially gigabits (billions of bits) per second compared to megabits (millions of bits) per second for cable and DSL. However, most FTTH ISPs provide different rate offerings where higher rates cost more money. Much of the core network is implemented by the optical fiber cable owned by major telecommunications companies.

Ethernet

Ethernet is the most common choice for access networks in corporate and university campuses. An Ethernet LAN typically uses twisted-pair copper wire to connect end users to an Ethernet switch, which is in turn connected to an edge router. End systems communicating over Ethernet divide a stream of data into shorter pieces called frames. Each frame contains source and destination MAC addresses which are the addresses given by the manufacturer to network interfaces. An Ethernet switch then outputs a frame onto the appropriate link based upon the MAC address. The frame also contains error-checking bits so that damaged frames can be detected and discarded. Ethernet can provide transmission rates of hundreds of megabits per second.

2.4.2 Long-Range Wireless Network Technologies

This section gives an overview of Worldwide Interoperability for Microwave Access (WiMax), cellular, and satellite technologies that can be used to build a **Wireless Wide Area Network (WWAN)**. A WWAN delivers Internet access to devices in a large area. These devices are typically cell phones or mobile devices, but WWAN cards are also available for laptops.

WiMax

WiMax is a wireless technology similar to Wi-Fi but operating at higher speeds and over a wider area designed to replace the use of cable or DSL. WiMax utilizes base stations that have both a transmitter and a receiver and an adaptive antenna system (AAS). The ASS antenna can focus its transmission energy in the direction of a receiver when transmitting and in the direction of the transmitter when receiving. WiMax stations can communicate with each other. A WiMax station might also have a high-bandwidth, wired connection to the Internet. WiMax customers can use a WiMax subscriber unit that connects to the WiMax network and provides Wi-Fi connectivity within the home. Or customers can connect to the WiMax network via a WiMax-enabled computer similar to how computers connect to Wi-Fi. WiMax operates on the same general principles as Wi-Fi; it sends data from one computer to another via radio signals. A computer (either a desktop or a laptop) equipped with WiMax would receive data from the WiMax base station. WiMax is also one of the versions of 4G wireless available in phones as Sprint's 4G technology, although WiMax started out as a way to deliver wireless broadband to homes and businesses. Figure 2-8 illustrates a WiMax network. Note that one of the base stations is connected to the wired Internet.

Cellular

Cellular phone communication works much the same way as other wireless communication. Signals carrying voice, text, and digital data are transmitted via radio waves from one device to another. In the case of cellular networks, the data is transmitted not to a nearby access point as it is with Wi-Fi or directly from device to device as is the case with Bluetooth, but instead data is transmitted to or received from a base transceiver station (BTS) that may be quite far from the cellular phone (Figure 2-9).

Figure 2-8

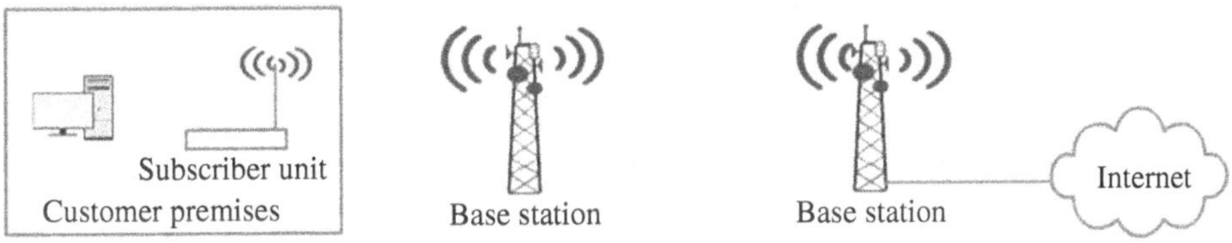

WiMax network.

Figure 2-9

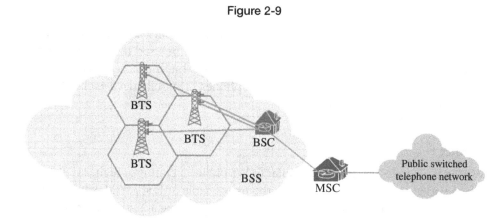

Cellular network architecture.

The term cellular is derived from the cellular design of the mobile network. The mobile phone network is divided into thousands of overlapping geographic areas called cells. A BTS is stored within each cell that provides service to each mobile device in the cell. The coverage area of the cell depends upon many factors including the transmitting power of the BTS and obstructions within the cell, such as obstructing building. The typical radius of a cell is between 2 and 20 km. A single base station controller (BSC) services tens of BTSs by allocating a radio channel and by handling the handoff of mobile communication from one BTS to another BTS when the signal between the current BTS and mobile device deteriorates. Together the tens of BTSs and the single BSC make up what is called a base station system (BSS). A switching office, called a mobile switching center (MSC), controls the BSS and connects the cellular network to the public switched telephone network.

Cellular technologies can be classified into generations. The 1G systems were analog and supported only voice communication. The 2G systems were designed to support digitized voice in order to provide higher-quality mobile voice communications. In addition, the transmission of digital data rather than analog data allows the frequency spectrum to be used more efficiently; thus the amount of bandwidth, that is, range of frequencies, required to transmit voice communication is smaller. Also, 2G supported the transmission of text messages. The 3G technologies provide both digital data and voice communication. Via 3G technologies, a portable device is automatically connected to the Internet; that is, there is no need to dial a number to connect. The 3G technologies allow someone to talk to anyone in the world with quality that is as good as the traditional television network. In addition, users can stream videos, surf the Internet, play games, participate in video conferences, and more. Unlike 3G technologies, 4G technologies are entirely packet based. This means that all voice and data are carried in IP datagrams. The 4G technologies also provide significantly higher upload and download rates over 3G; thus any app that requires transferring large amounts of data benefits from 4G. The 5G refers to the next generation of the mobile network technology. In addition to providing faster speeds, 5G networks will also meet the requirements created by the IoT, for example, hundreds of thousands of simultaneous connections to be supported for massive sensor deployments.

Satellite

A satellite network consists of three types of nodes: satellites, stations, and end hosts, such as satellite phones or satellite modems. The stations communicate directly with the orbiting satellites via radio signals. There are three categories of satellites based upon their orbits, which is the path it travels around the earth. Geostationary earth orbit (GEO) satellites permanently remain 36 000 km over a single spot on the Earth. The huge distance from the ground station to a GEO satellite causes a signification delay in the time that transmitted data takes to propagate from the station to the satellite. In spite of the delay, GEOs satellites are often used in areas without access to DSL or cable-based Internet. Three GEO satellites equidistant from each other can provide full global transmission.

Medium earth orbit (MEO) satellites are located at altitudes between 5000 and 15 000 km. The primary use of these satellites is for navigation, for example for the United States' Global Positioning System (GPS), Russia's Global Global Navigation Satellite System (GLONASS), and Galileo, the Global Navigation Satellite System (GNSS) created by the European Union and European Space Agency. MEO satellites travel overhead at all times, instead of tracking with a fixed point on Earth as GEO satellites do. MEO satellites can provide constant coverage through a constellation of several satellites that are closer to Earth, offering a significantly lower propagation delay than GEO satellites.

Low earth orbit (LEO) satellites have a circular orbit about 500–2000 km above the earth's surface. Because of the smaller altitude, they take much less time (about 90 minutes) to revolve around the earth than MEOs. In addition, LEO satellites change their positions relative to the ground position quickly; thus a large number of satellites are needed if an application requires uninterrupted connectivity. For this reason, LEO satellites are often part of a group of satellites working in concert known as a satellite constellation. Low earth orbiting satellites are less expensive to launch into orbit than geostationary satellites and, due to proximity to the ground, do not require as high a signal strength. LEO satellites communicate with each other as well as with ground stations. The International Space Station, the Space Shuttle, and the Hubble Space Telescope are all in LEO. LEO satellite communication may be used in the future to provide global access to the Internet (Gershgorn, 2015).

Satellite signals are transmitted far above the earth and do not rely on towers. Satellite phones and satellite base stations can receive the signals. Because they do not rely on towers, satellite signals are especially useful in remote areas. In addition, satellites are not damaged by disasters on earth such as earthquakes and thus satellite phones can be an important means for communication in an emergency. However, if a single satellite fails, communication can be lost entirely.

2.4.3 Short-Range Wireless Network Technologies

The technologies described in this section provide short-range connectivity ranging from a few centimeters (Near Field Communication or NFC) to hundreds of kilometers. However, the uses of these technologies tend to be quite different. Wi-Fi technology is typically used to allow end systems access to the Internet, although it can also be used to connect a laptop to a Wi-Fi printer or to share documents between two nearby computers. In general, Wi-Fi is used as a substitute for high-speed cabling, such as Ethernet; thus Wi-Fi is commonly used to build a **Wireless LAN (WLAN)**. Bluetooth technology is typically used to transfer data between two Bluetooth devices, for example, between a mobile phone and a hands-free headset. Like Wi-Fi, Bluetooth can also be used as an access point to the Internet, but provides that access at a much lower rate. Bluetooth, ZigBee, Dash7, RFID, and NFC are all technologies that can be used to build **Wireless Personal Area Networks (WPAN)**. ZigBee and Dash7 both consume less power and have a higher range than Bluetooth and thus are better choices for sensor nodes in smart city applications. RFID and NFC devices are used for extremely short-range data transmission of small packets of data making them suitable for tracking objects, including people and animals. This section describes each of these in more detail.

These technologies can also be used to build a **Wireless Sensor Network (WSN)**. A WSN is a wireless network consisting of a collection of sensors to monitor physical or environmental conditions. Nodes in the WSN system communicate with each other. One node provides wireless connectivity back to the Internet.

Wi-Fi

WLAN access based on IEEE 802.11 technology is known as Wi-Fi. Wi-Fi provides a low-power form of wireless transmission over short distances. The end system, usually a laptop or a cell phone, must be with a few tens of meters of the wireless router that serves as the access point. Typically, the wireless router is connected to a cable modem or DSL.

Bluetooth is a popular technology for building a WPAN known as a piconet. A piconet consists of a master device, up to seven active slave devices, and up to 255 inactive (parked) slave devices. The master device can bring an inactive device into active status at any time, after an active device is parked. The slave devices do not communicate with each other or with the Internet. All communication is through the master device. A simple example of a piconet is a fitness-monitoring device connected to a cell phone via the Bluetooth connection.

ZigBee defines technology for building a WPAN that is simpler and less expensive than Bluetooth. The ZigBee specification defines a radio protocol for communication among low-cost, low-power devices at a lower rate of transmission than Bluetooth devices. ZigBee has been successfully used in devices for control such as for lighting, irrigation, aerial vehicle (AV) systems, industrial equipment, security systems, and patient monitoring. For example, a ZigBee device can be

Figure 2-10

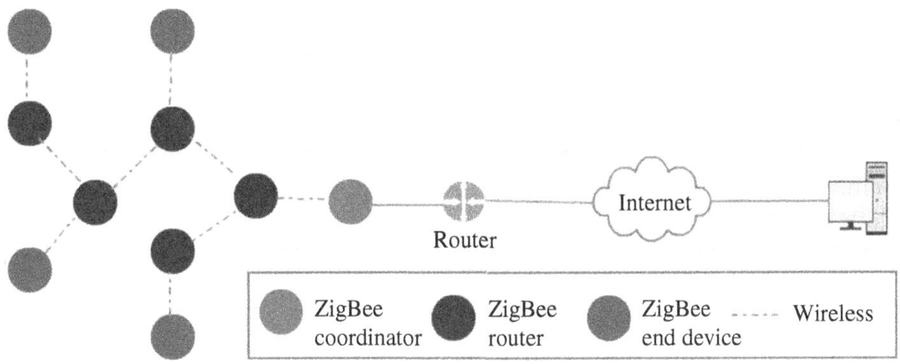

ZigBee wireless sensor network.

used to monitor a patient's blood pressure and heart rate and communicate the information to the hospital.

ZigBee devices are typically arranged in a mesh network where the connection is spread out among wireless nodes that can communicate with each other across a large area. The mesh network boosts data transmission range (up to 65 000 nodes can be on a single network) and provides greater fault tolerance if a node fails.

ZigBee nodes can be coordinators, routers, and end devices. Coordinators are comparable to Bluetooth master nodes and establish the network and store information like security keys that are used to encrypt transmitted data. ZigBee coordinators form the network by determining the PAN ID and the channel used for communication. Routers and end devices join the network. Routers act as intermediate nodes and relay data from other devices. End devices are low-power gadgets that can communicate with coordinators and routers but cannot transmit data to other end devices. End devices sleep most of the time in order to conserve batteries. Figure 2-10 illustrates a ZigBee WSN. The ZigBee end devices would contain sensors for things such as light, sound, temperature, pressure, gas, and so on.

Dash7

Dash7 is a long-range, low-power wireless communications standard for applications requiring modest bandwidth like sensor readings or providing the coordinates for location-based advertising. Dash7 excels at connecting things that move. Unlike Wi-Fi and Bluetooth, the "instant-on" capability of Dash7 allows connections with passing cars, buses, or people jogging. In addition, Dash7 operates at 433 MHz, which is a frequency that allows penetration through walls and supports ranges up to many kilometers. Like Bluetooth and ZigBee, Dash7 defines technology that can be used to build a WPAN where devices communicate in a master–slave relationship. However, Dash7 devices have a higher range and longer battery life.

Radio-Frequency Identification Systems

Radio-Frequency Identification (RFID) is a communication technology to uniquely identify tagged objects by transmitting radio signals. An RFID system consists of tags, a reader, and a database. The reader decodes the data stored in the tag and the data is transferred to the database for processing. RFID systems are widely used in manufacturing for tracking parts, in shipping, and in payment systems such as for toll roads. They are also being used in emergency management as described later.

RFID tags are either active or passive. Active RFID tags contain their own power source (i.e., a battery), giving them the ability to broadcast their tag. A reader within 100 m will be able to read the tag. Passive RFID tags do not have their own power source. Instead, the electromagnetic energy transmitted from an RFID reader causes the tag to activate. Because the radio waves must be strong enough to power the tags, the read range is smaller than it is for active tags. In particular, the reader must be within 25 m of the passive tag to activate and read the tag.

Near Field Communication

NFC is used in mobile devices for very short-range (10 cm or less) communication. Unlike RFID systems where an RFID device is either a tag or a reader, NFC is bidirectional; thus it is possible to share information between devices. The predominant current application of NFC is the digital wallet. A smartphone equipped with NFC can be used as a substitute for a credit card and can also be used to provide identification. In addition, since NFC communication is bidirectional, it can be used to share data (pictures, videos, contact information) between devices. Like RFID systems, NFC devices can be used for asset management; for example, in emergency response, NFC devices can be used to track people, animals, medical equipment, and so on.

2.5 The Internet and Emergency Management

In 2015, 67% of American homes had broadband Internet access (Horrigan and Duggan, 2015). This has slightly decreased from 2013 as more adults are using smartphones to access the Internet. About 13% of American adults reported in 2015 that their smartphone is the only device that they use to access the Internet; this is up from 8% in 2013. Overall access to the Internet continues to grow. Some 80% of American adults reported having either a smartphone or a home broadband subscription in 2015, compared with 78% who said this in 2013.

Being able to access the Internet has forever changed how news is produced and consumed. In the past, communication between newscasters and news consumers was one to many. Now, anyone with a phone and/or an Internet connection can contribute to the media conversation by calling into a talk show or posting to one of many available social media sites such as Facebook and Twitter.

In fact, the Internet enables government entities to serve as their own news bureaus. For example, during Hurricane Sandy, the New York Office of Emergency Management used Twitter and Facebook to provide hourly updates about evacuations, shelters, aid, and storm conditions. The Boston Police Department (BPD) used social media immediately after the Boston Marathon bombing to let people know what had occurred. The use of social media, in particular Twitter and Facebook, allowed the BPD to correct misinformation that was being spread by professional media outlets and social media sites. The public and professional news organizations alike soon realized that the most accurate information about the bombing was available on official BPD social media accounts. It is becoming increasingly more common that social media networks are a primary source of information for rescue authorities and victims following a natural or man-made disaster (Besaleva and Weaver, 2016).

The Internet has changed the hierarchical nature of information flow in an emergency situation. In the past, information flow in emergency management was top-down. Local officials would learn details about an emergency from their superiors if they needed to; likewise, community members would learn details from local officials. The Internet has changed the flow of information since the Internet is typically the source of information in an emergency and the information becomes available to all simultaneously. Misinformation and the misinterpretation of information on the Internet is a problem. However, for emergency management, the ability to communicate widely and quickly outweighs possible drawbacks.

The Internet is not immune to communication failures that occur during disasters but can sometimes stay intact or be repaired more quickly than other forms of communication. The most common cause of failure is physical damage to devices and network infrastructure (Richards, 2015). For example, hurricane force winds, floods, and seismic activity can potentially damage cell towers, power lines, and optical fiber cables. Damage to a cell tower will disrupt an area's wireless communication. A cell tower is expensive and time-consuming to repair and also requires getting a crew to the devastated area. Optical fiber cables can be even more challenging to repair because the cables are underground, making it more difficult to find the location of the damage and requiring excavation to pinpoint and repair the damage. Wireless links are also susceptible to disruption by heavy rain, snow, or fog.

Satellite-based emergency communication devices are typically the most reliable devices in an emergency situation because satellite communication is not affected by any localized conditions such as floods, power outages, fires, earthquakes, hurricanes, tornadoes, or other disasters. In addition, satellite coverage is universal. However, satellite phones are expensive and not widely used by the general public. In addition, if a single satellite fails, communication can be completely disabled and impossible to repair quickly.

In the absence of physical damage, the network infrastructure may still be unusable due to the volume of network traffic generated by those impacted by the disaster. When a disaster occurs, the network becomes inundated by videos and photos of the damage, friends and family attempting to communicate with loved ones in the impacted area, and communications between emergency personnel. Network nodes that receive data from many downstream networks, for example, a DSLAM device that receives DSL traffic from many customers, are often the failure points for congested network. If the network becomes too congested, messages can be lost entirely.

Communication failures are less likely when there is more than one type of path between the source and destination of the communication. This way if one path is destroyed during a disaster, the other path may still be intact. For example, if a customer has both broadband Internet access via DSL or cable and Internet access via the cellular network then if a break occurs in underground cables, the customer may still be able to access the Internet via the wireless link. However, this solution relies on the customer to purchase the needed redundancy. Indeed, the Pew Research Center found that the number of homes in the United States with broadband Internet access has slightly decreased in recent years as more adults are using only their smartphones to access the Internet (Horrigan and Duggan, 2015).

Broadband ISPs can provide more stability to their customers by complementing their own existing cable links with wireless links. The backup wireless solution must be as reliable and at least as high capacity as the wired connection, otherwise it too may be ineffective if the primary connection fails.

In an emergency situation in which communication has been destroyed, an ad hoc network can be quickly created to restore cellular communication (Richards, 2015). **Cellular on Wheels (COW) and Cellular on Light Trucks (COLT)** can be transported into an area to temporarily provide cellular service. A COW consists of networking equipment on a flat-bed trailer that has to be hooked to a truck tractor. A COLT is a self-contained truck that provides cellular and possibly Wi-Fi and portable charging stations for mobile devices. COLTs are used more often in the event of a natural disaster, as their independent operation can make them easier to deploy. As one example, COWs were deployed in the aftermath of Hurricane Katrina to provide critical phone service to rescue and recovery workers when the area's cellular networks were otherwise disabled.

FOR EXAMPLE

In October 2012, Hurricane Sandy devastated New York City, killing more than 100 people, crippling public transportation, cutting power to over 8 million homes, damaging infrastructure, and destroying entire communities. However, during that time AT&T, one of the country's leading network carriers, suffered no network problems (Bell, 2012). AT&T accomplished this impressive feat by sending COLTs and COWs to New York City, Long Island, and various locations in New Jersey. The trailers contained the exact same equipment as an AT&T central office, including their own power supply, and thus could be parked in a parking lot to become the central office. These mobile cellular towers were set up to provide cellular network access to Sandy victims.

2.6 IoT and Emergency Management

The **IoT** is a massive network of often battery-powered devices, estimated to reach 30 billion by 2020 (ABIResearch, 2013). These devices may connect to each other through the Internet, but more frequently they talk directly to each other through Bluetooth, ZigBee, or other wireless standards. Beyond this networking-oriented definition, IoT can be seen as a technology that enables decentralized systems of cooperating cyber–physical **Smart Objects** (SOs) which are physical objects, augmented with sensing/actuating, processing, storing, and networking capabilities. SOs may cooperate with other SOs and exchange information with human users and other computing devices.

The integration of SOs, people, physical environments, and computing devices is often called a **Cyber–Physical System (CPS)**. These include systems such as Smart Cities, Smart Grids, Smart Factories, Smart Buildings, Smart Homes, and Smart Cars. The terms CPS and IoT are often used interchangeably. However, IoT is more generally used to refer to the technology employed to provide connectivity to devices. IoT technology enables the development of a CPS, such as a Smart Car, that is, a car that could receive real-time traffic alerts and respond to them possibly without user intervention.

FOR EXAMPLE

In May 2016, Juniper Research named Singapore the "Global Smart City— 2016." The Singapore Smart City is empowered by an immense collection of sensors and cameras that are deployed across the city to monitor everything including the cleanliness of public spaces, crowd density, and the movements of registered vehicles. Sensor data is being fed into a system known as Virtual Singapore that is being built by the government's National Research Foundation with assistance from private–sector companies, universities, and other governmental departments. In addition to receiving sensor data, the system maintains a map that includes the exact dimensions of buildings, placement of windows, and the types of construction materials used.

At this point, applications for the data are being envisioned and developed including applications that:

▲ reroute buses based on where riders are gathering
▲ collect information about the bumpiness of bus rides from riders' cell phones to determine where road repairs need to be done
▲ detect smoking in prohibited areas
▲ automatically charge tolls based upon the movement of the registered vehicle
▲ provide parking information through an online map
▲ monitor the movements of elderly people in their homes to detect a potential emergency
▲ inform volunteers that can perform CPR of someone who has suffered from a cardiac arrest who is within 400 m of their location

To enable the development of applications, the Singapore government has created an initiative called "Smart Nation." This initiative seeks to engender a people-centric approach to creating applications by rallying citizens, industries, research institutions, and the government to participate in their creation. The government facilitates the development by sharing the extensive real-time public domain data collected via the vast network of sensors and cameras.

More precisely, IoT is the combination of billions of IP-enabled devices, RFID tags, WSNs, mobile apps, and cloud computing. **Cloud computing** refers to the practice of using servers that can be accessed via the Internet to store, process, and access data. A server is a computer that provides computing resources or data to other computers. If those two computers communicate via the Internet, then it is employing cloud computing and the server is located in what is called the cloud. For example, wireless sensor data can be sent to the cloud for storage and processing. Emergency personnel can then have access to the processed data via a mobile app.

WSNs are of particular importance to the field of emergency management since sensors can be used to detect environmental parameters that may indicate an emergency situation (Benkhelifa et al., 2014). For example, changes in atmosphere and temperature can be used to detect a forest or building fire. The presence of a toxic gas may indicate an explosion. Vibrations may indicate an earthquake. In addition, during rescue and recovery, the number of Bluetooth devices in the area can be used to estimate the number of victims. If a company uses an RFID system or NFC for tracking entrance into a building, that data can be used to determine the number of people in a building in the event of a disaster.

One of the key tasks of emergency management is tagging/tracking and RFID systems can support this important task. An urgent problem at the emergency scene is the overwhelming number of victims that must be monitored, tracked, and managed by first responders and volunteers. In addition, the equipment deployed at the emergency scene, as well as other resources to support victims, needs to be managed and distributed appropriately. The process of managing humans and other objects during emergencies is composed of the following tasks (Ahmed, 2015):

▲ Marking or tagging of humans and objects
▲ Using tags to track humans/objects
▲ Using tags for object management before, during, and after emergencies.

In particular, RFID systems can be used to identify an object within a group of similar objects and to provide real-time information about that object's position.

FOR EXAMPLE

Hurricane Katrina exposed a number of problems dealing with the evacuation of citizens. In 2005, when Katrina loomed in the Gulf, most New Orleanians did leave town, but more than 100 000 residents were left behind. Many of those that stayed lacked a car and money for transportation or had no one outside of the city that they could turn to for shelter. In addition, some residents, not having Internet access, relied on television for information about the storm. Television stations were slower at informing viewers how bad the storm would be. Still others were disabled or suffering from a chronic disease, which made evacuation more difficult. The city failed to inform its most vulnerable residents about the seriousness of the impending storm and they failed to facilitate their evacuation.

Many of the evacuees of Hurricane Katrina were moved to Texas. Unfortunately, Hurricane Rita hit some of the areas to which Hurricane Katrina victims were evacuated, causing those victims to be evacuated again. It became very difficult for emergency personnel to keep track of who was being evacuated and where they were being evacuated. Many of the victims of the storm were separated from their families including a large number of parents separated from their children. Special needs people were particularly vulnerable. It sometimes took weeks for families to find their loved ones.

After experiencing the evacuation mishaps of hurricanes Katrina and Rita, Texas Governor Rick Perry spearheaded a program that uses RFID, GPS, and bar code technology to automate the evacuation process of elderly, sick, disabled, or able-bodied individuals or families who have no access to transportation during an emergency. Evacuees meet at embarkation centers, which are located in towns and cities. At these centers, adults and children are issued wristbands and pets receive special tags affixed to their collars. Each wristband and tag contains a bar code and/or an RFID. The IDs issued to the pets and children are associated in a back-end database with those of their guardians. Assets, such as medical equipment, are also tagged. Bar code scanners or RFID readers are used to read the wristbands of evacuees boarding buses at the various embarkation centers. GPS receivers inside of buses are used to track the location of the bus and the evacuees inside of them. When evacuees leave the bus, a bar code scanner or RFID reader is used to read tags of evacuees and the database is updated to indicate who disembarked at that site.

WSNs, **Unmanned Aerial Vehicles (UAVs)**, and **Unmanned Ground Vehicles (UGVs)** can be used for disaster preparedness, damage assessment, and disaster response and recovery (Erdelj and Natalizio, 2016). WSNs and UAVs can be used for structural and environmental monitoring to provide information to forecast an impending disaster. For example, sensors can be used to detect slope movement that can predict a landslide (Frigerio et al., 2014). However, to enable disaster preparedness often a WSN is deployed to an inhospitable location that can cause a sensor to fail. For example, flood water or shifting terrain can damage a WSN node. WSNs require multihop communication to allow transmitted data to reach a master node; thus a single failed node can cause the system to be inoperable. This is where a UAV or UGV can be helpful. A UAV/UGV can be sent to the site of a disaster to monitor the environment when the WSN fails or even to connect to the WSN if there are failings in some part of the infrastructure (Ueyma et al., 2014).

During disaster response and recovery, WSNs, UAVs, and UGVs can be used to search for victims of the disaster. For example, sensors placed inside of a building can be helpful in determining the location of victims in the event of a building collapse (Pogkas et al., 2007). UAVs can be used to search for victims and to establish a communication infrastructure when the power lines, cell phone towers, and antennas have been damaged.

SUMMARY

The Internet allows residents and professional emergency responders to share information and coordinate activities to prepare for and respond to emergencies and major disasters. The Internet can play a particularly vital role in response and recovery as other forms of communication often fail. In addition, the Internet and IoT technologies are playing an increasingly more important role in all phases of emergency management. For example, a WSN can be deployed to detect impending disasters such as a building collapse or landslide, thus allowing an evacuation to occur before the disaster happens, reducing the impact of the disaster. In addition, WSN, UAV, UGV can be used to for disaster assessment and recovery.

This chapter discussed the technologies that enable communication over the Internet and the technologies behind the IoT. In addition, the chapter discussed how networks can fail during an emergency and what can be done to avoid or recover from a communications failure. Finally, we discussed how these technologies are used for emergency management.

KEY TERMS

Access network	The portion of a network that connects an end system to the edge router.
Broadband Internet service	Internet service that utilizes a range of frequencies for transmitting data thus supporting a high rate of transmission.
Cellular on wheels (COW) and Cellular on light truck (COLT)	Portable networking infrastructure that can be moved into a disaster area to quickly restore communications.
Checksum	Bits in a packet header that are used to detect errors in the packet.

Circuit switching	Network communication that involves reserving resources to support a connection between a source and destination end system in communication links and switches before a message is sent. All messages that are part of the connection will travel through those reserved resources.
Cloud computing	Refers to the use of remote powerful computers, known as servers, that are accessed via the Internet to store, process, and access data.
Core network	The portion of a network that connects the access networks.
Cyber–physical system (CPS)	An integration of Smart Objects, people, physical environments, and computing devices such as a Smart City.
Internet	Internet is a Wide Area Network (WAN) that spans the entire world. The two main protocols that enable communication on the Internet are TCP and IP (TCP/IP).
Internet exchange points (IXPs)	Physical points at which the backbone networks owned by large telecommunication companies connect.
Internet of Things (IoT)	Refers to the idea that any object can be connected to the Internet.
Internet Service Provider (ISP)	Company that provides services for accessing the Internet.
Local area network (LAN)	Network that connects end systems in a single geographic area.
Metropolitan area network (MAN)	Network that spans a city or town.
Network	Network is a collection of end systems, communication links, and connecting devices that allows software running on the end systems to communicate.
Packet switching	Network communication that involves dividing a message into packets that are sent separately, possibly across different paths, and reassembled at the destination.
Personal area network (PAN)	Network that spans a very small area, typically less than 10 m.
Router	Connecting device on a network. The router uses the IP address of the destination packet and a forwarding table that is accessed with the IP address to determine the outgoing link.
Smart object	Physical object that can sense, process, store, and communicate data.

Switching	The technique used by a connecting device to choose the outgoing link.
Unmanned aerial vehicle (UAV)	An aircraft that can be navigated without a human pilot on board.
Unmanned ground vehicle (UGV)	Vehicle that travels across the ground and can be navigated without a human driver on board.
Virtual private network (VPN)	Private network created on top of the Internet by encrypting the data sent by the end systems on the network.
Wide area network (WAN)	Network that spans a wide geographic region such as a state, country, or even the world.
Wired network	Network in which the communication links are built from a physical medium such as twisted-pair copper wire or optical fiber.
Wireless network	Network in which data is transmitted through the air.
Wireless local area network (WLAN)	Local Area Network that is built using wireless technology such as Wi-Fi.
Wireless personal area network (WPAN)	Personal Area Network that is built using wireless technology such as Bluetooth, ZigBee, Dash7, NFC, and RFID.
Wireless sensor network (WSN)	Network of low-power nodes that gather information about their environment and wirelessly transmit that information to other nodes.
Wireless wide area network (WWAN)	Network that spans a large geographic region by using wireless technologies such as WiMax, Cellular, and Satellite.

ASSESS YOUR UNDERSTANDING

Go to www.wiley.com/go/pine/tech&emergmgmt_2e to evaluate your knowledge of using technology. This website contains MCQ's, self checks, review questions, applying this chapter and you try it.

References

ABIResearch. (2013). More than 30 billion devices will wirelessly connect to the Internet of everything in 2020. https://www.abiresearch.com/press/more-than-30-billion-devices-will-wirelessly-conne/ (accessed April 23, 2017).

Ahmed, A. (2015). Role of GIS, Rfid and handheld computers in emergency management: An exploratory case study analysis. *JISTEM—Journal of Information Systems and Technology Management*, 12(1), 3–27. Epub April 2015. https://dx.doi.org/10.4301/S1807-17752015000100001.

Bell, L. (2012). AT&T reveals how the network survived Hurricane Sandy. *The Inquirer*, December 2012. http://www.theinquirer.net/inquirer/feature/2231811/at-t-talks-about-its-disaster-recovery-strategy-during-hurricane-sandy (accessed April 23, 2017).

Benkhelifa, I., Nouali-Taboudjemat, N., & Moussaoui, S. (2014). Disaster manage projects using wireless sensor networks: An overview. In 28th International Conference on Advanced Information Networking and Applications Workshops, Gwangju, Korea, May 13–16, 2014.

Besaleva, L., & Weaver, A. (2016). Applications of social networks and crowd-sourcing for disaster management improvement. *Computer*, *49*, 47–53.

EJC. (2012) It happened again: Media and twitter during earthquakes in Japan. *Emergency Journalism*, December 2012. http://emergencyjournalism.net/it-happened-again-media-and-twitter-during-earthquakes-in-japan/ (accessed April 23, 2017).

Erdelj, M., & Natalizio, E. (2016). UAV-assisted disaster management: Applications and open issues. In 2016 International Workshop on Wireless Sensor, Actuator and Robot Networks—ICNC Workshop, Kauai, Hawaii, USA, February 15–18, 2016.

Frigerio, S., Schenato, L., Bossi, G., Cavalli, M., Mantovani, M., Marcato, G., & Pasuto, A. (2014). A web-based platform for automatic and continuous landslide monitoring: The Rotolon (Eastern Italian Alps) case study. *Computers & Geosciences*, *63*, 96–105.

Gershgorn, D. (2015). Samsung wants to blanket the earth in satellite internet. *Popular Science*, August 2015. http://www.popsci.com/samsung-wants-launch-thousands-satellites-bring-everyone-earth-internet (accessed May 6, 2017).

Horrigan, J., & Duggan, M. (2015). Home Broadband 2015. Pew Research Center. http://www.pewinternet.org/2015/12/21/home-broadband-2015/ (accessed April 23, 2017).

Pogkas, N., Karastergios, G. E., Antonopoulos, C. P., Koubias, S., & Papadopoulos, G. (2007). Architecture design and implementation of an Ad-Hoc network for disaster relief operations. *IEEE Transactions on Industrial Informatics*, *3*(1), 63–72.

Richards, C. (2015). When communications infrastructure fails during a disaster. *Disaster Recovery Journal*, November 2015. http://www.drj.com/articles/online-exclusive/when-communications-infrastructure-fails-during-a-disaster.html (accessed April 23, 2017).

Ueyma, J., Freitas, H., Faical, B. S., Filho, G. P. R., Fini, P., Pessin, G., Gomes, P. H., & Villas, L. A. (2014). Exploiting the use of unmanned aerial vehicles to provide resilience in wireless sensor networks. *IEEE Communications Magazine*, *52*(12), 81–87.

3

CYBER SECURITY

Cindy Norris

Department of Computer Science, Appalachian State University, Boone, NC, USA

Starting Point

Go to www.wiley.com/go/pine/tech&emergmgmt_2e to assess your knowledge of cyber security.
(Determine where you need to concentrate your effort.)

What You'll Learn in This Chapter

▲ How cyber security attacks can have devastating consequences
▲ Why the growth of the Internet has resulted in a greater potential for cyber attacks
▲ The various types of cyber criminals
▲ Different avenues for cyber attacks
▲ Categorizations of malware
▲ Five mechanisms for cyber defense
▲ Mechanisms for data security
▲ Steps to recover from a cyber attack

After Studying This Chapter, You'll Be Able To

▲ Explain why the implementation of the Internet of Things (IoT) concept has increased the risk of cyber attacks.
▲ Explain the difference between a state-sponsored cyber criminal, hacktivist, and individual threat actor.
▲ Explain what an attack vector is.
▲ Compare the various types of attack vectors.
▲ Distinguish between malware according to how it propagates.
▲ Describe the different types of malware payloads.
▲ Explain the top five mechanisms for cyber defense.
▲ Describe methods for keeping data secure.
▲ Describe the steps to recover from a cyber attack.

Technology and Emergency Management, Second Edition. John C. Pine.
© 2018 John Wiley & Sons, Inc. Published 2018 by John Wiley & Sons, Inc.
Companion website: www.wiley.com/go/pine/tech&emergmgmt_2e

Goals and Outcomes

▲ Understand the importance of keeping the software on your computer up to date

▲ Understand the risks of visiting malicious Web sites and opening malicious e-mail attachments

▲ Be able to inform your organization of simple measures for cyber defense and data security

INTRODUCTION

A developed country's computer networks are now critical resources needed for daily life. An attack on a nation's computing infrastructure can damage the economy, threaten security, and put lives at risk. Indeed, an attack on key computer systems can potentially be as damaging as a natural disaster. In addition, emergency managers rely on computer networks to share information and coordinate and implement response and recovery activities. Any damage to computer networks, whether caused by a natural disaster or a cyber attack, can hinder the efforts of emergency personnel. Thus, it is imperative that organizations integrate cyber security awareness into their emergency management plans. In particular, organizations need plans to:

▲ prevent unauthorized access to computer systems,
▲ detect when unauthorized access is attempted,
▲ keep data secure, and
▲ recover from attacks.

The attacks that have occurred demonstrate the potential for devastating consequences:

▲ On March 10, 1997, a teenaged hacker broke into a Bell Atlantic computer system, causing a crash that disabled the phone system at the local Worcester, Massachusetts, airport. The crash disabled the phone service at the airport control tower, airport security, the airport fire department, the weather service, and the carriers that use the airport. In addition, the tower's main radio transmitter and another transmitter that activates runway lights were disabled, as well as a printer that controllers use to monitor flight progress. Although no accidents or close calls resulted from the outage, the area manager for the airport's air traffic control company, Joseph Hogan, stated "We dodged a bullet that day" (Thomas, 1998).

▲ In 2000, Australian Vitek Boden hacked into the Maroochy Shire, Queensland, computerized waste management system and caused millions of liters of raw sewage to spill out into local parks and rivers polluting the environment and killing marine life. Boden who was an employee of the company that had installed the waste management system conducted a series of electronic attacks on the Maroochy Shire sewage control system after a rejected job application (Smith, 2001).

▲ In 2003, CSX Corporation, the third-largest railroad company in North America, temporarily stopped service after its control systems were attacked by the Sobig computer virus. The virus disrupted the telecommunications network upon which the signaling and dispatching systems rely. When the virus was discovered, the company curtailed rail service throughout the CSX network. CSX operates about 1600 trains a day. The computer systems were disabled for about 8 hours (Guth and Machalaba, 2003).

▲ In 2006, traffic engineers Gabriel Murillo and Kartik Patel hacked into the LA traffic control system slowing traffic at key intersections as part of a labor protest. The engineers programmed the signals so that red lights would be extremely long on the most congested approaches to the intersections, causing gridlock. Fortunately, no accidents occurred as a result (Grad, 2009).

▲ In 2008, a teenager in Lodz, Poland, modified a TV remote control so that it could be used to control wireless switch junctions on the city's tram system. According to Miroslaw Micor, a spokesman for the Lodz police, the teenager "studied the trams and the tracks for a long time and then built a device that looked like a TV remote control and used it to maneuver the trams and the track." Four trams were derailed, and others had to make emergency stops that left passengers hurt. Twelve people were injured in one of the incidents (Leyden, 2008).

▲ In 2015, cyber attacks were responsible for plunging 80 000 homes in the Ivano-Frankivsk region of Ukraine into darkness. These were the first cyber attacks known to be coordinated to cause power outages. The cause of that outage was Black Energy malware that was delivered via a Microsoft Office attachment to specifically targeted e-mails. This malware allowed attackers to gain control of the grid's industrial control systems (ICSs) and supervisory control and data acquisition (SCADA) components. Power was restored after power companies switched to manual operation (Jennings, 2016).

In recent years, due to the growth of the Internet and the implementation of the idea known as the Internet of Things (IoT), ICSs have become more susceptible to cyber attacks. The IoT is the idea that anything can be connected to the Internet. Specifically, IoT is the combination of billions of IP (Internet protocol)-enabled devices, Radio-Frequency Identification (RFID) tags, wireless sensor networks, mobile apps, and cloud computing. Expanding a control system network by increasing the number of sensor and controller nodes and making that network accessible via the Internet raises the number of ways in which that network can be attacked.

Because of the increased threat of cyber attack, emergency management agencies and industries are looking for graduates with cyber security and emergency management experience (Clement, 2011). This chapter provides an overview of cyber security topics: who is performing cyber attacks, how they are performed, categories of malware, recommendations for keeping a cyber systems and data secure, and how to recover from a cyber attack. Although the material in this chapter won't make you a cyber security expert, you will develop a better understanding of cyber security issues and how to defend against cyber attacks.

3.1 Sources of Attacks

All sources of attacks are ultimately human. The attack may be automated, for example, a worm can spread without human interaction, but it takes a human to implement and initiate the attack before it can spread on its own. The cyber criminals posing the greatest risk can be grouped into three broad categories: state-sponsored threat actors, hacktivists, and individual threat actors (Holland, 2016).

State-sponsored or **nation-state cyber criminals** are those performing the cyber attack with the support of their government. Hostile governments initiate these attacks to steal intellectual property, gain access to military intelligence, or otherwise harm a rival nation. In recent years, a number of countries have announced their intent to launch cyber offensive attacks. These include the United States, China, the United Kingdom, Israel, North Korean, Iran, and Russia. Typically these attacks are performed after weeks of researching the target organization and multiple methods are used. Often the attack is initiated by sending personalized e-mails to executives in the organization with an attachment of interest that is carrying malware.

A **hacktivist** performs an attack to promote a social or political agenda. One well-known hacktivist is Aaron Swartz who downloaded millions of documents from the scholarly database JSTOR. Swartz was a supporter of Open Access, which is the belief that research should be available free online and without restriction. Swartz was charged with numerous federal crimes, including wire fraud, computer fraud, and unlawfully obtaining information from a protected computer. Facing potential incarceration for alleged criminal offenses for which the victims, MIT and JSTOR, declined to pursue civil litigation, Swartz died by committing suicide on January 11, 2013.

Another well-known hacktivist organization is Anonymous. Anonymous is a decentralized organization that uses illegal or legal digital tools in the pursuit of political ends. Anonymous has performed numerous cyber attacks including a distributed denial of service attack (DDoS) against PayPal for terminating the WikiLeaks donation account as well as many attacks that have targeted the Web sites of organizations and individuals (Bay Area Rapid Transit, Donald Trump, ISIS, HBGarry security firm, US Department of Justice, and others).

Individual threat actors commit cyber crimes for sport or financial gain. In fact most cyber attacks are committed for financial reasons. The 2016 Data

Breach Investigations Report provided by Verizon indicates that 80% of the investigated cyber crimes in 2015 were committed for money. Espionage is a distant second at about 10%. The other reasons were "Fun," "Ideology," and "Grudge" (Verizon, 2016).

3.2 Attack Vectors

The original source of a cyber attack is always a human. Beyond that, a cyber attack is enabled by a tool or avenue that opens up the target to a cyber attack. The path or means by which an attacker can gain access to a computer or network in order to initiate the cyber attack is known as the **attack vector**. This section describes the majority of the documented attack vectors employed in 2015 (Verizon, 2016).

3.2.1 Vulnerabilities

A software vulnerability is a flaw in software that allows a cyber attacker to execute exploit code. Typically, the exploit code installs malware in some location on the target machine. One example of a software vulnerability is buffer overflow. Input to a program is stored in a holding location, called a buffer. If more input is provided than the buffer can hold, an overflow can occur overwriting important pieces of the executing program. Cyber attackers can use this to their advantage to cause exploit code to be executed. The Verizon study reported that really old, known vulnerabilities continue to be exploited. This indicates that computer users are often not diligent about applying software patches that would repair vulnerabilities like buffer overflow.

3.2.2 Phishing

A **phishing** attack involves duping an individual to click on a link within an e-mail or opening an attached document. This action could then cause malware to be installed or the link could lead to a site that requests private information. **Spear phishing** is a more sophisticated form of phishing in which the e-mail appears to have come from a known and trusted associate. The e-mail is spoofed so that the e-mail header makes it appear as if the e-mail is from a trusted source rather than the attacker. A spear phishing attack is typically preceded by reconnaissance of the organization to be attacked. The attacker may precede the spear phishing attack by pretexting, which involves presenting oneself as someone else in order to obtain useful information. This information can then be used to manipulate the recipient into falling for the spear phishing attack.

Phishing attacks can be very effective. The Verizon study reports that 30% of recipients open phishing messages and 12% open the attachment or click on the link. Phishing attacks also happen very quickly. The median time for opening the malicious e-mail is 1 minute, 40 seconds. The median time to open the attachment or click on the link is 3 minutes, 45 seconds (Verizon, 2016).

3.2.3 Stolen Credentials

Another avenue used by cyber criminals to gain access to a computer system is to steal the credentials (username and password) needed to do so. One way to steal credentials is to guess the password, which is why users are encouraged to create long passwords with special characters. Hardware devices (e.g., a Wi-Fi router) often arrive with a default password, which can be an avenue for an attack if not changed. In addition, malware software can collect credentials by recording keystrokes. The Verizon study reported that 63% of data breaches involved weak, default, or stolen passwords.

3.2.4 Web Applications

Visiting a Web site can expose a user to malware. For example, the Web site may trick a user into downloading malware while the user believes the download is some desired software or document. Or it is possible that a Web site is a spoof of a legitimate Web site frequented by the user and thus trick the user into entering private information.

A more sophisticated attack is known as a **drive-by download** in which malware is downloaded by simply visiting a Web site. Specifically, visiting the Web site causes exploit code to be executed, which downloads the malware to the user's computer. The Web site itself is typically not actually hosted by the cyber criminal. Instead, cyber criminals find Web sites that have vulnerabilities and exploit those vulnerabilities to enable the cyber attack. For example, most Web sites use scripts to make the page interactive. The script is automatically executed when the page is loaded into the browser. If the Web site allows visitors to enter comments that are viewed by other visitors, the cyber criminal could enter a script containing exploit code as a comment that is then executed when someone else views the page containing the embedded comment. For example, the attacker could enter something like what is given here as a comment on the vulnerable Web site.

```
<script>downloadMalware();</script>
```

When another visitor views the comment, the function "downloadMalware" is executed thus infecting their machine. This particular attack is known as **cross-site scripting (XSS)**.

In general, a Web application can be used as an attack vector if it contains vulnerabilities that open it up for exploitation. For example, the XSS attack described in the last paragraph would not be possible if the Web application checked the user's input. Another common attack that exploits vulnerabilities in a Web application is known as Structured Query Language (**SQL**) **injection**. In this type of attack, the cyber criminal provides input via a Web site that is used to access an SQL database. A database stores data. For example, a database maintained by an e-commerce Web site could hold customer names, usernames, addresses, passwords, and credit card information. If the Web application doesn't validate the user input, the cyber criminal could provide input that deletes or retrieves the entire contents of the database. For example, suppose a visitor provides a username to a

Web application that is then used to access a database table. The statement that builds the query that is used to access that table could be something like this:

`"SELECT * FROM TABLE WHERE ID ="+uname`

where uname represents the username entered by the Web site visitor. The * is a wildcard that is used to grab all of the rows in the database table where ID is equal to the provided username. If the visitor enters a valid username, such as *smithcd*, then the query that is built is something like this:

`"SELECT * FROM TABLE WHERE ID=smithcd"`

In this case, all is good and the query will return all of the rows in the table where ID is equal to *smithcd*. However, if the visitor enters *hacked OR 1=1* as the username then the query that is built is this:

`"SELECT * FROM TABLE WHERE ID=hacked OR 1=1"`

This query grabs the rows from the database table where either the ID is equal to hacked or 1 is equal to 1. Since 1 is equal to 1 is always true, the query will grab all of the rows in the table. This attack would not be possible if the Web application checked the user input and recognized that a username of *hacked OR 1=1* is not a valid one. Thus, the hack is possible because of a vulnerability in the Web site.

3.2.5 Point of Sale Intrusions

A **point of sale (POS) device** is an electronic device used to process credit cards or debit cards at retail locations. Connected to the device is a POS reader that is used to read magnetic strip data or Europay, MasterCard, and Visa (EMV) chip data. These devices are popular targets for cyber criminals to obtain credit card information. There are two methods for obtaining that information that don't require physical access to the POS device. One method is to access the POS server, which is the computer system that holds customer information and is used to verify customer purchases and credit card information. In the past, the POS server was a common target for a "smash and grab" attack in which a cyber criminal would install malware on the server that would grab credit card information as it was processed. This attack was effective because the POS server is visible to the Internet and the POS server software would come with a default login that was then exploited by the criminal.

A second method for obtaining credit card information is to install malware directly on the POS device. In small businesses, the POS device may simply be a tablet that is used both for processing payments and for reading e-mail or checking social media. These extra uses introduce the risk of malware being installed on the device that obtains the credit card information as it is being scanned and sends it to the cyber criminal. A dedicated computer would help reduce this vulnerability.

3.2.6 Payment Card Skimmers

A **payment card skimmer** is a hardware approach to attacking POS and ATM devices. The payment card skimmer reads the magnetic strip data when the card is swiped and stores the information on the skimmer. In order for this to be effective, the bad guy needs to have physical access to the device both to install the skimmer and to later retrieve the skimmer. The recent shift to EMV chip technology is in response to the ease of hacking magnetic strips. EMV chip technology is harder to hack, but not impossible. In 2011 and 2012, five French citizens were able to use stolen cards with EMV chip technologies to steal about $680 000 by modifying the stolen cards to circumvent the PIN number requirement. Specifically, the cyber criminals inserted a second chip in the card that accepts any PIN number. After inserting the card, the original EMV chip responds to the authentication request. When a PIN number is entered (any PIN number), the second chip responds to indicate the PIN is correct. This type of attack is known as a **Man in the Middle attack**. In this case, the second chip is between the first chip and the POS device (Jain, 2015).

3.2.7 Insider and Privilege Misuse

An employee who has access to sensitive data or privileged access to computer systems can commit or enable a cyber attack. For example, an employee could deliberately install malware or download sensitive data onto a USB drive.

3.2.8 Physical Theft and Loss

Laptops, cell phones, tablets, USB drives, and so on, are regularly lost or stolen. Typically, it is easy to bypass the protection of the password on those devices gaining access to personal information such as accounts and passwords. The best way to protect private information on these devices is to encrypt the device's drive and removable media.

3.2.9 Denial of Service Attacks

A **denial of service (DoS) attack** overwhelms computing systems so that legitimate users will be unable to use the system. For example, when you type a URL into a Web browser, you cause a request to be sent to a Web server. A Web server can only handle a finite number of requests before it begins to respond slowly or not at all. A typical DoS service is to send a flood of requests to a Web server that will disable its ability to respond to a legitimate user. A DDoS attack uses multiple computers to launch the attack. Malware installed on the computers sends requests to the target machine.

3.3 Overview of Malware

Malware is an abbreviation for malicious software. Most of the attack vectors described in the last section utilized some form of malware; thus malware is arguably one of the most significant threats to computer systems. Specifically, malware is software designed to somehow disrupt a computer, for example, disable activities, steal information or money, participate in a DoS attack, propagate, destroy information, or simply annoy the user by popping up ads. Two methods of categorizing malware are by how the malware propagates and by what actions the malware takes (Stallings and Brown, 2012).

3.3.1 Malware Propagation

How does malware spread to reach desired targets? This section categories malware according to how it spreads; however, keep in mind that malware can utilize more than one propagation technique to increase its ability to spread.

Viruses

A computer **virus** is malware that infects another program by modifying it. A typical modification of the host program is to add code that copies the virus to other programs or onto certain areas of a computer's disk. The copy is not necessarily identical to the original version. Like a biological virus, the computer virus morphs, usually to avoid detection. When the host program is executed, the virus code is also executed with the same privileges as the host program. For example, if the host program executes with the privileges of the system administrator then the virus executes with those same privileges and can thus wreak significant damage, for example, deleting files. Some viruses destroy the host program altogether by rewriting the host program with a copy of itself. A virus requires the assistance of a human to activate; specifically, a human must execute the program that the virus has infected.

Worms

Like a virus, a **worm** also replicates when it is executed. However, unlike a virus, a worm does not require human involvement to replicate and is not part of a host program. Instead, a worm spreads by exploiting a vulnerability in the host system. Because worms spread without a human's assistance, a worm can be much more damaging than a virus. For example, a worm may e-mail a copy of itself to everyone on the computer user's e-mail contact list. When those contacts open the attached worm, it executes and spreads. Or, a worm could use the file transfer software on a computer to transfer itself to another system.

Trojan

A **Trojan** is malware that looks legitimate. It doesn't spread on its own but rather via a social engineering attack where a user is tricked into executing the malware. For example, unsolicited junk e-mail known as spam e-mail may contain an attachment that when opened installs malware on the user's system. Or, a computer game or another application downloaded from a malicious Web site could contain a Trojan. Unlike viruses and worms, Trojans do not replicate when executed. Instead, when the user executes the software containing the Trojan, the malware "payload" is executed that begins the cyber attack.

3.3.2 Malware Payload

A second categorization of malware is by the harmful action that the malware takes. This is called the **payload**. It is possible that the malware carries no payload and the only thing it does is spread. More often the malware carries one or more payloads that damage data or steal information or money.

System Corruption

Some malware damages the data and/or programs on the host computer, sometimes for financial gain. For example, **ransomware** is malware that encrypts user's data and demands payment for the key that can be used to unencrypt it. Malware that deletes data or overwrites the BIOS code also falls in this category. The BIOS code is used to initially start up the computer; thus overwriting this code can make the computer unusable.

FOR EXAMPLE

In January 2003, the Slammer worm shut down the safety monitoring system at the Davis-Besse nuclear power plant in Ohio for nearly 5 hours. The Slammer worm entered via an unsecured network of a Davis-Besse contractor and then through a T1 (high-speed dedicated line) line to the Davis-Besse corporate network. The T1 line was used to access the business network without going through the plant's firewall that would have blocked the Slammer virus. From the business network, the Slammer worm was able to spread to the plant network.

The worm exploited a vulnerability in Microsoft's SQL Server software. Once a machine was infected, it would scan additional machines to infect by randomly generating IP addresses and transmitting packets over the network to those IP addresses. The packets identified port number 1434, which is the port that the SQL Server software used to receive data. If the server software was not patched (as was the case for the David-Besse plant network), the target host would be infected. The worm itself did not contain a malicious payload. However, the amount of scanning performed by the worm to seek additional machines to infect created more congestion then the network could handle; thus the worm essentially performed a DoS attack.

At the David-Besse plant network, the congestion created by the worm crashed the Safety Parameter Display System, which is the plant's display panel used for monitoring the most critical safety indicators, that is, the coolant systems, the core temperature systems, and the external radiation sensors. Fortunately, the attack did not pose a safety hazard because operations had been suspended months earlier due to a hole in a reactor head. In addition, the monitoring system had an analog backup that wasn't impacted by the worm. However, the case does indicate a growing cyber security problem where the interconnection of networks, in this case a plant network and a business network, can expose critical control and safety systems to cyber threats (Moore et al., 2003; Poulsen, 2003).

Zombies and Bots

A **zombie or bot** is malware that uses the host machine to participate in cyber attacks. For example, a bot may participate in a DDoS attack, send spam e-mail, spread malware, manipulate online polls and games, and so on.

Information Theft

Keyloggers and spyware are malware that capture information while the computer is being used. **Keylogger** malware captures keystrokes, specifically looking for keystrokes that correspond to usernames and passwords. **Spyware** captures information about how the host machine is being used such as what Web pages are being visited. In addition, spyware can cause some page requests to be redirected so that instead of displaying the page the user intended such as a banking page, a similar page is displayed that can be used to obtain private account information. When using a Web browser, remember to check the URL in the address bar to make sure you are visiting the site you intended!

Rootkits

A **rootkit** is a set of programs that allow a cyber criminal access to the computer on which they are running. Using the rootkit, a cyber criminal could potentially view the contents of any files on the machine, run programs, delete and modify files, create and delete accounts, send and receive data from the network, in general, do anything that the system administrator could do. In addition, rootkits are designed to be invisible, for example, by modifying the operating system program that displays what programs are running to not display the rootkit programs.

3.4 Securing Cyber Systems

All four phases of emergency management are supported by the cyber infrastructure, that is, the computer hardware and software that process, store, and communicate information. Mitigation and preparedness can be supported by the use of software to predict and model disasters. Communication networks are vital for the phases of response and recovery. Emergency personnel rely on communication software and hardware to ensure that resources are deployed to the correct location when they are needed. Thus, it is important that emergency management agencies can protect their own cyber systems. This section discusses the five top mechanisms (what they call "Foundational Cyber Hygiene") recommended by the Center for Internet Security for effective cyber defense (https://www.cisecurity.org/critical-controls.cfm).

It is becoming increasingly common for employees to bring their own devices (laptops, smartphones, USB drives, etc.) to their workplaces and connect them to the company network. An organization's system administrator may be very diligent at making sure that patches and security updates are applied to the internal computing systems. However, this diligence doesn't necessarily extend to the devices of employees. If these devices are compromised by malware, then connecting them to the network can introduce that malware to the company's cyber infrastructure. Thus, the top security control is to *maintain an inventory of authorized and unauthorized devices*. In other words, organizations need to be aware of what devices are connecting to the company network and that only approved devices are allowed to do so. This effort can be aided by software that regularly scans the network to identify the devices connected to it.

Second, attackers attempt to spread malware through Web pages, documents, media files, and programs. Visiting hostile Web sites, downloading and executing Trojans, opening infected documents are all activities that can compromise a computer system. Once a single machine on a network is compromised, the malware can spread to other computers on the network. Computers that are particularly vulnerable are those that are running software that is not up to date. Thus, another security control is to *maintain an inventory of authorized and unauthorized software*. Only authorized (whitelisted) software known to be secure can be executed. Unauthorized (blacklisted) software should be prevented from being installed.

Whitelisting tools can be used to keep an inventory of the applications and ensure that the installed programs are the most secure versions. These whitelisting tools are typically bundled with other tools to support cyber security. Anti-virus and anti-spyware software detects and removes malware by looking for patterns on the computer that indicate the presence of malware. It is important to keep this software up to date since software vendors find new malware regularly. **Firewall** software keeps damaging elements off a computer or network by looking for specific types of network packets that should be blocked. **Intrusion Detection Systems (IDSs)** monitor the network for malicious activity while **Intrusion Prevention Systems (IPSs)** monitor as well as attempt to block the attack. For example, an IDS may detect that a user is logged onto the computer system at odd hours or multiple times or that a large amount of data is being transmitted to a remote site. These activities could indicate that the system has been compromised.

Computing devices are delivered in a default state with a fixed set of software, open ports for network traffic, and default accounts with default passwords. This default state can make the device vulnerable. Thus to make these devices secure, a strong initial configuration must be developed and installed. Thus, the third recommended security control is to provide *secure configurations for hardware and software on mobile devices, laptops, workstations, and servers*. Resources are available for organizations needing to develop secure configurations for their systems including securing benchmarks developed by the Center for Internet Security (https://benchmarks.cisecurity.org) and the National Checklist Program sponsored by the US National Institute of Standards and Technology (http://www.nist.gov/itl/csd/scm/ncp.cfm).

The cyber infrastructure is in a constant state of change. New software and software updates are being deployed, vulnerabilities in existing software and devices are being discovered, and new hardware devices are being used to connect to computer networks. Security analysts are discovering vulnerabilities in the software and vendors are developing patches. Information about vulnerabilities is available to both users and cyber attackers simultaneously. There is a continual race between users to protect against the exploitation of vulnerabilities and cyber attackers to design and deploy malware that exploits vulnerabilities. Thus, the fourth recommended security control is to perform *continuous vulnerability assessment and remediation*. A large number of tools are available that can scan for vulnerabilities, determine what software needs to be updated, and apply patches.

Administrative (i.e., *super*) users have a lot more power on a computer system than regular users. Administrators can create accounts, delete accounts, change passwords, access and delete any files on the machine, and install and execute any software. Some of the potential activities performed by malware can only be performed if the user that begins the execution of the malware has administrative privileges. In addition, some operating systems only allow software to be installed on the machine if the user doing the installing has administrative privileges. This can protect the machine from the installation of malware if, for example, a user is tricked into clicking a link that would normally cause malware to be installed. Attacking those users with administrative privileges can result in much greater damage than attacking users without those privileges. Thus, the fifth recommended security control is the *controlled use of administrative privileges*. In particular, users should have no more privileges than what they need to complete their computing tasks. Administrative accounts should only be used when necessary. In addition, administrators should not use their administrative accounts for performing tasks that can open a system up for attack such as Web surfing or reading e-mail.

Beyond this Foundational Cyber Hygiene, many experts recommend the importance of Security Awareness Training (SAT) given that many cyber attacks are at least partially socially engineered (Mijares, 2015). A social engineering attack involves human interaction, for example, enticing a human to click on a link in an e-mail (i.e., a phishing attack). Social engineering attacks have become increasingly more sophisticated with the rise in social media Web sites. For example, a cyber criminal could create a fake LinkedIn profile as part of a spear phishing attack and send very legitimate looking e-mail with a malicious attachment from the LinkedIn account. The more aware an employee is of these types of attacks, the less likely he or she is to be tricked.

3.5 Securing Data

Organizations typically keep sensitive information about customers and employees in a database that can be accessed by one or more software applications. Examples of the type of information that is stored include:

▲ Name, address, social security number, bank account number, credit card information
▲ Company financial records
▲ Medical records
▲ Product information

In addition, sensitive information is often communicated via e-mail. These e-mail messages are stored on a personal computer and/or the e-mail server. An e-mail server is a machine that receives and delivers e-mail over a network. When you send an e-mail, the message is sent to your e-mail server which then sends the message to the e-mail server of the user identified in the "TO" field. E-mail messages are retrieved from the e-mail server when they are read, but not necessarily deleted from the e-mail server. A cyber criminal may be able to access those e-mails by attacking the e-mail server or by attacking the machine used to read the e-mail.

Data security refers to protecting data from unauthorized access and from corruption. Many cyber attacks are performed specifically with the goal of accessing protected data and these attacks occur regularly. In 2015, 2260 security incidents resulted in data loss, which is 3.5% of all reported incidents with most successful attacks performed on financial institutions (Verizon, 2016).

The foundational cyber hygiene described in the previous section can help keep data secure. Beyond that, experts recommend other techniques specifically for data security (Lord, 2016). Some of these recommendations are:

▲ Developing a data classification policy. Some data is less sensitive than others. Organizations need to determine which data is the most sensitive and if compromised would cause the greatest amount of risk.

▲ Encrypting sensitive data before sending it over an untrusted network. **Encryption** involves converting the data into an unreadable form using a key that is also needed for decryption. If the data is sent over an untrusted network, cyber criminals may be able to read the data during transit. However, if the data is encrypted using a secure encryption algorithm and the key needed for decryption is not available to the cyber criminal, the cyber criminal will be long dead before being successful at guessing the key and decrypting.

▲ Encrypting data stored in the cloud. Data that is stored in the cloud is in the hands of another organization. Sensitive data needs to be encrypted before uploading it to the cloud.

▲ Limiting access to internal data. Edward Snowden was able to download sensitive data onto a thumb drive (from his office computer) because nothing was in place to prevent that. Organizations cannot "minimize the human dimension of security" (Lord, 2016).

▲ Performing regular backups and verifying that the backups are viable. A **backup** is a second copy of the data. If the data is damaged by a cyber attack or hardware failure, a backup will enable the data to be restored.

▲ Storing passwords as a hash. A **hash** is the transformation of a string into another value. The process that creates the hash is called **hashing**. Unlike encryption, a hash is one-way; that is, a hash can be created from a string such as a password, but the hash cannot be used to obtain the string. Thus, hashing can be used for passwords. The password entered by the user can be hashed and that hash can be compared to the hash stored in the database. Storing a password as a hash will prevent a cyber criminal from accessing a user account if a data breach does occur. However, this does not circumvent the need to create secure passwords since weak passwords can be guessed, then hashed, and then compared to the hash in the stolen data. A secure password is at least 16 characters, and contains a combination of numbers, symbols, uppercase letters, lowercase letters, and spaces. It should not contain usernames, dictionary words, pronouns, known sequences, or be repetitive.

▲ Using a Virtual Private Network (VPN). More employees are accessing corporate data from remote locations with their own devices. Using a VPN to access the data will ensure that the data that is transmitted from corporate servers to employee devices is encrypted.

3.6 Cyber Security Attack Recovery

IDS and IPS software can aid the detection of an ongoing cyber attack. Beyond that, these signs can indicate a cyber attack:

▲ Slow connections to the Internet. This can indicate an ongoing DoS or DDoS attack where a machine on the local network is either being sent an onslaught of requests or running a zombie that is making an onslaught of requests.

▲ Machine that runs slower than usual, boots up more slowly, or crashes frequently.

▲ An increased number of popups. This can indicate the presence of spyware. You should be particularly leery of popups that ask for personal information.

▲ Browser redirection. The display of a Web site different from the one that you requested can also indicate the presence of spyware.

▲ Files and folders that can no longer be accessed; the appearance of new files, folders, and icons; software that no longer runs properly. This can indicate that malware has corrupted your system.

After the attack has been detected, what steps should be taken to recover? Specific tasks will depend upon the type of cyber attack and the severity of the attack. If the cyber attack is significant in that it impacts a large number of victims or critical infrastructure, the attack should be reported to law enforcement. Otherwise, a local incident response team should handle the cyber attack by:

▲ Determining the origin and the type of the attack. How many machines are involved? Has a data breech occurred? Anything that is discovered needs to be carefully logged so that the vulnerabilities that enabled the attack can be repaired. It may be necessary to create an image (an exact copy) of storage devices to allow the cyber attack to be studied further at a later point. This can also provide evidence at a later trial if needed.

▲ Minimizing additional damage. Disconnect infected machines from the network to prevent the attack from spreading. Configure the firewall to block network traffic that is the result of a DoS attack.

▲ Changing all passwords. The cyber attack could result from the cyber criminal gaining unauthorized access. Changing all of the passwords, including those on routers, can prevent further access.

▲ Updating anti-spyware, anti-virus, IDS, and IPS software and applying security patches to application and operating system software. It may be necessary to reinstall a clean version of the operating system.

▲ Conducting a vulnerability scan before reconnecting the impacted systems to the network. Vulnerability scanning software assesses computers, networks, and software for weaknesses.

SUMMARY

We are headed toward a ubiquitous cyber infrastructure that extends into every household, business, and government organization. Everyday devices from laptops to lighting can connect to the Internet. Unfortunately, a ubiquitous cyber infrastructure introduces more means for cyber attacks and no country is cyber-ready. Cyber attacks can simply be an inconvenience that requires the replacement of a credit card or can place lives in danger. This chapter provided an introduction to cyber security that provides insight into how to keep cyber systems secure.

KEY TERMS

Attack vector	Avenue used by a cyber criminal to gain access to a machine.
Backup	A backup is a copy of the files and folders on the storage device.
Cross-site scripting (XSS)	Technique for enabling a drive-by download that involves injecting script code into a Web site that is automatically executed when the Web site is visited.
Denial of service attack	Cyber attack that involves overwhelming a computer system so that it is unable to respond to legitimate traffic.
Drive-by download	Cyber attack in which malware is installed on a machine while it is used to visit a Web site.
Encryption	Technique that takes a string and a key and generates an equivalent value. Encryption is two-way in that the original input can be regenerated using a decryption algorithm and the key.
Firewall	Software and/or hardware that blocks unauthorized access to a computer network.
Hacktivist	Someone who performs a cyber attack to achieve a political or social agenda.

Hashing	Technique that takes a string such as a password and generates an equivalent value. Hashing is one-way in that the hash that is created cannot be used to recreate the original string.
Individual threat actor	Someone who performs a cyber attack for sport or financial gain.
Intrusion detection system	Software and/or hardware that monitors a computer network for malicious activity.
Intrusion prevention system	Software and/or hardware that monitors and blocks a computer network from malicious activity.
Keylogger	Malware that records keys as they are being typed.
Man in the middle attack	Attack in which a device in the middle of two other parties supplies communication in a way that the two parties believe they are communicating with each other.
Nation-state cyber criminal	Someone who performs cyber attacks with the support of his or her government.
Payload	The harmful action performed by malware.
Payment card skimmer	Device that attaches to a point of sale device or ATM card reader that reads the credit card information stored in the magnetic strip.
Phishing	Technique of tricking someone to click on a link or open an e-mail attachment that then provides the means for the cyber attack.
Point of sale (POS) device	Device that can be used to scan a credit card.
Ransomware	Malware payload that encrypts users' data and demands payment for the key that can be used to decrypt it.
Rootkit	Malware that is a set of tools which enable an unauthorized user to gain control of a computer system without being detected.
Spear phishing	A very targeted phishing attack in which the cyber criminal attempts to learn about and establish a relationship with the target so that the phishing attack is more likely to succeed.
Spyware	Malware that records how a machine is being used, for example, what Web pages are being visited.
SQL injection	Technique for accessing an SQL database in which unchecked user input is used as part of an SQL query to obtain invalid access to the database.
Trojan	Malware that is hidden inside an apparently legitimate computer program.

Virus	Malware that infects a program by modifying it and propagates when the program is executed.
Worm	Malware that propagates on its own, for example, by transmitting itself to other computer systems.
Zombie, bot	Malware that works with other zombies to perform a cyber attack.

ASSESS YOUR UNDERSTANDING

Go to www.wiley.com/go/pine/tech&emergmgmt_2e to evaluate your knowledge of using technology. This website contains MCQ's, self checks, review questions, applying this chapter and you try it.

References

Clement, K. E. (2011). The essentials of emergency management and homeland security graduate education programs: Design, development, and future. *Journal of Homeland Security and Emergency Management*, 8(2), ISSN (Online) 1547-7355, DOI: 10.2202/1547-7355.1902.

Grad, S. (2009). Engineers who hacked into L.A. traffic signal computer, jamming streets, sentenced. *L.A. Now*. http://latimesblogs.latimes.com/lanow/2009/12/engineers-who-hacked-in-la-traffic-signal-computers-jamming-traffic-sentenced.html (accessed April 23, 2017).

Guth, R. A. & Machalaba, D. (2003). Computer viruses disrupt railroad and air traffic. *The Wall Street Journal*. http://www.wsj.com/articles/SB106140797740336000 (accessed April 23, 2017).

Holland, J. F. (2016). 3 sources of cyberattacks—and 3 preventive steps government can take (industry perspective). *Government Technology*. http://www.govtech.com/opinion/3-Sources-of-Cyberattacks-and-3-Preventive-Steps-Government-Can-Take.html (accessed April 23, 2017).

Jain, K. (2015). How hackers can hack your chip-and-PIN credit cards. *The Hacker News*. http://thehackernews.com/2015/10/hacking-chip-n-pin-cards.html (accessed April 23, 2017).

Jennings, R. (2016). Ukraine power outage was a cyberattack—U.S. doesn't finger Russia (officially). *Computer World*. http://www.computerworld.com/article/3039772/security/ukraine-power-cyberattack-russia-itbwcw.html (accessed April 23, 2017).

Leyden, J. (2008). Polish teen derails tram after hacking train network: Turns city network into Hornby set. *The Register*. http://www.theregister.co.uk/2008/01/11/tram_hack/ (accessed April 23, 2017).

Lord, N. (2016). Sensitive data: 34 experts reveal the biggest mistakes companies make with data security. *Digital Guardian*. https://digitalguardian.com/blog/

expert-guide-securing-sensitive-data-34-experts-reveal-biggest-mistakes-companies-make-data (accessed April 23, 2017).

Mijares, A. (2015). Social engineering: Employees could be your weakest link. *Computer World.* http://www.computerworld.com/article/2996606/cybercrime-hacking/social-engineering-employees-could-be-your-weakest-link.html (accessed April 23, 2017).

Moore, D., Paxson, V., Savage, S., Shannon, C., Staniford, S., & Weaver, N. (2003). Inside the slammer worm. *IEEE Security & Privacy, 1*(4), 33–39.

Poulsen, K. (2003). Slammer worm crashed Ohio nuke plant network. *Security Focus.* http://www.securityfocus.com/news/6767 (accessed April 23, 2017).

Smith, T. (2001). Hacker jailed for revenge sewage attacks: Job rejection caused a bit of a stink. *The Register.* http://www.theregister.co.uk/2001/10/31/hacker_jailed_for_revenge_sewage/ (accessed April 23, 2017).

Stallings, W. & Brown, L. (2012). *Computer Security: Principles and Practice,* 2nd ed. Upper Saddle River, NJ: Pearson Education, Inc.

Thomas, P. (1998). Teen hacker faces federal charges: Caused computer crash that disabled Massachusetts airport. *CNN Interactive.* http://www.cnn.com/TECH/computing/9803/18/juvenile.hacker/index.html?eref=sitesearch (accessed April 23, 2017).

Verizon. (2016). Verizon 2016 Data Breach Investigations Report. http://www.verizonenterprise.com/verizon-insights-lab/dbir/2016/ (accessed April 23, 2017).

4

SOCIAL MEDIA AND EMERGENCY MANAGEMENT

Josh Kastrinsky

Coastal Resilience Center of Excellence, University of North Carolina at Chapel Hill, Chapel Hill, NC, USA

Starting Point

Go to www.wiley.com/go/pine/tech&emergmgmt_2e to assess your knowledge of warning systems.
Determine where to concentrate your effort.

What You'll Learn in This Chapter

▲ What social media is and how it has evolved
▲ How social media and mass media differ
▲ What a disaster is and how social media has shaped in response to it
▲ How social media is used to prepare for mass emergencies
▲ How social media has been used to communicate during and after events
▲ What concerns are there about the use of social media to coordinate disaster response

After Studying This Chapter, You'll Be Able To

▲ Identify different types of social media used in disasters.
▲ Understand how social media usage patterns during events have changed over time.
▲ Understand how the model of interaction between emergency officials and the public has changed over time.

Goals and Outcomes

▲ Understand how emergency managers interact with the public during disasters
▲ Understand how crowdsourced information has altered situational awareness during disasters

Technology and Emergency Management, Second Edition. John C. Pine.
© 2018 John Wiley & Sons, Inc. Published 2018 by John Wiley & Sons, Inc.
Companion website: www.wiley.com/go/pine/tech&emergmgmt_2e

INTRODUCTION

Technology grows and changes rapidly. Tools that did not exist even 5 years ago are now primary modes of communication for millions of individuals. So said Craig Fugate, Administrator of the Federal Emergency Management Agency (FEMA), in a 2011 speech to the US Senate's Committee on Homeland Security and Government Affairs (Lieberman, 2011).

Digital tools such as *YouTube*, Facebook, *Twitter*, and others were not created for the purpose of preparing for, responding to, or recovering from emergencies and disasters, Fugate said. However, "our success in fulfilling our mission at FEMA is highly dependent upon our ability to communicate with the individuals, families and communities we serve. For that reason, social media is extremely valuable to the work we do, and we are fortunate to have partners in the social media community with us here today who see the value of using these tools to increase public safety" (Lieberman, 2011).

This statement is emblematic of a sea change in how emergency managers view the role of social media in disaster events. As **social networking** tools have changed over the last 15–20 years, first responders and government agencies have modified their views on digital communication—and on the public's role in responding to natural hazards and other disaster events. Long known for the command-and-control style of reporting and action, emergency managers have begun utilizing the public's ability to communicate information from nearly anywhere to people nearly everywhere as part of emergency response. The public is treated as more of a resource than a liability (Lieberman, 2011).

Rather than trying to convince the public to adjust to the way FEMA communicates, Fugate said, the agency must adapt to the way the public communicates by leveraging the tools they use on a daily basis. By viewing them as a powerful, self-organizing, and "collectively intelligent" force, **information and communication technology (ICT)**, including social media, can play a transformational role in crisis events (Palen et al., 2010). Viewing a civil society that can be improved by ICT is based on social and behavioral knowledge about how people respond to disasters, rather than on simplified and mythical portrayals of people unable to help themselves.

4.1 Situational Awareness, Emergency Communications, and the Public Realm

Fugate's message was that social media provides the tools needed to minimize the communication gap between first responders and the public, and to participate in an active, ongoing dialogue. Fugate stressed that the public should be able to easily communicate with emergency managers, to act as the "'first' first responders" (Lieberman, 2011). The sooner emergency managers are able to ascertain the on-the-ground reality of a situation, the better they are able to coordinate response efforts.

By leveraging the public's **collective intelligence**, emergency authorities could better understand "the big picture"—better known as **situational awareness** during critical situations—and thus make the best, most informed decisions possible for deploying aid and rescue and recovery operations (Yin et al., 2012). Social media's emergence as a part of everyday life, along with the wide availability and ubiquity of smartphones, makes it possible for nearly anyone to report on the occurrence of hazards. These same people can report on location of evacuation centers and road closures, orchestrate fundraising and volunteering opportunities, and identify the location and safety of family and friends (Bird et al., 2012).

Bird et al. write that while social media will not replace traditional forms of hazard and risk communication, they provide another useful tool that shares the responsibility of reducing risk, facilitates community involvement, and empowers people to take action.

Nonemergency management personnel are usually the first to respond in any disaster situation affecting their community (Díaz et al., 2013). They rely on existing social structures and authority relationships that they know from daily life. Armed with smartphones, there responders can now become first reporters as well (Hughes, 2012). They seek reliable information using any means possible to optimize for local conditions (Palen et al., 2010).

Researchers have deemed that social networks are important to a community's resilience, the ability to respond to and recover from natural or human-caused disasters. **Interventions**—activities designed to change or improve conditions in a community—are facilitated by community leaders taking advantage of such networks to send and receive information (Magsino, 2009).

Social media can also broaden the reach of conventional media (National Research Council, 2011). They allow a community to leverage the trust that people place in their connections.

A 2002 Congressional statute mandated the federal-level implementation of the **National Incident Management System (NIMS)**, a quasi-military organizational structure built upon the 36-year-old Incident Command System used in wildfire suppression (Palen and Liu, 2007). NIMS is built on a chain-of-command model that divides responsibility of labor and supports interjurisdictional coordination. A quasi-military response to disaster frames disaster as a problem of restoring law and order, not one where the public welfare, health, and community ties need to be restored and maintained, which in large part happens through the very involvement of the public itself.

It is well-established through research that no single system will reach the entire population or be suited for all circumstances (National Research Council, 2011). But, given that many people keep wireless devices within 3 feet of them all the times, social media can be a solution to the problem of reaching large segment of the population.

Social media can, however, complicate the job of emergency managers as easily as it can aid them (National Research Council, 2011). People on the ground may be the source of both the first reports and the most detailed reports (including pictures and video), and can make such information widely available to the public using social media. While government agencies are generally risk-averse, social media provides the opportunity to enhance public relations efforts and capabilities and can improve the public's trust of government response (National Research

Council, 2013b). This requires advance planning, experimenting with various workflows and technologies to perfect the rapid dissemination of information.

4.2 What Is Social Media?

While systems like NIMS are mass media channels, social media is differentiated in one key way: **Social media** is any type of online-based communication that allows for a two-way path of information sharing, and in which communities are established for that sharing. Social media services are generally free and opt-in, while many mass media systems are designed to be opt-out. Mass media reaches people over a defined distance and can be tailored for specific subsets of a population; social media has a broader reach and can be tailored even further (National Research Council, 2011).

Social media, also known as **Social Networking Sites** (SNSs), allow individuals to construct a public or semipublic profile, develop a list of other users, and learn about the network of individuals (White et al., 2009). Part of the wave of changes online that came to be known as Web 2.0, social networks improve resilience within communities and can improve preparedness for disasters (Díaz et al., 2013).

Boyd and Ellison (2007) define social media as "web-based services that allow individuals to (1) construct a public or semi-public profile within a bounded system, (2) articulate a list of other users with whom they share a connection, and (3) view their list of connections and those made by others within the system." The difference between these technologies and other standard forms of ICTs are users are able to make their views, perceptions, and knowledge public via the system. This forms ties with other individuals who may have similar interests, needs, or problems.

Traditional media outlets' work has also been impacted by social media (Hughes, 2012). Traditional print and broadcast media have seen major cutbacks and staff shortages. Often, one member per media outlet is filming scenes, conducting on-camera reports and managing social media, evening the field with citizen responders (Latonero and Shklovski, 2011).

4.2.1 The Birth of Web 2.0

Magsino (2009) points to 2004 being a pivotal date in the role of social media. A new vision for the internet began to take shape during the Web 2.0 Conference in 2004. Web 2.0 represents a culture shift, with the Internet being controlled by users from the bottom and providing an interactive environment that fosters innovation. Users became active participants rather than observers.

Within 4 years, 62% of Americans had used wireless technology; by 2013, the penetration rate had exceeded 100%. (It should be noted that these figures account for each wireless device per person being 100%, meaning ownership of multiple devices per person results in counts above 100%.) A 2015 Pew Research survey found that smartphone penetration was about 65% (Telecoms.com, 2014). The Wireless Association reported more than 290 million cellular phone US subscribers by mid-2010, a greater than 90% penetration rate (National Research Council, 2011).

The first generation of the Internet was centered on personal and organizational Web sites where individuals sought information. Web 2.0 provides technology to support mass collaboration (White et al., 2009).

Citizen journalism, where nonprofessionals contributed to situational awareness during emergencies, helped elevate the role of social media in the public realm. The Indian Ocean tsunami of December 26, 2004, and Hurricane Katrina's landfall on August 29, 2005, spurred the creation of many blogs, use of photo and video sharing and other online venues where people made offers of housing, jobs, and emotional support (Palen and Liu, 2007).

Magsino also noted that a 2008 study found that social networks were most commonly used by people under the age of 25 and, perhaps surprisingly, over the age of 50. Social media can be accessed by computer, tablets, smartphones and cellular phones, and mobile phone text messaging (short message service (SMS)) (Lindsay, 2011). A 2009 study commissioned by the American Red Cross found that social media are also commonly used by individuals and communities to warn others of unsafe areas or situations, inform friends and family that someone is safe, and raise funds for disaster relief.

Palen and Liu (2007) identified three types of information pathways as being predominant in the Web 2.0 era: Communications within the public affected by a crisis; communications between members of the public who are affected by the crisis and those outside of the crisis zone; and communications between **official public information officers** (PIOs) and members of the public. Notably, only one of those three includes official sources of information.

Social media's value is predicated on frequent contributions of small knowledge chunks in various forms that are easy to acquire, share, and use (Yates and Paquette, 2011). People are natural information seekers, and will seek it from multiple sources, relying primarily on their own social networks to validate and interpret information coming from formal sources, and then to calculate their own response measures (Palen et al., 2010).

4.3 Types of Social Media Used in Disasters

Social media are divided into several types, based on the platform and user engagement method. They include

- ▲ *Blogs:* Public messaging platforms such as *WordPress*, *Blogger*, and *Tumblr* that sometimes allow for comments.
- ▲ *Chatrooms/Discussion forums:* Strings of grouped messages, usually involving established accounts.
- ▲ *Wikis:* Web sites that allow people to openly contribute by adding and/or editing content, enable broad participation in the creation and dissemination of information (Palen and Liu, 2007).
- ▲ *Photo channels:* Sites like Flickr where users can tag (provide key words or labels for) photos posted by themselves and others (White et al., 2009).
- ▲ *Video channels:* Examples include YouTube and Vimeo.

▲ *Facebook:* The largest social network, with more than 1.7 billion users. Users create profiles for themselves or organizations and share information by sending messages or posting to a "wall."

▲ *Others:* In the nature of social media, some sites' usage rises and falls within a few years. Examples of formerly widely used networks include *MySpace* and *Bebo.*

▲ *Twitter:* The most-studied social network in regard to disasters. A form of "micro-blogging"—lightweight, mediated communication where users can broadcast short messages to their networks and direct these messages to specific people within networks (Latonero and Shklovski, 2011). Users of Twitter send short (up to 140 characters) messages or "tweet" to their networks of "followers"— people who chose to be updated when the person they "follow" adds a new message to the stream. Twitter users send "tweets" to their followers, and users can also "retweet" or pass along messages originating from others.

Twitter includes search functions so users can search the site for prevalence of key words, phrases, topics, trends, or individuals (Latonero and Shklovski, 2011). Twitter gave individuals the unprecedented ability to rapidly broadcast and exchange small amounts of information with large audiences regardless of distance.

Although Twitter is Internet-based, its primary focus is on integration with mobile/cellular devices, which creates the potential of an alternative communications system apart from traditional telephony, radio, and television. This and other SNSs are accessed with increasing frequency from application programming interfaces, known as APIs.

A 2009 study of Twitter content during a crisis found that message content could be categorized as follows: 37% of the messages provided information (warnings, updates, answers); 34% were commentary; 26% dealt with personal impact or requests for information; and 4% were promotions of available media coverage or products and services (National Research Council, 2011).

Although most people think of Twitter as a social network, it can also be viewed as a full-spectrum media ecosystem (National Research Council, 2013b). One important finding from this work was that a small number of "elite" users were followed by half of all Twitter users.

Approximately half of this information reaches users indirectly. A lot of information did not come directly from the media source but instead indirectly through other accounts, which were labeled opinion leaders by researchers (National Research Council, 2013b). Opinion leaders were consuming much more content than normal users but also tweeting more and had a higher number of followers. These results suggest that many social media users will receive alerts from a nonauthoritative source.

Twitter users may provide personal status updates; inquire about the well-being of others; and ask about road closures and evacuation routes, property damage, sheltering options for people and animals among other inquiries and statements. They may offer support and/or prayer and request monetary and/or material donations (Vieweg, 2012).

4.4 Mass Alert Systems

A mass alert system is not considered a social network under the definitions provided earlier (National Research Council, 2011). The Warning, Alert, and Response Network (WARN) Act of 2006, which established a national all-hazards alert system and calls for the use of multiple technologies, including wireless telecommunications, was motivated in part by a desire to leverage new technologies to increase the reach of existing, one-way alerts and warnings.

The Department of Homeland Security's Commercial Mobile Alert System (CMAS) was developed to issue presidential alerts, imminent threat alerts, and child abduction/America's Missing: Broadcast Emergency Response (AMBER) alerts. Opt-out functionality would not be possible under the planned program. Text was limited (beyond the heading) to 90 characters per message, in contrast to Twitter's 140 message that can also include images and video (National Research Council, 2011). The program is now known as Wireless Emergency Alerts (WEAs).

Less is known about the efficacy of similar SMS systems in disaster situations. SMS are opt-in services provided via mobile phone plans which are used to contact users in local jurisdictions with hyperlocal messaging, though they are subscribed to by a smaller subset of the overall population (National Research Council, 2011).

Cellular broadcast, the means through which WEA operates, offers two principal advantages over SMS. A single broadcast message can reach each active cell phone within range of a given cellular tower, reducing the network capacity required for message delivery compared to that required for sending messages to each subscriber. Because cellular broadcast uses a data channel separate from that used for other messages and calls, it is unaffected by network congestion (National Research Council, 2011).

This is important because cellular networks can become damaged or overloaded in the very crisis situations in which alerts are most needed (National Research Council, 2011). Another advantage of cellular broadcast over SMS is that, because messages can be localized to cellular towers, alerts can be geographically targeted, and targeted by actual subscriber location rather than by telephone area code or home service area. In the case of WEA, this capability is to be used to localize messages by county or equivalent jurisdiction—"immunity to network connection"; it does not include URLs because of concerns about overload (National Research Council, 2011).

Most mobile devices have the capability to access wireless hot spots such as those found in coffee shops, bookstores, and public buildings. These semipublic wireless networks have much more capacity than that of cellular wireless networks.

4.5 Mass Media and Social Media Use in Virginia Tech Shooting Response

Several types of messaging grew in use in the aftermath of the Virginia Polytechnic Institute shootings of 2007 (National Research Council, 2011). On April 16, 2007, a lone shooter killed 32 people and wounded 17 in two separate incidents approximately 2 hours apart. During the event, e-mails from the university were used to send longer, more detailed messages to students, and displays showing the messages were present in most classrooms.

In the field of social media communications in disasters, the Virginia Tech shooting was a first in collecting mass amounts of social media data to study patterns (Palen et al., 2009).

This field of study, known as crisis informatics, explores emergency response among not only official responders, but also members of the public (Palen et al., 2009). Crisis informatics views emergency response as an expanded social system, where information is disseminated within and between official and public channels and entities.

In spite of these improvements, social media can provide unfiltered, more immediate information than mass media options (National Research Council, 2011). Long before an alert is delivered by an official source, information about the event will most likely already be available on social media sites, such as Twitter or Facebook, that support online social interaction, including the widespread sharing of people's observations about current events. Social media postings include not only text but images and video, which are readily captured using mobile phones.

As a result, those directly affected by a disaster can also become key sources of information about the event (National Research Council, 2011). These tools also change conventional news gathering—reporters can use cell phones to interview people at the scene of an event or to gather both still images and video quickly. One potential consequence of the use of these new tools is that the personal experience of those caught up in a disaster, who may be experiencing psychological trauma and stress, can now be shared widely. Even those not physically present can vicariously experience the traumatic nature of events.

WEA and similar systems have additional drawbacks: Without the inclusion of text-to-speech capabilities, they cannot be used by those who are blind. Past research has shown that people respond to alerts and warnings by seeking additional information to confirm the event, determine their risk, and decide on their next action. Because of this, social media may be used as a second and confirming source during an alert or warning (National Research Council 2011). The program was intended to provide alerts and warnings to over 80% of the American population on mobile devices (cell phones and pagers) (National Research Council, 2011). No system was put in place to track who received the alerts (Magsino, 2009).

Conversely, someone receiving an alert on a cell phone would seek additional information by texting or placing telephone calls to family or friends, using social networks, browsing news Web sites or searching online—activities that might end up using more capacity than would be needed if people followed a link to official information (National Research Council, 2011).

According to a 2011 American Red Cross study, although one in six subjects reported that they had used social media to find information about an emergency, television continues to be their primary source of information during these events (National Research Council, 2013b). Further, more than 80% of those interviewed indicated that they were willing to post information about a disaster on social media sites, including images or video clips. Of those who would post requests for help, 80% expected a response within an hour.

However, only 15% believed that emergency management agencies were actively following social media during emergencies. That is, although many believed that emergency officials should be following their feeds, few believed that they actually were.

Since PIOs are likely to first encounter information generated by members of the public, and therefore to appreciate the active role members of the public play in response, they could be the most able to act on such information and instigate organizational change from, in essence, the bottom-up (Palen and Liu, 2007).

4.5.1 Information Communication Technologies

Palen and Liu (2007) also observed that not only can crisis situations benefit from informed **ICT** development, ICT development can benefit by working within crisis settings. Though disaster situations are special sociological conditions, they sometimes affect all aspects of a society though the disadvantaged are disproportionately affected—and activity, sometimes exposing features not used under normal conditions that might be able to benefit from ICT support. Crisis settings, therefore, are not only important situations for which to design, they are also important situations from which to design (Yates and Paquette, 2011).

4.6 What Is a Disaster?

Scholars refer to disasters, or "mass emergencies," as not only natural hazards but mass unrest, protests, and other sociopolitical events. Historically, disasters have been addressed within emergency management in the command-and-control style of response. Social media has changed that approach, making the focus more bottom-up than top-down.

"Disaster" is a term typically used when existing resources are overwhelmed. Mass emergencies do not include those that do not exceed capacities of local agencies and do not significantly affect the built environment or social order (Vieweg, 2012).

Protests are considered a **mass disruption event**—an event affecting a large number of people that causes disruption to normal social routines (Starbird et al., 2012). Examples of mass disruption events include natural disasters, acts of terrorism, mass emergencies, extreme weather events, and political protests. A disaster can often be viewed as not only one large emergency, but multiple "mini-crises" or catastrophes that emerge over a period of time (Yates and Paquette, 2011).

The NIMS, established in 2004 by the Department of Homeland Security, aims to be a single, consistent organizational approach to all US domestic incident management and disaster prevention, preparedness, response, recovery, and mitigation programs and activities (Hughes, 2012). However, several researchers describe the model as authoritative and inflexible.

The use of social media during a mass emergency is often first associated with civil unrest (from Twitter's role in the postelection events in Iran in 2009 to confrontations between police and protestors playing out over live-streaming services in the mid-2010s). However, its use before, during, and after natural hazard events offers many insights into the evolution of communication models.

Emergency management—the response to a natural or man-made event—is a process comprising four phases: preparedness, response, recovery, and mitigation (Díaz et al., 2013). During these events, the public can act as "intelligent sensors" to collect information, sending data to emergency managers via tweets, phone calls, or other methods. Emergency management organizations identify **trusted sensors,** people whose data can be directly processed because they are reliable (Díaz et al., 2013).

Shortly after its inception in 2006, Twitter took a large role in nonofficial reporting of disasters. According to the Web site *TechCrunch*, information regarding the 2008 terrorist attacks in Mumbai was shared worldwide in nearly real time using the service—faster than news agencies such as CNN reported the events (Magsino, 2009). As seen in domestic natural disasters such as flooding in Georgia and Tennessee in 2009–2010, disaster survivors often have little with them but their phones (Lieberman, 2011). Because of this, FEMA leadership have put greater emphasis on accessing services via mobile Web sites.

During mass emergencies, affected populations construct an understanding of the situation based on incomplete information, including the status of a hazard, damage done to buildings and infrastructure, the location of an evacuation center, and the number and location of injured people and/or animals (Vieweg, 2012). This provides decision makers with information that contributes to an understanding of emergency situations, and can help them decide what actions to take.

Complete information is not attained during mass emergency, or else it would not be a mass emergency (Palen et al., 2011). However, the more information people have and the better their situational awareness, the better equipped they are to make tactical, strategic decisions. Palen et al. write that research shows the need for individuals with different specialties and knowledge to collaborate to develop the most effective plans.

Research on Twitter use during mass emergencies shows that despite the lack of a formal system to communicate information during mass emergency, people turn to Twitter to broadcast information that can potentially contribute to situational awareness (Vieweg et al., 2010).

4.7 Usage Patterns of Social Media Over Time

The use of SNSs waxes and wanes with changes in popularity and new technologies. It also changes according to major events that showcase the networking capabilities of services not previously used to such scale. Twitter emerged during several mass disturbance events in 2008–2010 that were independent of natural hazards, and crowdfunding sites gained increased notoriety in the aftermath of the 2010 earthquake in Haiti.

FOR EXAMPLE

The August 2007 Minneapolis Bridge collapse brought new public attention to the possibilities of Twitter among members of the public, and increasingly, among traditional news media (Palen et al., 2010). Its use represented "that innovation for emergencies could greatly benefit by reframing disaster response as a set of socially-distributed information activities that support powerful, parallel, socio-technical processing of problems in times of change and disruption." These technologies, Palen writes, allow a wide group of people to gain situational awareness and build resilience in the face of threat (Palen et al., 2010).

In many cases, the rise of one SNS coincides with the fall of another. The ubiquity of MySpace in the mid-2000s has transitioned into the more widespread use of Facebook and Twitter, which themselves are being supplanted by fast-growing social networks like *Instagram (a product of Facebook) and Snapchat.*

FOR EXAMPLE

The move of social media from computers to smartphones also led to major changes. During the Queensland, Australia, floods of 2010–2011, researchers began noting that residents affected by the flooding were just as likely to use their cell phones to access the Internet as landline computers (Bird et al., 2012). This trend continued, and Internet access by smartphone now exceeds 50% of all Internet access, even in developing countries (Pew Global, 2016). As of the 2010–2011 events, Australia's cell phone penetration rates lagged behind only Singapore (Bird et al., 2012). As smartphones are increasingly used to access online content, Bird et al. speculate that the importance of social media as a source of information will only grow.

While social media penetration has grown rapidly in the past decade-plus, with Facebook and Twitter taking a growing share of users, some emergency management agencies have been more open to using the technology than others (Chavez et al., 2010). Among those Chavez et al. surveyed, several said Twitter was best suited for their purposes. Its mobile accessibility and the ability to receive tweets via text message make the format more useful than Facebook, which is passive, according to emergency management officials in the city of Evanston, Illinois.

The reach of traditional reverse 911 systems is changing as fewer people subscribe to landline phones, and may be away from home when natural hazards occur (Chavez et al., 2010). To use a Twitter alert system, residents need follow the Twitter page to get emergency tweets. Several municipalities, including Moorhead, Minnesota, surveyed by Chavez et al. found that providing real-time updates via Facebook and Twitter was easier for staff than updating the town's static flood information Web page.

The traditional emergency management agency's response to the public during emergencies has been through the press release, which includes a formal structure, selected quotations and statistics about an event (Hughes, 2012). This has been replaced by a system in which information often emerges in small pieces, so a press release is now often redundant.

That informal system often centers around Twitter. A 2009 study by the Pew Internet & American Life Project found that 19% of all Internet users share updates about themselves on Twitter or another similar service (Latonero and Shklovski, 2011). During the Iranian student protests of 2009, the US Department of State reportedly asked Twitter management to delay a scheduled maintenance so users of Twitter in Iran could continue their mobilizing of protests via the site. During the revolutionary protests in Egypt in the spring of 2011, users reportedly employed Twitter (and Google) as an ad hoc distributed communication system, until the government shut down Internet access countrywide.

As of Fugate's 2011 speech, FEMA utilized YouTube, Facebook, and Twitter to communicate with the public. FEMA has 16 separate Twitter accounts, including one run by the Administrator himself (@CraigatFEMA) through early 2017. Each FEMA regional office also posts on its own Twitter account, providing localized information on FEMA activities (Lieberman, 2011).

In a 2011 report, the National Research Council pointed to cell phones as a means of complementing existing emergency warning technology such as radio, television, and weather radios. However, "the ability to target messages to a cell phone's actual location makes it possible to target more precisely those individuals who would be most at risk in a crisis situation." Cell phones were seen as ways to fill communication gaps, but the gap has only grown with reduced staffing capabilities of traditional media outlets (National Research Council, 2011).

Social media have the advantage of being **"persistent forms" of communication**: They are visible, recordable, and/or transferable to other people over time (Palen and Liu, 2007). In disaster settings, this description also applies to missing person fliers posted around an impact area, SMS messages inquiring about the safety of a friend, chalked messages or pictures on a sidewalk, and spray-painted messages on buildings, among others.

High penetration rates for Internet access, and the prolific diffusion of cell phones, have aided the persistence of electronic communications. When traditional communications technologies go down, Voice Over Internet Protocol (VoIP) service, e-mail, and text messaging services remain available for managing an emergency and for providing information to the media and public (Palen and Liu, 2007).

In events that cover wide areas (like hurricanes) and can occur and die out quickly (like wildfires), sources of information from multiple eyes-on-the-ground can be more helpful than official news sources because the information can provide a more local context and rapid updates for those who need to make decisions about how to act (Palen et al., 2009).

The Internet has changed how people gather information—in times of mass emergency and otherwise (Palen et al., 2009). Twenty-five years ago, news producers were usually regarded as the only credible information source for the public during a disaster event.

When faced with a mass emergency, people are prone to increased information seeking—Twitter complements this behavior by providing the potential for up-to-the-second information from a vast extent of sources. However, social media present the opportunities for rumors to spread (Palen et al., 2009). Rumors are a person-to-person communication that takes place through informal channels, involving information that is unverified by official sources. When institutional sources are unable to provide necessary information, people generate rumors.

Much of the information communicated via Twitter during mass emergency can be viewed as **rumor**—information that is not verified by an official source which is sent via an informal channel and which provides a collective picture of an event. It is difficult to know how to react or what actions to take, so people work to make "good enough" decisions and they may incorporate information communicated via Twitter in that process (Palen et al., 2009).

The publically available nature of the information shared via Twitter is causing emergency managers to take note, and some are realizing the positive impact microblogging services can have (Palen et al., 2009). Using the example of the 2010 San Bruno, California, fire, FEMA Administrator Fugate stated that the agency achieved better situational awareness from Twitter before they received official information, a drastic change from just a few years before (Lieberman, 2011).

Palen et al. state that Twitterers tend to take on one of three roles: information source, information seeker, or friend. The types of information shared on Twitter have been studied and divided into 32 separate categories (Palen et al., 2009).

Within the Twitter universe, directing messages directly to other user using the "@" symbol is an important action to make sure one's communications are being seen through the massive quantity of available messages on the platform (Palen et al., 2009). Because Twitter communications are constructed through the written word, they are often conversational and informal in nature, making it more of an extension of existing behavior than a new language to learn (Palen et al., 2009). Hashtags can be used to filter information to help narrow the focus of search. They were an important basis for the eventual organizing of activities (Starbird, 2010).

In most urban areas, different types of networks, such as fixed-line, Wi-Fi, cellular, and WiMax, can provide overlapping coverage for Internet connectivity (Yin et al., 2012). So, during times of crises, when a certain type of telecommunication infrastructure is destroyed, people can still use other means to keep in touch via social media.

4.8 Social Media's Growth and the Role of Traditional Sources

Social media has expanded access to resources and increased the speed at which information can be distributed and exchanged (Hughes, 2012). Improved Internet speed and increased Internet penetration rates have been matched by the expansion of the number of tools available to the public, from photo- and video-sharing services to microblogging sites that are the center of much recent research.

With this growth in Internet access, proliferation of smartphones and availability of new means to share information with the world, the hierarchical patterns typically used by emergency management institutions—top-down, control-and-command—have been challenged by a system in which nonresponders have growing capabilities to report and contribute to situational awareness.

4.8.1 Role of Social Media in Disasters

Latonero and Shklovski (2011) write that the new media traditionally play the role of conduit between emergency managers and the public. However, this role has changed as people's usual reaction to emergency events—to seek further information about the situation by whatever means available—has been met by social media's ever-improving ability to provide large quantities of information.

4.8.2 Use of Social Media by People Affected by Crisis

Dissatisfaction with traditional media is one of the more frequent reasons cited for why people affected by crisis situations turn to social media in search of information. When standard mass-messaging communications networks went down, social media helped fill the void. In 2008 during Hurricane Gustav, a Community Emergency Response Team (CERT) used social media to send mass e-mail notifications to team members through Facebook when its call notification system went down. The CERT group also updated status messages to notify first responders and citizens of developments as the incident unfolded (Lindsay, 2011).

By understanding how information is spread, and by understanding how trust is built between practitioners and the public and private sectors, practitioners may efficiently use networks to spread helpful messages and control rumors. Identifying the behavioral characteristics of those networks most effective at organizing themselves around hazards could help community leaders foster those characteristics in the networks within their own communities (Magsino, 2009).

4.9 Use of Social Media for Preparedness and Planning

Social media has limitations. In addition to being used more frequently by a younger demographic than traditional communication channels, it is often an amplifier of official channels and may not be a good option for slower-moving local governments because they end up appearing even slower (Chavez et al., 2010). Social media may not reach especially vulnerable audiences like those with disabilities, people without cell phones, people with low incomes, and people in rural communities.

FEMA Administrator Fugate has called social "imperative to emergency management, because the public uses these communication tools regularly....We must use social media tools to more fully engage the public as a critical partner in our efforts" (Díaz et al., 2013).

Starbird and Palen's (2010) research demonstrates that Twitter users overwhelmingly retweet messages from official information sources such as emergency management or news media organizations.

PIOs, in interviews with researchers, expressed that social media expands not only the scope and type of PIO work activity, but also the "information pathways" that exist between PIOs, the media, and members of the public (Hughes, 2012). This collective intelligence, called "crowdsourcing," is the gathering of a collection of resources, capacities, and a progression to increasingly more defined tasks and even organizational identity in response to an event (Starbird, 2010).

This, in turn, can aid **community resilience**—the ability of a community or social unit to withstand external shocks, such as disasters, to its infrastructure, which emerges from a community's ability to adapt to stress and return to healthy functioning (Magsino, 2009). The speed with which a community can mobilize and use resources during and following a disaster is strongly dependent on its abilities to adapt to change. The strength of social networks is a factor: A disaster that has little impact on a community at one time can have a much larger impact at another time. Many of the same capacities and characteristics that allow a community to continue functioning during a disaster are those that allow a community to thrive during normal times.

Preparedness for natural hazards can be hampered by the incentive for postdisaster funding (Magsino, 2009). Although research findings from the Multi-hazard Mitigation Council indicate that communities can expect a four-to-one return for every dollar spent on disaster mitigation, communities often do not take advantage of the expected savings. The return is not realized unless a disaster occurs and a reduction in recovery costs is observed. Additionally, mitigation planning may be thwarted by an inability to decide where mitigation is needed. A community may mitigate in the wrong way or be prepared for the wrong disaster. Under these circumstances, a community may suffer during a disaster and see no return on its investment.

4.9.1 Expansion of Communication Networks

A study commissioned by the American Red Cross found that roughly half of the respondents would sign up for e-mails, text alerts, or other applications for emergency information to help them during an emergency situation (Lindsay, 2011). However, according to Administrator Fugate, only half of American households have emergency kits in their home, and only 40% of American households have an emergency plan in place. Although not a substitute for emergency kits or plans, providing lifesaving directives and information at the onset of an incident, or during an incident, could help underprepared citizens.

4.10 Use of Social Media Before and During Mass Emergencies

Twitter communication during times of emergency and crisis falls into four broad categories (Latonero and Shklovski, 2011):

1. Self-generated messages about the crisis posted to users' social networks.
2. Users **retweeting messages** received from members of their social networks, traditional media, unofficial and official sources.

3. Emergency management professionals using the service in either official or unofficial capacities to send messages to the public in affected communities or the public at large.
4. Emergency management professionals monitoring feeds from the public to gather information during times of emergency, and to exchange information with other organizations involved in crisis response.

4.10.1 Emergency Managers' Use of Social Media in Response

Social media accounts provide emergency managers with their own media outlets, through which they can reach a very specific audience—their followers—with messages on preparedness and action to be taken (Chavez et al., 2010). This is important because emergency managers have now become the PIOs, a role that includes monitoring the public information arena during an emergency, quelling false rumors, and correcting misinformation (Hughes, 2012). This new role of "listener," coupled with a shortened (some would say round-the-clock) new cycle, increases pressure on PIOs to address inaccuracies and monitor information on a constant basis.

Hughes and Palen (2012) noted that media outlets are not bound by the same rules of confirmations and approvals as PIOs, creating frustration on the part of officials as they are forced to sit out ongoing discussion on social media when they are unable to comment fully absent official confirmation of facts being reported.

4.10.2 Emergency Managers in Listening Mode

Díaz et al. (2013) note that, when in that listening mode, many emergency managers preferred videos and pictures to inform of situations in disaster areas. Texts or voice messages were less useful as many citizens do not provide relevant information to evaluate the situation.

4.10.3 Managing the Use of Twitter or Facebook

Other PIOs use tools such as Twitter or Facebook to send incident updates to reduce the number of inquiries from the media and others. Directing the media and the public to a Web site seems to also reduce the number of phone calls to information hotlines (Hughes, 2012).

4.10.4 Information-Vetting Dynamics

Information exchange relies on extensive self-organizing and **information-vetting** as well as on the emergence of personalities that become information hubs to the rapidly growing legions of their followers. Moreover, Starbird and Palen (2010) show that people seek out and even privilege official information, augmenting rather than discounting statements issued by emergency services and mass media outlets (Starbird and Palen, 2010). This consistently observed privileging of information from official sources on Twitter suggests that traditional broadcast media are not only retaining their importance for disseminating emergency information, but also that this information can now be given extra weight and legitimization through the word-of-mouth nature of Twitter (Latonero and Shklovski, 2011).

FOR EXAMPLE

Facebook has been noted as a main source of information during some mass emergencies. Most people responding to a survey about their Facebook usage during the Queensland, Australia, floods found the event-related pages through an invitation from a friend or a Facebook search (Bird et al., 2012). Nearly two-thirds used the pages to find out information about their own community, while others found the pages to learn more about the communities of families and friends. Almost all (97%) reported information back to family and friends, and fewer than 40% of respondents found conflicting or inaccurate information.

These online communities were self-policing to quell the spread of rumors. Moderators of pages set up during the Queensland flooding often provided official confirmation of reports, and discussion on those pages was efficient at correcting misleading or incomplete information (Bird et al., 2012).

4.10.5 Building Resiliency

Building resiliency into social networks requires an understanding of how networks evolve during normal times, and during times of stress. Understanding how networks change when stressed, and how to promote positive changes that allow the networks to function during a disaster, is important (Magsino, 2009).

Emergency managers can also employ a **Virtual Operations Support Team** (VOST), which consists of trusted digital volunteers who extend the resources of an incident management team by performing online tasks that can be done remotely (Hughes, 2012). This includes monitoring social media and posting information to Web and social media sites. These support structures began emerging around 2011 in response to the growth of social media's role in disaster response (Hughes, 2012).

This kind of interactivity involves staff time and attention that is unusual with large government organizations. Validation of information available on Twitter and via other social media is a persistent and difficult question (Palen et al., 2009).

Information is carried out in communities in different ways. Because weather forecasts allow alerts and warnings to be issued days in advance, many information outlets, including print media, are useful for carrying messages about hurricanes or winter storms (National Research Council, 2011). People also consider social cues such as whether their neighbors are evacuating or whether local businesses are closing, and environmental cues such as whether they can see evidence of the

Figure 4-1

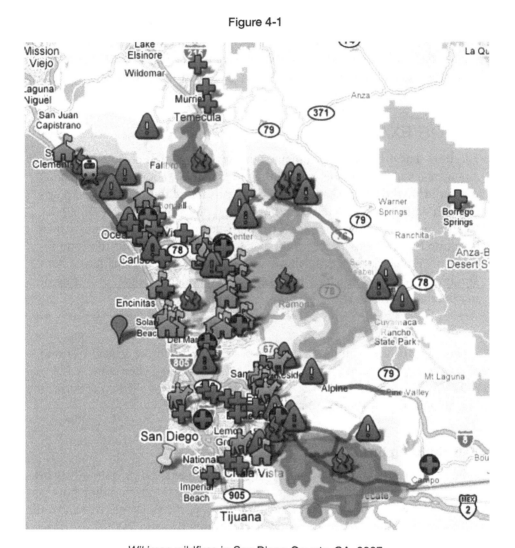

Wikimap wildfires in San Diego County, CA, 2007.

reported hazard. Effective warning messages are clear, specific, accurate, and truthful, and they consistently use authoritative language to explain the hazard, what actions should be taken, and when they should be taken (National Research Council, 2011).

During hazard events, older technologies have often proven to be resilient— for example, during Hurricane Charley in 2004, a local radio station's building was destroyed, and yet the station was operating again within 5 hours (Figure 4-1).

4.10.6 Changing Nature of Social Behaviors

Social behaviors have been shown to change. For example, research has shown that during a disaster or mass emergency situation, people have a greater willingness

Figure 4-2

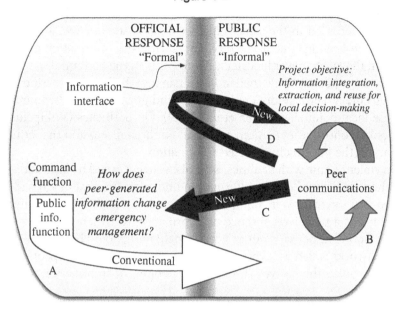

Crisis response as a social system: high-level schematic of conventional and new ICT-enabled information pathways.

to follow individuals who are different from themselves than they do under normal circumstances. Also, they tend to seek firsthand, "on the ground" information (National Research Council, 2013b).

Those who are inside the crisis zone as well as those on the outside are compelled to help not only through supplying physical labor, goods, and psychological support, but also by playing critical roles in information dissemination (Palen et al., 2010) (Figure 4-2).

FOR EXAMPLE

Virginia Tech Shootings as an Example of Collective Intelligence

During the 2007 Virginia Tech events, research has shown that a large, unmanageable number of social media pages that sprout up related to the same events, particularly on Facebook, have limited filtering options to coalesce response efforts (Palen et al., 2009).

Over a set of Web sites that were the focal points for this information, members of the international public began trying to determine who the victims of the crisis were as it unfolded (Palen et al., 2009). People reported personal information they knew themselves or had seen posted elsewhere by others and began to create and expand on lists of the known victims.

Any interesting phenomena occurred during the emergency: The total compiled information across all lists was a correct identification of the 32 victims, before Virginia Tech officially released names to the public. The names were not always reported in the same sequence across lists, nor was any list fully complete, indicating concurrent problem solving and information gathering. However, they were never incorrect. Participants in the list-building activities self-policed, and they knew that adding a name to the list was a serious statement. Accuracy, verification, credentialing, and gravitas ruled the interaction on these focal point sites (Palen et al., 2009). On both sites (Wikipedia and Facebook), contributors participated in an editorial discussion that critiqued accuracy of the informally gathered information.

As a violent crime with fatalities, officials were governed by laws and ethics about how they could release information until after the next of kin had been notified and forensics were completed (Palen et al., 2009). This created the conditions of a perceived absence of information to which members of the public responded perhaps out of need to help and cope. The activity within social networks was not governed by those same conventions; people could rapidly organize themselves through the pooling of information around a focused task.

Though tweets sent by those local to an event could be a resource both for responders and for those affected, most Twitter activity during mass disruption events is generated by the remote crowd. Tweets from the remote crowd can be seen as noise that must be filtered, but another perspective considers crowd activity as a filtering and recommendation mechanism (Starbird et al., 2012).

These activities bear a great resemblance to a term coined by the news media in response to the ubiquity of information-sharing platforms among the public (Starbird et al., 2012). Individuals could seek information about people and property, synthesize information, and coordinate action.

Twitter's appeal in particular comes from its short message, broadcast, public nature: most posts can be seen by anyone which means that interactions are not "walled" away to a restricted group (Starbird et al., 2012). Users can also make Twitter lists of other Twitterers, grouped by conversation topic or some other user-defined classification, and publicize these lists to other users to "follow." These include the retweet mechanism (RT @username) to permit message forwarding with upstream author attribution and the hashtag (#keyword) to support information search and group formation.

Derivative information—information in the form of reposts or pointers to information available elsewhere—is so abundant that it is commonly viewed as a form of "noise" that must be filtered out to arrive at the signal of good data (Starbird et al., 2012). An alternative perspective is to view derivative information as a valuable part of the information ecosystem that can be treated as meta-data, or information about information that might be able to provide a road map for navigating the noisy information space, even as it simultaneously contributes to that noise.

4.11 Issues Arising from the Use of Social Media by Emergency Managers During Events

During the Queensland flooding, three-quarters of respondents to the survey administered by Bird et al. said they used government or media Facebook pages as their main source of information, despite the time lag necessary for official sources to confirm information. Facebook groups and pages, in contrast, provided real-time information that was not always accurate (Bird et al., 2012). This problem, however, was overcome by references to official sources on these chat threads to resolve rumors and open questions.

Diaz et al. noted that mid-size emergency management agencies might have problems adapting to use of social media because of the sheer quantity of messages involved during a disaster event, as well as the need to respond quickly while doing their core jobs.

4.11.1 Changing Role of PIO

PIOs find that with social media they can distribute information directly to the public, effectively bypassing the media (Hughes, 2012). This distribution channel grants new control of the outgoing message, though the public via social media gives that message a life that may persist after the message is no longer accurate. The role of PIOs is changing from gatekeeper to translator.

While PIOs act as conduits and arbiters of information, they are usually not the ones making the most immediate impact on the ground. Members of the public in the immediate and surrounding area of a disaster provide relief in the form of shelter, clothing, blankets, and food (Palen and Liu, 2007). Victims of disasters—to the extent that they can—are themselves often among the volunteers. Faith-based organizations provide planned relief services including, for example, child day care while parents complete insurance claims paperwork, as well as emergent services.

4.12 Using Social Media to Establish Information on Damages and Recovery

Social media brings new challenges in how to sift relevant information from the sheer volume of data being broadcast over time. User-generated content is naturally "noisy" and uses different language than conventional print communication documents (Yin et al., 2012).

Vast amounts of data can be parsed, however, by the **collective intelligence** of social media users. Crowdsourcing allows capable crowds to participate in various tasks, from simply "validating" a piece of information or photograph as worthwhile to complicated editing and management, such as those found in virtual communities that provide information—from Wikipedia to Digg (Gao et al., 2011). This type of interaction continues to validate the involvement of the public in emergency response.

Some services build on existing systems to synthesize information. Ushahidi is a social media network that integrates data from multiple sources—phones, Web applications, e-mail, and social media sites such as Twitter and Facebook—to provide an up-to-date, publicly available crisis map that is also available to relief organizations (Gao et al., 2011).

Gao et al. found that the **crowdsourcing** approach has several benefits: immediate capture of status reports, data geotagging, filtering, and analyzing through automated software. Many of these applications do not have security features for relief organizations; their content is available for public viewing. A fraudulent message could spread quickly with good camouflage, especially in a chaotic disaster environment, unless better incentives for verification are present (Gao et al., 2011).

True to Fugate's words, members of the public have changed their relationship with the institution of emergency response through social media (Hughes, 2012). The public's information may be relevant to responders: Some have value as data, as long as those data can be effectively received.

4.12.1 Evolving Networks

Social media tools could be used to understand how networks emerge and evolve in a disaster situation, and may help identify the sustainable linkages among them. Given enough data, the commonalities and important characteristics that allowed these networks and linkages to survive can be discovered. However, accessing and using public data for the purpose of studying or constructing networks of networks is often challenging (Magsino, 2009).

Networks form based on how the physical characteristics of the disaster affect the built and social environment, which in turn results in different arrangements for communications (Palen and Liu, 2007). Networks form to seek and provide relief assistance (information about housing, food, jobs, transportation help). **Peer-to-peer communication** can also be emotive and evaluative (including expressions of anger, grief, humor, wishes of support, political statements, and religious content) and evolve over time as more information about an event emerges.

4.12.2 Expanding Information Relevant to a Specific Event

Lindsay (2011) argues that having a platform for each type of mass emergency would be advantageous because FEMA could provide a wide range of information relevant to the specific event, including evacuation details, food, water and shelter locations, as well as links to other sites or actual locations where residents could find and obtain other essential needs. Social media could also be used to provide timely response and recovery updates to keep citizens informed of developments as the incident unfolds. The same Web site could later serve as an information portal for recovery and ultimately be retained after the recovery and serve as a historical document.

4.12.3 Expanded Communication Benefits

One benefit of two-way communication is helping officials compile lists of the dead and injured, and contact information of victims' friends and family members (Lindsay, 2011). Researchers studying the use of Twitter during the March 2011 Japanese earthquake and tsunami found that those with Twitter accounts tweeted for assistance when they could not use a phone. Younger people are more likely not only to use social networking, but are also to request help through social media, believe agencies should monitor their postings, and have high expectations that agencies will respond quickly to their requests.

If FEMA adopted social media use for recovery, the agency could provide information concerning what types of individual assistance are available to individuals and households, including how to apply for assistance, announcing application deadlines, and providing information and links to other agencies and organizations that provide recovery assistance (Lindsay, 2011). Social media could be used to accelerate the damage estimate process by transmitting images of damaged structures from cell phones.

High-resolution aerial and satellite images online, through Google's Crisis Response application, provided a valuable resource to people in the 2005–2006 Gulf Coast hurricane season (Palen and Liu, 2007). Such capabilities can help the formal response effort in collecting and providing information useful to the public (as it now depends, in practice, on the media help to do) but can also place additional demands on the formal response effort to do additional verification.

During response efforts, a virtual volunteer organization assigns multiple volunteers to the task of "media monitoring," an activity that includes identifying and creating lists of on-the-ground Twitterers. For volunteers like these, the use of techniques that increase the signal-to-noise ratio in the data has the potential to drastically reduce the amount of work they must do (Starbird et al., 2012).

4.13 The Advantages and Fallbacks of Geotargeting

Social media also serves recovery by providing geographic data on users. **Geotargeting** is a two-step process: The first is the geo-definition of the targeted area (e.g., a county or a geographic polygon). The second is the geo-delivery of the message to recipients within the targeted area (National Research Council, 2013a).

Both steps are prone to imprecision. In the case of geo-definition, some alerting systems only allow the definition of an area down to the county level, even if the actual affected area is only a section within it. In the case of geo-delivery, receipt of wireless transmissions cannot be limited precisely to a specific region. Additionally, there are legal concerns about the use of information (National Research Council, 2013a).

The less precise the geotargeting, the more likely the recipient will ignore the alert, or choose to opt out of the alerting system, because they are not sure whether the message applies to them (National Research Council, 2013a).

Some types of geolocation-dependent messaging, such as "reverse-911" systems, can dial groups of landline telephone subscribers and can achieve a high degree of precision because they are capable of calling subscribers located within a specific polygon. On the other hand, wireless-based systems, such as the Emergency Alert System (EAS), are inherently less precise because of the wireless fencing issue. In the case of the national WEA system, alerts are transmitted to cellular phones using cellular broadcast technology (National Research Council, 2013a).

Fewer than 5% of all tweets used are accurately geocoded (National Research Council, 2013b). Second, the key word detection algorithms have approximately a 10% false rate. Detection thresholds can be positively adjusted, but there will always be trade-offs between false positives and false negatives.

National Oceanic and Atmospheric Administration (NOAA) weather radio uses dedicated radio frequencies and special-purpose receivers (National Research Council, 2013a). It delivers weather and other hazard alerts and allows users to limit alarms to only those alerts designated for their location by specifying regions that are largely aligned with counties or portions of counties.

4.14 Social Media Companies' Contribution to Emergency Response

In his 2011 testimony, Fugate said he had met with representatives from Apple, Craigslist, Facebook, Google, Microsoft, and Twitter to continue the discussion on how to "harness ever-changing capabilities of the digital world to better serve the public" (Lieberman, 2011). As part of the pivot toward involving the public more in disaster response, social media networks have adapted to include emergency-related tools.

Facebook supports several emergency-related organizations, including Information Systems for Crisis Response and Management (ISCRAM), the Humanitarian Free and Open Source Software (FOSS) Project, as well as numerous universities with disaster-related programs (Magsino, 2009).

4.14.1 Information Dissemination and Feedback

Social media can be used somewhat passively to disseminate information and receive user feedback via incoming messages, wall posts, and polls. To date, this is how most emergency management organizations, including the FEMA, use social media (Magsino, 2009).

Some of the same methods used by these digital pioneers are under discussion for use at the federal government level: smartphone-friendly mobile versions of FEMA Web sites to allow users to access information and request assistance and using social media to facilitate communication between the public, first responders, volunteer groups, the private sector. and all levels of government.

Another approach involves the systematic use of social media as an emergency management tool. Systematic usage might include using the medium to conduct emergency communications and issue warnings, using social media to receive victim requests for assistance, monitoring user activities to establish situational awareness, and using uploaded images to create damage estimates, among others (Magsino, 2009).

FOR EXAMPLE

MySpace Contribution in a Disaster

The Sydney Morning Herald in Australia reported that as Hurricane Gustav approached the Louisiana border in 2008, DHS officials reached out to MySpace and requested a fast-track disaster notification system. MySpace developed a "widget" that linked profile pages to federal information, allowing tracking of those impacted by the storm (White et al., 2009).

4.15 Concerns About and Limitations of Social Media Usage in Disasters

Social networking tools are easily used by those with both honest and dishonest intent. Some terrorist organizations are known to use tools such as Twitter and Google Earth to update their networks (Magsino, 2009). The challenge for emergency management practitioners is to synthesize and analyze the large volume of information available and determine whether the information is correct, actionable, or requires response. Many believe this information sharing, despite its risks, is the strength of the Internet (Magsino, 2009).

4.15.1 Misleading Information

Bad information can be long-lived and can persist even on successful social institutions such as Wikipedia, where entries are subject to constant review by members (Magsino, 2009). Even considering content error, these institutions remain successful because within their bottom-up organizational structures ways are available to manage data, look for and fix problems, and recognize and resolve attacks on the system. For application in the disaster management community, it is essential that systems and networks are functioning before a disaster in order for them to be effective during and following a disaster (Magsino, 2009). Spread of inaccurate information could endanger first responders, and malicious use of social media during an incident could range from mischievous pranks to acts of terrorism.

Research notes that not only are emergency management and other officials often concerned about misleading information being put out to the public, they are also concerned about the potential for existing systems to be overloaded by message volume (Magsino, 2009). Although social media may improve some aspects of emergency and disaster response, overreliance on the technology could be problematic under prolonged power outages.

4.15.2 Dependable Networks

In the aftermath of Hurricane Katrina in 2005, some people had cell phones, but coverage was limited, and finding places to charge them was difficult.

Emergency shelter landline phone banks still had lengthy waits nearly one month later (Palen and Liu, 2007).

4.15.3 Reliable Information Sources

If the information source is not identified in the message, the message is unlikely to be deemed as trustworthy. A weather alert issued by the National Weather Service is generally viewed by the public as having a high degree of credibility, but verified sources of information on less familiar hazards may not be considered as trustworthy compared to the same information relayed by a trusted government source (National Research Council, 2011).

4.15.4 Communicating with a Broad Audience

Social media is not always designed for a universal audience. People with disabilities have important communications needs, often using mobile devices as a lifeline, not only during medical emergencies but also daily to further independence and access to services (Magsino, 2009). Affordability and accessibility have to be considered in developing warning systems and designing new technologies. A technology that is out of reach for a large segment of the population loses a great deal of its usefulness.

Systems like WEA have relatively small audiences, since participation is opt-in. The system is used mostly by those who are most interested in receiving such alerting information. Geographic disparity of social media users means that it is more difficult to match local information to those participating in the conversation of an event.

4.15.5 Managing a Large Quantity of Data

The quantity of data being monitored by emergency managers during events is difficult to overstate. Filtering tools would improve their ability to better do their job, but progress toward such automated tools will rely on advances in natural-language processing (National Research Council, 2013b).

A certain hierarchy exists within social media spheres: Messages that are propagated have a chance of receiving attention; those that are not die out quickly (National Research Council, 2013b). During natural disasters, misinformation typically stems from constant rereporting of old news, although there is a possibility that awareness of limited resources could create an incentive and a desire to share misinformation so as to provide oneself with supplies before others.

For example, although the reach of an official message may be widened greatly if it is redistributed, the message might have been modified in ways not anticipated or desired by its originators. Rumors typically continue to spread despite having been found to be false—a problem that is not unique to the Internet or social media (National Research Council, 2013b).

Another shortcoming of social media is the need for someone in the emergency management operations to assess the tidal wave of information available. Content published on social media is intrinsically noisy and arrives at a high rate, making it difficult for watch officers to manually monitor and analyze such texts. Watch officers are typically time-constrained, whereas the information they are seeking is both time-critical and infrequent in text streams (Yin et al., 2012).

4.16 The Future of Social Media in Disasters

Many scholars studying the growth in social media usage during mass emergencies write of the need to constantly monitor and respond to changing information in social media streams. This takes staff time. Some emergency responders, like the Los Angeles Fire Department (LAFD), studied by Latonero and Shklovski (2011), have shown how this can be done if resources are allocated in a certain way.

Brian Humphrey, who is a paramedic-trained firefighter at the LAFD, had served as a PIO for 17 of his 24 years at the department as of the study. *Wired* magazine wrote that Humphrey is "single-handedly hauling the city's fire department into the Web 2.0 era" (Latonero and Shklovski, 2011).

4.16.1 New Role for the Public in a Crisis

Humphrey's vision for the future of social media for emergency management, described in the study, is a system where each member of the public is enabled with the technological means to transmit information about a fire, crisis, or disaster directly to emergency management professionals. Interactivity is a means to a mutual communicative relationship between individuals and emergency management professionals with systems of information verification in place to facilitate mutual trust.

Yet, not all emergency management organizations share Humphrey's vision of social media's implementation for real-time interactivity and listening to the public (Latonero and Shklovski, 2011). For example, FEMA states it has been using Twitter "as a means to offer information about the agency's mission, efforts and perspective." FEMA's purpose seems to lean more on the one-way dissemination model of media usage, not "listening."

4.16.2 Dynamic Nature of Social Media

The ad hoc and intuitive manner by which social media messages are vetted during events indicates a dynamic and flexible evaluation process (Latonero and Shklovski, 2011). However, there is a strong potential for PIOs to be overwhelmed by the amount and types of information.

In the future, emergency management- and government-developed social media tools can be better integrated with a user's existing social networking tools so that a different, unfamiliar tool is not needed during an event, and for leveraging users' existing social networks (National Research Council, 2011). The success of citizen science initiatives, a form of crowdsourcing that harnesses individual observations to assist in scholarly research, suggests that similar techniques could be very useful in harnessing the public for help in coping with disasters (National Research Council, 2013b).

4.16.3 Social Media as a Valuable Resource

Though news tweeters local to disaster events provide only a small portion of total tweets on an event, this information can be a valuable resource for emergency responders, event planners, affected people, journalists, and the digitally converging crowd. Locals may have knowledge about geographic or cultural features of the affected area that could be useful to those responding from outside the area (Starbird and Palen, 2010). Starbird and Palen (2010) found that people were more likely to retweet accounts of those who were local to the event, even when local accounts only made up a small portion of event-related tweets (Starbird et al., 2012).

4.16.4 Self-correcting Nature of Social Media

The future also indicates a greater level of trust in the collective intelligence and self-correcting behavior of social media users. Studying the propagation of rumors on Twitter in the wake of the Chilean earthquake in 2010, researchers found that tweets containing false information were more likely to be challenged by other Twitterers (Starbird and Palen, 2010).

4.16.5 Accuracy of Information

The accuracy of information, which is of utmost importance when managing emergency response, needs to be constantly checked and validated, which is very difficult given the amount of data that can flow into these systems (Yates and Paquette, 2011). Identity, whether personal or role-based, is an important component of social media since each knowledge contribution "comes from" and is "received by" someone. Social media may help emergency management organizations to better identify knowledge boundaries that exist that are knowledge-based rather than functionally based (Yates and Paquette, 2011).

Many scholars have pointed to the need for mass emergency-specific social media tools. An emergency domain social network is not envisioned to replace existing organizations; rather, it would be a common ground meeting place for organizations and people to come together to share information and find potential collaborators with needed expertise (White et al., 2009).

Including profiles could help to verify the "credentials" of the reporting users—similar to those used by some social networks to identify commenters—and the use of groups within such a system like neighborhood and community groups would help to filter the information according to locale (White et al., 2009).

4.16.6 Threats of Technology Failure

The same threats facing current emergency response would continue into the future if an emergency management-specific network were to be developed. The threat of technology failure, hackers, stalkers, viruses, flaming, usability issues, uncertainty of information quality, and information overload are still at the forefront of minds among emergency managers (White et al., 2009). As younger people are more likely to use such a system to its fullest capability, the acceptance of a social network devoted to the emergency domain may take time as the emergency domain becomes more populated with younger professionals.

The competition among the current generation of social networking systems, and the relatively quick turnover of user bases from one system to another, means that they attempt to capture the user into one system and this makes it difficult for individuals to integrate their activities in different systems (White et al., 2009).

The future of emergency management institutions will be operating in a world where activity by members of the public generates information on a far more expanded, rapid scale, with information production activity happening at even greater magnitudes than such disruptive events already trigger (Palen et al., 2009).

4.16.7 Case Example: Crowdfunding and Remote Emergency Response: 2010 Haitian Earthquake as a Case Study

In January 2010, a magnitude 7.0 earthquake struck Haiti, with an epicenter about 25 miles west of the capital, Port-au-Prince. The event caused at least 100,000 deaths—the exact figure is a matter of dispute. In just 48 hours, the Red Cross received $8 million in donations directly from text message which exemplifies one benefit of the powerful capability of social media sites (Gao et al., 2011).

Although social media can positively impact disaster relief efforts, it does not provide an inherent coordination capability for easily pulling together and sharing information, resources, and plans among disparate relief organizations. Nevertheless, crowdsourcing applications based on social media applications such as *Twitter* and *Ushahidi* offer a powerful capability for collecting information from disaster scenes and visualizing data for relief decision making (Gao et al., 2011).

As reported by FEMA Administrator Fugate, even when an area's physical infrastructure was completely destroyed, the cellular tower bounced back quickly, allowing survivors to request help from local first responders and emergency managers to relay important disaster-related information via social media sites (Yin et al., 2012).

Cell phones proved to be a lifeline after the earthquake. Even if the physical infrastructure of an area was completely destroyed, the cellular infrastructure may have been able to bounce back quickly, allowing emergency managers to relay important disaster-related information and enabling the public to request help from local first responders (Lieberman, 2011).

Millions of tweets were sent referencing the 2010 Haiti earthquake during the early aftermath of that event (Starbird et al., 2012). Though a portion of these data comes directly from the ground in the form of citizen reports from affected people or relayed by "proxy" accounts, a majority of these communications are derivative—information in the form of reposts or pointers to information available elsewhere (Starbird et al., 2012).

A noted behavior of "digital volunteers" in the aftermath of the Haiti earthquake is the process of self-organizing in the information space of a microblogging environment, where collaborators were newly found and distributed across continents (Starbird, 2010). Only a small percentage of the population of Haiti were Twitter users, so the event-related syntax that emerged was used primarily by those viewing the events from afar. Many Twitterers located around the world emerged as "translators"—those who translated information from multiple sources into the syntax and tweeted it out to their followers.

4.16.8 Examining the Use of Social Media in Haiti

Haiti was the entry point for several Twitter users, who tend to engage in a new social network during crisis events (Starbird, 2010). Many begin using the network with a single cause—a person or place with specific needs—and later branched out to communicating about other needs and issues. Many of the people studied by Starbird (2010) began tweeting for Haiti as a way of volunteering their time—sometimes entire waking days—from areas far removed from the event. Many of the people involved in crowdsourcing information actually joined Twitter around the time of the earthquake, adopting the newer technology to assist with recovery.

The ability to leverage existing connections was a powerful part of the work process for the digital volunteers studied by Starbird (2010). Though a few Twitterers had nonsocial network connections with one or two users they communicated with online, a clear majority replied that they had never previously connected with these other Twitterers. Some became "remote operators": provided public updates for broadcasting or seeking a wide range of help; addressed tweets for making connections, directing information, and challenging misinformation; sent Direct Messages for moving resources, exchanging other contact info, and confronting possible hoaxers (Starbird, 2010).

Long-standing research on the sociology of disaster suggests that the desire to help in times of crisis is age-old, and in fact is a behavior in disaster response that is critical to response and recovery. Large numbers of people are known to converge onto the site in the wake of a disaster event to observe or to help (Starbird, 2010). Organizations that did not exist prior to a major disruption of the social order are emergent organizations—groups of people that previously had no standing structure or defined tasks (Starbird, 2010). Emergent groups are usually self-organizing, and come about in disaster settings to meet some unmet need.

One example provided by Starbird is Humanity Road, a virtual organization that was sparked by digital volunteering activities during the 2009 political unrest in Iran, but then formalized during the Haiti event.

On the ground, things went less smoothly as aid was coordinated. Responders were forced to deal with lined-up jumbo jets at the airport waiting to deliver supplies and aid workers, shortages of medical supplies, prison escapes and contaminated wetlands, on top of their primary mission of humanitarian aid (Yates and Paquette, 2011).

Responders on the ground used SharePoint, a collaborative Web site that could be considered "social," to organize response activities. It was not deemed a success, because without a preexisting hierarchy of pages and folders, new users were unsure where to add their knowledge (Yates and Paquette, 2011). Also, since the tasks and even the tone of the response changed as days passed, a prebuilt structure imposed a different classification on users that they did not like. With wikis, the most significant knowledge management challenge was the extent to which the wikis grew unchecked—and unwieldy—as more and more users added knowledge yet little shaping of the knowledge ensued (Yates and Paquette, 2011).

4.17 Looking Forward

FEMA Administrator Fugate said, in his 2011 Senate testimony, "We value two-way communication not only because it allows us to send important disaster-related information to the people who need it, but also because it allows us to incorporate critical updates from the individuals who experience the on-the-ground reality of a disaster." The nature of emergency management makes time a critical resource. The sooner emergency managers are able to comprehend the full scope of the disaster, the better able they are to support citizens and first responders (Lieberman, 2011).

Fugate expresses a strong trust in community involvement in preparedness, response, and recovery efforts. Rather than asking the public to change the way they communicate to fit FEMA's system, FEMA would try to change the way they do business to fit the way the public communicates online. The goal is to reach the largest possible audience to share important information as well as to engage a larger community as part of the emergency management infrastructure (Lieberman, 2011).

Social media technologies hold great promise for leveraging public participation in disaster response, especially when used within formal organizations to support open, collaborative knowledge sharing and reuse. When properly employed, the benefits of social media support are faster decision cycles and more complete knowledge resources. Whether or not these lessons can be duplicated in other crises or emergencies is an open question, as each circumstance offers unique challenges (Yates and Paquette, 2011).

KEY TERMS

Collective intelligence	A group of social media users such as in crowdsourcing which allows capable crowds to participate in various tasks, from simply "validating" a piece of information or photograph as worthwhile to complicated editing and management, such as those found in virtual communities that provide information—from Wikipedia to Digg (Gao et al., 2011).
Community resilience	The ability of a community or social unit to withstand external shocks, such as disasters, to its infrastructure, which emerges from a community's ability to adapt to stress and return to healthy functioning (Magsino, 2009).

Crowdsourcing	The practice of obtaining information or input by enlisting the services of a large number of people, typically via the Internet.
Derivative information	Information in the form of reposts or pointers to information available elsewhere—so abundant that it is commonly viewed as a form of "noise" that must be filtered out to arrive at the signal of good data (Starbird et al., 2012).
Geotargeting	Defining geographically an area through satellite or Internet-based means (e.g., a county or a geographic polygon) and the delivery of a message to recipients within the targeted area (National Research Council, 2013a).
ICTs	Information and communication technologies is a broad term that includes many communication devices and applications that include radio, television, cellular phones, computer and network hardware and software, and satellite communication systems.
Information-vetting	The process of confirming information that has been obtained so as to determine its usefulness.
Interventions	Activities designed to change or improve conditions in a community—facilitated by community leaders taking advantage of such networks to send and receive information (Magsino, 2009).
Mass disruption event	An event affecting a large number of people that causes disruption to normal social routines (Starbird et al., 2012).
National Incident Management System (NIMS)	A quasi-military organizational structure built upon the 36-year-old Incident Command System used in wildfire suppression (Palen and Liu, 2007). It was established in 2004 by the Department of Homeland Security and aims to be a single, consistent organizational approach to all US domestic incident management and disaster prevention, preparedness, response, recovery, and mitigation programs and activities (Hughes, 2012). A required part of the ICS is the coordination of public information by the POI (Public Information Officer).
Networks	Linkages between people and institutions, often formed through repeated connections or a shared purpose or interest.
Peer-to-peer communication	A decentralized communications network in which each party has the capacity to initiate and receive communication. This type of model is in contrast to a centralized model in which the information is controlled and provided to network members.

Persistent forms of communication	Communication that is visible, recordable, and/or transferable to other people over time (Palen and Liu, 2007).
Public information officer	A designated communications coordinator or spokesperson for a government organization who provide information to the media and the public.
Retweeting	The act of forwarding messages via *Twitter* received from members of a social network, traditional media, unofficial and official sources to others.
Rumor	Information that is not verified by an official source which is sent via an informal channel and which attempts to provide a collective picture of an event. It is difficult to know how to react or what actions to take, so people work to make "good enough" decisions and they may incorporate information communicated via Twitter in that process (Palen et al., 2009).
Situational awareness	The process of identifying, processing, and comprehending information so as to understand what is happening in their environment/community.
Social media	Any type of online-based communication that allows for a two-way path of information-sharing, and in which communities are established for that sharing. Social Media is a web-based service that allows individuals to (1) construct a public or semi-public profile within a bounded system, (2) articulate a list of other users with whom they share a connection, and (3) view their list of connections and those made by others within the system. (See Section 4.3 for further details on types of social media.)
Social networking sites (SNSs)	Also known as social media; allows individuals to construct a public or semipublic profile, develop a list of other users, and learn about the network of individuals (White et al., 2009).
Trusted sensors	People whose data can be directly processed because they are reliable (Díaz et al., 2013).
Virtual Operations Support Team (VOST)	A group which consists of trusted digital volunteers who extend the resources of an incident management team by performing online tasks that can be done remotely (Hughes, 2012).

ASSESS YOUR UNDERSTANDING

Go to www.wiley.com/go/pine/tech&emergmgmt_2e to evaluate your knowledge of using technology. This website contains MCQ's, self checks, review questions, applying this chapter and you try it.

References

Bird, D., Ling, M., & Haynes, K. (2012). Flooding Facebook-the use of social media during the Queensland and Victorian floods. *Australian Journal of Emergency Management*, 27(1), 27–33. http://doi.org/10.1017/CBO9781107415324.004

Boyd, D. M., & Ellison, N. B. (2007). Social network sites: Definition, history, and scholarship. *Journal of Computer-Mediated Communication*, 13(1), 210–230. Doi:10.1111/j.1083-6101.2007.00393.x.

Chavez, C., Repas, M. A., Stefaniak, T. L., & Chavez, C. (2010). *A New Way to Communicate with Residents: Local Government Use of Social Media to Prepare for Emergencies: An ICMA Report* (pp. 1–13). Washington, DC: ICMA.

Díaz, P., Aedo, I., Romano, M., & Onorati, T. (2013). Supporting Citizens 2.0 in disasters response. In *7th International Conference on Methodologies, Technologies and Tools Enabling E-Government (MeTTeG 2013)*, Pontevedra, Spain, October, pp. 79–88.

Gao, H., Barbier, G., & Goolsby, R. (2011). Harnessing the crowdsourcing power of social media for disaster relief. *CSDL Home IEEE Intelligent Systems*, 26(3), 10–14.

Hughes, A. L. P. (2012). The evolving role of the public information officer. *Journal of Homeland Security & Emergency Management*, 9(1), 1–20. http://doi.org/10.1515/1547-7355.1976 (accessed April 24, 2017).

Hughes, A., & Palen, L. (2012). The evolving role of the public information officer: An examination of social media in emergency management. *Journal of Homeland Security & Emergency Management*, 9(1), 1–20. http://doi.org/10.1515/1547-7355.1976 (accessed May 11, 2017).

Latonero, M., & Shklovski, I. (2011). Emergency management, twitter, and social media evangelism. *International Journal of Information Systems for Crisis Response and Management*, 3(4), 1–16. http://doi.org/10.4018/jiscrm.2011100101 (accessed April 24, 2017).

Lieberman, J. I. (2011). Understanding the power of social media as a communication tool in the aftermath of disasters. In *Committee on Homeland Security and Governmental Affairs United States Senate One Hundred Twelfth Congress*, pp. 1–126. Retrieved from http://scholar.google.com/scholar?hl=en&btnG=Search&q=intitle:UNDERSTANDING+THE+POWER+OF+SOCIAL+MEDIA+AS+A+COMMUNICATION+TOOL+IN+THE+AFTERMATH+OF+DISASTERS#0 (accessed April 24, 2017).

Lindsay, B. (2011). Social media and disasters: Current uses, future options, and policy considerations. *Journal of Current Issues in Media and Telecommunications*, 2(4), 287–297. https://digital.library.unt.edu/ark:/67531/metadc93902/ (accessed May 10, 2017).

Magsino, S. L. (2009). *Applications of Social Network Analysis for Building Community Disaster Resilience: Workshop Summary*. Washington, DC: National Research Council. https://www.abebooks.com/servlet/BookDetailsPL?bi=8639713616&searchurl=bi%3D0%26ds%3D30%26bx%3Doff%26sortby%3D17%26isbn%3D9780309140942%26recentlyadded%3Dall (accessed May 11, 2017).

National Research Council. (2011). Public Response to Alerts and Warnings on Mobile Devices: Summary of a Workshop on Current Knowledge and Research

Gaps. Retrieved from http://www.nap.edu/catalog/13076.html%5Cnhttp://
books.google.com/books?hl=en&lr=&id=L1RwsYceJ2AC&oi=
fnd&pg=PT1&dq=Public+Response+to+Alerts+and+Warnings+on+
Mobile+Devices:+Summary+of+a+Workshop+on+Current+Knowledge+and+
Research+Gaps& (accessed April 24, 2017).

National Research Council. (2013a). *Geotargeted Alerts and Warnings : Report of a
Workshop on Current Knowledge and Research Gaps.* Committee on Geotargeted
Disaster Alerts and Warnings: A Workshop on Current Knowledge and Research
Gaps; Computer Science and Sciences; National Research Council. Washington,
DC: National Research Council.

National Research Council. (2013b). Public Response to Alerts and Warnings Using
Social Media: Report of a Workshop on Current Knowledge and Research Gaps.
Retrieved from http://www.nap.edu/catalog.php?record_id=15853 (accessed
April 24, 2017).

Palen, L., & Liu, S. B. (2007). Citizen communications in crisis: Anticipating a
future of ICT-supported public participation. *Natural Hazards,* 727–736.
http://doi.org/10.1145/1240624.1240736 (accessed April 24, 2017).

Palen, L., Vieweg, S., Liu, S. B., & Hughes, A. L. (2009). Crisis in a networked
world. *Social Science Computer Review,* 27(4), 467–480. http://doi.org/
10.1177/0894439309332302 (accessed April 24, 2017).

Palen, L., Anderson, K. M., Mark, G., Martin, J., Sicker, D., Palmer, M., & Grunwald,
D. (2010). A vision for technology-mediated support for public participation &
assistance in mass emergencies & disasters. In *Proceedings of the 2010 ACMBCS
Visions of Computer Science Conference,* pp. 1–12. Retrieved from http://portal.
acm.org/citation.cfm?id=1811182.1811194 (accessed April 24, 2017).

Palen, L., Vieweg, S., & Anderson, K. M. (2011). Supporting the "Everyday
Analyst" in Safety- and Time-Critical Situations. *The Information Society Journal,*
27(1), 52–62.

Pew Global. (2016). http://www.pewglobal.org/2016/02/22/smartphone-ownership-
and-internet-usage-continues-to-climb-in-emerging-economies/ (accessed April
24, 2017).

Starbird, K. (2010). Self-Organizing by Digital Volunteers in Times of Crisis. In
29th Annual Chi Conference on Human Factors in Computing Systems,
Vancouver, BC, Canada, May 7–12, 2011.

Starbird, K., & Palen, L. (2010). Pass it on? Retweeting in mass emergency. In
*Proceedings of the International Conference on Information Systems for Crisis Response
and Management,* Seattle, WA.

Starbird, K., Muzny, G., & Palen, L. (2012). Learning from the crowd : Collaborative
filtering techniques for identifying on-the-ground Twitterers during mass disrup-
tions. In *ISCRAM,* Lisbon, Portugal, April 2011, pp. 1–10.

Telecoms.com. (April 2014). *US Smartphone Penetration Still Only 64%—Survey.*
http://telecoms.com/414662/us-smartphone-penetration-still-only-64-survey
(accessed April 24, 2017).

Vieweg, S., Hughes, A. L., Starbird, K., & Palen, L. (2010). Microblogging during
two natural hazards events: What twitter may contribute to situational awareness.
In *Proceedings of CHI 2010,* Atlanta, GA, April 10–15, 2010, pp. 1079–1088.

Vieweg, S. E. (2012). *Situational Awareness in Mass Emergency: A Behavioral and Linguistic Analysis of Microblogged Communications* (Doctoral dissertation). University of Colorado at Boulder, Boulder.

White, C., Plotnick, L., Kushma, J., Hiltz, S. R., & Turoff, M. (2009). An online social network for emergency management. *International Journal of Emergency Management*, 6(3/4), 369–382. http://doi.org/10.1504/IJEM.2009.031572 (accessed April 24, 2017).

Yates, D., & Paquette, S. (2011). Emergency knowledge management and social media technologies: A case study of the 2010 Haitian earthquake. *International Journal of Information Management*, 31(1), 6–13. http://doi.org/10.1016/j.ijinfomgt.2010.10.001 (accessed April 24, 2017).

Yin, J., Lampert, A., Cameron, M., Robinson, B., & Power, R. (2012). Using social media to enhance emergency situational awareness. *CSDL Home IEEE Intelligent Systems*, 27(6), 52–59.

5

GEOSPATIAL TECHNOLOGIES AND EMERGENCY MANAGEMENT

Jacqueline W. Curtis and Andrew Curtis

Department of Geography, Kent State University, Kent, OH, USA

Starting Point

Go to www.wiley.com/go/pine/tech&emergmgmt_2e to assess your knowledge of GIS and GPS tools.
Determine where you need to concentrate your effort.

What You'll Learn in This Chapter

▲ The nature and elements of geospatial technologies (GT) and their application to emergency management
▲ What data are being created, how we use them, and how we share what we know to create more resilient communities
▲ Appreciate the need to refine at the local level the general picture of social vulnerability from American Community Survey (ACS) data
▲ The use of GT to inform emergency management practitioners and the public

After Studying This Chapter, You'll Be Able To

▲ Describe appropriate uses of GT for identifying where are people and resources, where are our hazards, and where hazards and our people and resources interact.
▲ Clarify the limitations of ACS population data.
▲ Determine ways of identifying critical built and social infrastructure.
▲ Identify tools for understanding the spatial patterns of population and resources and their use in emergency management.
▲ Identify tools for understanding the human-hazard interface and then using it to guide emergency management activities.

Technology and Emergency Management, Second Edition. John C. Pine.
© 2018 John Wiley & Sons, Inc. Published 2018 by John Wiley & Sons, Inc.
Companion website: www.wiley.com/go/pine/tech&emergmgmt_2e

Goals and Outcomes

▲ Assess GT resources and the best way to use them in emergency planning and response

▲ Understand the value of utilizing buffers in analyzing exposures to hazards

▲ Clarify the nature of socially vulnerable populations in communities

▲ Determine appropriate methods for identifying mobile populations that are vulnerable to hazards

▲ Assess the benefits and limitations of using ACS data in emergency planning, response, and long-term recovery

▲ Assess emerging GT resources such as Google Street View and Spatial Video Geonarrative (SVG) in emergency management

▲ Develop the ability to identify resources for hazard zonation and their use in emergency planning and response

INTRODUCTION

Where is the flooding and how deep are the floodwaters here or there? Where do we land our helicopter safely and to serve the most people? Where do we enact an evacuation order? What pieces of critical infrastructure have been damaged? Where are the bodies and how do we get to them with the flooded or damaged roads? Where should we target our public education initiatives? Where are the repetitive loss properties in our community that are in need of structural mitigation? These are just a few of the many important questions that emergency management must answer. Some of these questions are dealt with on a daily basis, such as those regarding planning/preparedness and mitigation activities, while others are infrequent occurrences resulting from a disaster event. In either case, effective answers to these questions can be achieved with the assistance of **geospatial technologies (GT).**

This includes **Geographic Information Systems (GIS),** but also a whole suite of other approaches for data collection, analysis, visualization, and dissemination. It is also important to note that although GIS has a number of definitions, for the purpose of this chapter it can be summarized as software that enables creation and manipulation, analysis, visualization, and dissemination of spatial data. At its most basic level it provides dynamically linked windows between a map of these spatial data and an underlying database that holds all of the attributes of these data (e.g., latitude and longitude, as well as any other characteristics of each location).

Spatial data are *anything* with an associated location. Take a moment to think about what that really means. Of course, traditional data come to mind, such as transportation networks, census data, and hazard zones. However, with the proliferation of Global Positioning System (GPS)-enabled sensors and smartphones, anything from photos to tweets, air quality to noise pollution, can be assigned a coordinate and mapped. This advance, along with the spreading use of unmanned aerial vehicles (drones), and even of GIS, digital globes, and other mapping applications, means that we are currently in an unprecedented time of awareness, production, and use of spatial data.

5.1 Geospatial Technologies and Emergency Management

This chapter is about emergent GT that can improve upon traditional uses of GIS in planning/preparedness, response, recovery, and mitigation activities. In this chapter, we will examine existing and emergent GT applications in emergency management, as well as the promise and pitfalls that accompany this rapidly expanding technology. We will address questions on what data are being created, how do we make sense of them, and how do we share what we know to create more resilient communities?

Before addressing these topics and for the sake of transparency, it is worth noting that these issues are personal ones for us. They are not based solely on objective and disconnected observations of academics, but rather are colored by the combination of our research, teaching, and personal experiences over the past decade. We are geographers by training and hazards had always been in our background, but on August 29, 2005, everything changed. Hazards forever moved from a topic of study, to the forefront of every aspect of our lives. Many important accounts of Hurricane Katrina have been documented and adding our own personal experiences of the storm is not necessary. However, our professional perspective is of value here. Louisiana State University (LSU) students, faculty, and alumni with GIS experience were asked to help support the Louisiana State Emergency Operations Center (EOC) "GIS Desk." This entailed round-the-clock use of GIS to support the many needs in response and then in short-term recovery. We were a part of the team that answered this call and the experience quickly and dramatically initiated us into the world of emergency management. Indeed, we continue to work with all levels of government, non-profits, and researchers even many years after this event (Curtis et al., 2006a). It left an indelible mark on who we are, on our teaching, and on what we prioritize in our research. What became evident from our involvement in all phases of this event was the true power and need for GT to support effective emergency management. It does not have to be complicated or expensive, just targeted to what is needed and how to meet those needs. With this context to the chapter, we hope that you will have an open mind to the possibilities of GT in your daily professional activities.

5.1.1 Elements of GT

Even with our focus on technology, keep in mind that successful use of GT in emergency management requires the presence of several key pieces such as:

- ▲ Installation of the best software for the job,
- ▲ Having the technological infrastructure to run the relevant programs and make maps, and
- ▲ People to manage the system. At its core are great people who are technically well-trained, flexible, and good natured, as well as being well-versed in cartography.

After all, though GT has great potential power for assisting emergency management in making good decisions, they are just tools. The power of these tools comes from the people who know how to use them effectively.

5.1.2 Use of GT to Answer Questions in Emergency Management

With this background, the subsequent material will focus on three questions ubiquitous across emergency management that are often answered with some form of mapping:

1. where are our people and resources,
2. where are our hazards, and
3. where do these variables potentially interact?

Each of these guiding questions will be followed with a discussion and examples of standard approaches and issues, but will then pivot to identification of where adaptation of emergent forms of GT can augment and improve upon these standard applications. Of course, the rapid pace of GT development and even novel uses of existing approaches means that any text will not be able to comprehensively address this topic. Therefore, we are specifically focusing on effective "tried and true" approaches that we ourselves have used with our colleagues in emergency management.

We want to present what is relevant and accessible, knowing that there is a great deal of GT in development that is not widely available or user-friendly in their current states, but may become so in the future. This is an exciting time to work in the intersection of GT and emergency management! So with this framework and its caveats, at the completion of this chapter, the reader will be able to think more critically and creatively about the role of GT in emergency management.

5.2 GT Across the Human–Hazard Interface

5.2.1 Our People

Arguably the most common source of data used to locate people is the census. In the case of the United States, the decennial census and the sample data that are collected at 1-, 3-, and 5-year intervals through the **American Community Survey (ACS)** provide a nationally ubiquitous set of observations on the residential locations of a population, as well as social and economic characteristics for a particular time and a particular place. Many of the geographic scales at which these data are available are nested, meaning that, for example, blocks build into block groups, which build into tracts, while counties build into states. As the same data are collected for the same time periods, and for the same geographic scales, US Census data enable comparative studies across places, as well as examination of change over time in one place. Looking to the needs of emergency management, it is evident why these characteristics often result in use of census data for planning activities, as well as in monitoring recovery.

5.2.2 Limitations of Census Data

In terms of planning, census data have largely been used as one way to identify locations of **socially vulnerable populations** who, for example, would need preparedness materials in languages other than English or who would need priority assistance in evacuation. Indeed, census data are a main component in Federal Emergency Management Agency's (FEMA) HAZUS-MH software, in construction of the Social Vulnerability Index (SoVI) (Cutter et al., 2003), and in the development of State Hazard Mitigation Plans (SHMPs).

Despite the large number of variables in and the national ubiquity of census data, using this source in mapping for planning and recovery activities also has limitations. For example, what is collected in the census might not necessarily be exactly what is needed to answer a particular question, such as where are pregnant women located in our county or city? Pregnancy creates health vulnerability both for the mother and for her unborn child. However, the census does not collect these data, and, even if it did, this is such a dynamic situation that the gap between when the data would be collected and when they would be available for use make them unreliable. Identifying people with mobility impairment is another need that is not well-served with census data. Of course, there are proxies that can be utilized, such as age. These are populations who need to be checked on and assisted in when evacuation becomes necessary, but their exact locations need to be known to successfully accomplish this objective; knowing their residential census tract or even block is insufficient. Therefore, the variables collected in the census can create a general picture of social vulnerability, but should be refined at the local level through partnerships with social services and other entities who serve these populations.

The term "reside" also raises another limitation of census data. The demographic characteristics collected in the census are linked to the location where the person lists as his/her home address. When the person is a homeowner, that address is likely reliable; however, consider the large population who rents and those who are homeless. These populations are more likely to be mobile, which means that there is a greater likelihood that where their data are placed geographically may not be relevant after the time gap when the data are released. In the case of the homeless, there is an even more basic question of if their data are collected at all, as is true for illegal immigrants. Think about the challenge of locating **mobile populations** in terms of the importance of these data for planning and response in particular. How might we use GT to assist in this process? Later in the chapter, we will introduce the use of GPS-enabled video that can be used to survey the local social environment to identify such dynamic populations.

Furthermore, even for the population who has a stable home address, how much time do they spend at home and if they are not at home, where are they (Bhaduri et al., 2007; Kobayashi et al., 2011)? This information is vital when estimating the number of people who will be affected by a rapid-onset event, such as a tornado. If it occurs at night, early morning, or weekends, the number of people who reportedly live in an area as indicated by the census will likely be closer to reality than if the tornado strikes during work or school hours in the middle of the week. In places with large seasonal variation in population, such as beach destinations, the census population data may be unreliable for months out of each year, necessitating a locally initiated population count to improve the data.

FOR EXAMPLE

Let's look at the Tuscaloosa-Birmingham EF4 tornado on April 27, 2011. An overlay of population data from the census with the tornado path is one way to estimate impacted population (Figure 5-1). Consider how a simple overlay in Google Earth of census blocks might be used, and in particular the benefits and limitations of such an approach. Underneath these blocks is imagery from April 28, 2011, which clearly shows the damage scar created by the tornado.

Notice the variation in both size of the blocks and the distribution of structures within these blocks in comparison with the damage scar. The geography of damage is not necessarily well-suited for even this finest of census scales. Even at this scale, rarely is an entire block damaged, and in many cases it is only a fractional part of a block that is impacted. This is a result of the nature of tornadoes; census data for estimating impact might be more appropriate for more regional scale events, such as a hurricane. However, even in the aftermath of Hurricane Katrina, it was clear that flooding could vary in small spaces depending on characteristics of both the physical and built environments (Figure 5-2).

Figure 5-1

Google Earth overlay of Tuscaloosa census blocks with posttornado
aerial imagery, 2011.

Figure 5-2

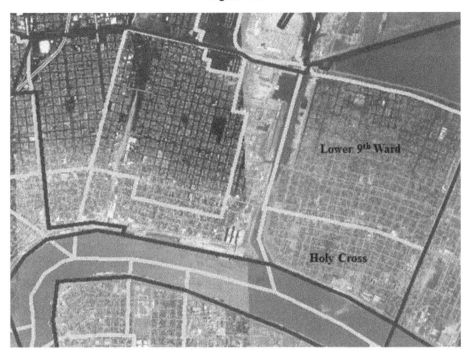

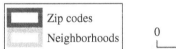

A comparison of administrative scales with flooding in Hurricane Katrina, New Orleans, 2005.

Figure 5-3

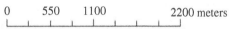

FEWER CHILDREN	Parishes hardest hit by Hurricane Katrina saw steep declines in the number of children between 2000 and 2010, new census data show.							
	Jefferson	**Orleans**	**Plaquemines**	**St. Bernard**	**St. Charles**	**St. John**	**St. Tammany**	**Region**
Overall population change, 2000 to 2010	–5.0%	–29.1%	–13.9%	–46.6%	9.8%	6.7%	22.2%	–11.3%
Change in population of children younger than 18	–15.5%	–43.4%	–19.0%	–45.9%	–2.5%	8.0%	10.5%	–22.5%
Source: U.S. Census								THE TIMES-PICAYUNE

Census data on child population change by parish for the impacted region (2000–2010). http://www.nola.com/katrina/index.ssf/2011/02/child_population_in_new_orlean.html.

These issues are primarily a concern of using the census in preparedness and response activities, but the census has both benefits and limitations in understanding recovery as well, especially long-term recovery. For example, in longer-term analysis of population postevent, the census can be a powerful source for identifying changes over time and for specific populations (Figure 5-3).

This overview and examples show that in sum, yes, the census is a good place to start when mapping population data related to planning, recovery planning, and even to some degree in monitoring long-term recovery as well. However, its limitations should be considered, as well as the potential integration of GT, such as aerial imagery, to enhance the census data.

Given the limits of census data, it is important to note the existence of emergent resources that have been developed which can improve upon census data, such as LandScan (Bhaduri et al., 2007). However, also note that observations of aerial images alone can provide powerful augmentation of improving understanding of population distribution. Of course, this approach is better suited for small area studies. The census and applications such as LandScan are developed for scales ranging from national to global.

5.3 Our Resources

Locating our resources is a more straightforward task than pinning down a dynamic population. Usually, the first resources of concern are our critical infrastructure. This dataset often relies on geocoded data of resources and is a priority dataset for all levels of emergency management. Clearly, it is essential to know locations of resources such as power plants and hospitals, but it is equally important to know the characteristics of these resources, such as how many beds does the hospital have, what trauma level is it? This need to know location along with capacity is true of most critical infrastructure. Take shelters, for example. Is it located in an area that is not at risk to flooding or wildfire or tsunami (Wood and Good, 2004)? Equally important, are the transportation routes connecting this resource to the community also low risk for being impacted by a natural disaster? What is the square footage of the shelter, how many people can it humanely accommodate? In mapping critical infrastructure, there are three main aspects that need to be addressed: location, capacity, context.

5.3.1 Understanding Critical Infrastructure

Location may remain relatively static for these infrastructural items, but capacity less so. Take, for example, a hospital. Although there will be a certain number of beds, those already occupied preevent will clearly reduce this capacity. Linking back to the previous discussion on mapping population, depending on the type and timing of event, and the type of hospital, not only the capacity but the need for capacity at that specific location, or even accessibility to it, might change (Curtis et al., 2012). Furthermore, the context in which the critical resources are located may change in an event. For example, a structure may be built to code due to its proximity to the Cascadia Subduction Zone (CSZ), but what if the surrounding buildings are high risk for failure in an earthquake, perhaps as identified by rapid visual screening (Applied Technology Council (ATC), 1988; Wood and Good, 2004). Such screenings can be conducted through walking or dashboard audits. However, more recent advances in GT have leveraged GPS-enabled video cameras

Figure 5-4

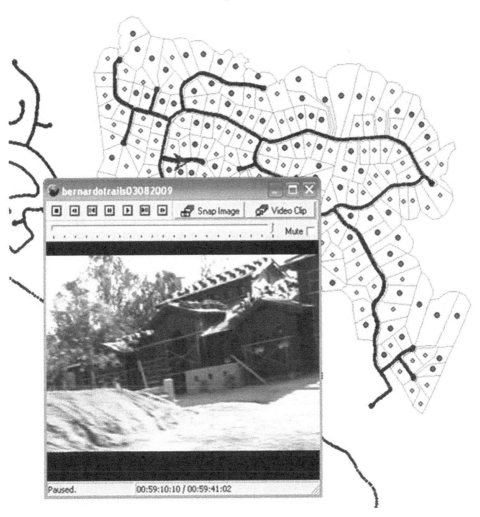

Example of spatial video to collect and map the built environment context.

(spatial video) (Curtis et al., 2013) as well as the use of Google Street View (Mabon, 2016) to spatially code characteristics of the built environment pertinent to the needs of emergency management (Figure 5-4).

5.3.2 Understanding Critical Social Infrastructure

In addition to what is traditionally considered critical infrastructure, there is growing acknowledgement that critical *social* infrastructure is also important, especially in recovery planning. For example, roads are a part of critical infrastructure and must necessarily be reconstructed if damaged in order for a community to recover from an event. However, the roads are important not in and of themselves, but because they connect people to the resources that form the fabric of their communities, such as faith-based entities (e.g., churches, synagogues, mosques), libraries, schools, parks, grocery stores, pharmacies, and health clinics. Only devoting time to documentation of traditional critical infrastructure data will not be wholly effective in realistic recovery planning that will actually result in recovery. Furthermore, these entities should be included in education about their risks and structural and nonstructural mitigation activities that will help protect them and assist in decision making. Including the community as partners identifying infrastructure that is critical to them is essential and well-suited for facilitation through mapping activities (Mills, 2009; O'Sullivan et al., 2013).

5.3.3 Resources of Social Importance

So far, we have focused on data that answers the questions of where are our people and our resources? There are clearly good reasons that sources such as the US Census are commonly used to identify the geography of local populations and that critical infrastructure data are geocoded to know the locations, capacity, and context. Though less commonly undertaken, it also makes sense to identify resources of social importance to the community. To this point, these data can be mapped based on secondary sources (i.e., someone else has already collected the data—government database, phone directory, etc.). However, there are some important datasets that simply do not exist in mappable form, ready for download and input into GIS. For example, in areas of flood risk, which structures have been elevated to account for base flood elevations and which are built on slab foundations? In areas at risk to tropical cyclones, which structures have hurricane shutters or roof clamps? Perhaps local permit data will include these variables, but not necessarily. However, all of these mitigation features are visible from the street. Therefore, using built environment surveys can be a useful investment in time and human resources to document the spatial patterns of these infrastructure improvements, or lack thereof. Built environment surveys can be as simple as walking down the street with a notepad or field map, noting presence/absence of specific features; it can include a digital survey form with GPS-enabled data input and photography.

Since Hurricane Katrina in 2005, advances have been made with using GPS-enabled video (spatial video) to drive streets and then code the observable features of interest in GIS or even in Google Earth. This approach was initiated to address the need for systematic and replicable damage assessment at a regional scale, but then was subsequently utilized to monitor recovery. For example, this approach was used to identify the uneven patterns or rebuilding in neighborhoods across New Orleans, as well as to document cultural resources at the same time (Mills et al., 2010). Since then, the technology needed to conduct spatial video surveys has dramatically decreased in size and in price, and increased in ease of use. However, there is an even less expensive approach that is being tested, **Google Street View (GSV)**, which can be virtually "driven" and then each structure coded based on variables of interest (e.g., structural mitigation features) (Curtis et al., 2013).

5.3.4 Spatial Video Geonarrative

Recently, spatial video has been further advanced to include participant commentary to describe and explain what is directly observable in the built environment. This approach is termed **spatial video geonarrative (SVG)** (Figure 5-5). This advance is important because the meaning for what is being seen cannot always be known from observation alone. For example, it may appear that a home is being

Figure 5-5

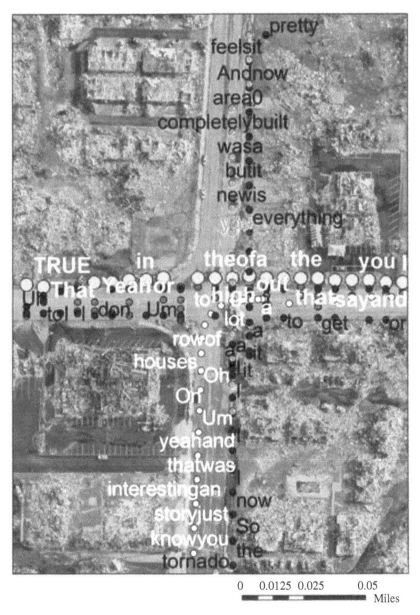

Example of spatial video geonarrative in a postdisaster environment (Curtis et al., 2015).

rebuilt after a disaster, and then it becomes clear that the property is inhabited. However, just because the structure is back does not mean that the residents are those who lived there before the event. Furthermore, what was an owner-occupied unit may become a renter-occupied unit. These differences have implications for the long-term sustainability of the community and its recovery. SVG enables local residents or expert practitioners to talk about their knowledge of individual properties and then this audio commentary is geocoded as is the image. The result is both a map of built environment conditions and an explanation of why they appear the way that they do.

5.4 Understanding Our Hazards

Understanding the spatial patterns of population and resources for the purposes of emergency management has been steadily improving through integration of GT. The same is true for improved knowledge of the geography of natural hazards. There are a few common ways of identifying these risk areas, such as mapping casualties from past events and delineating **hazard zones** by specific type of event. Furthermore, there is growing research into mapping the public perception of where these zones are located in order to compare perception to reality. Clearly, there are potential implications for using such data to educate communities and improve their preparedness and engagement in mitigation.

5.4.1 Natural Hazards Casualties in the United States

Starting with the locations of past event casualties, National Oceanic and Atmospheric Administration (NOAA) provides statistics on weather fatalities each year for the past 76 years (http://www.nws.noaa.gov/om/hazstats.shtml). Its US Summaries from 1995 include weather events under the classifications of convection (e.g., lightning, tornado, thunderstorm wind, and hail), extreme temperatures (e.g., cold and heat), flood (e.g., flash flood and river flood), marine (e.g., coastal storm, tsunami, and rip current), tropical cyclones (e.g., tropical storm/hurricane), winter (e.g., winter storm, ice avalanche), and other (e.g., drought, dust storm, dust devil, rain, fog, high wind, waterspout, fire weather, mud slide, volcanic ash, miscellaneous). The annual reports also present a summary of all fatalities by age and gender as well as by month and by state for fatalities, injuries, property damage, crop damage, and total damage for all weather events. Fatalities are then reported by state, by weather type, and then by location (e.g., ballfield, boating, business, camping, heavy equipment/construction, golfing, in water, long span roof, mobile/trailer home, other, outside/open areas, permanent home, school, telephone, under tree, and vehicle/towed trailer). Some data are also available for multiple hazards at the county scale (Borden and Cutter 2008). However, there are also less consistent and perhaps even ethically questionable sources on outcomes from past events, such as maps provided by news outlets (Curtis et al., 2006b).

5.4.2 Hazard Zonation

Knowing where people have been impacted in the past is only one way to understand where our hazards are located, and certainly it has limitations in terms of scale and data availability, just to name a few. More commonly, a dataset that is widely used in emergency management is **hazard zonation.** This only makes sense as in planning activities it is important to know where people are in relation to risk. Certainly, some types of natural hazards are more suited for zonation, such as floods where the risk is usually tightly concentrated in the floodplain or tsunamis with the accompanying tsunami inundation zone (Table 5-1). However, at the other end of the spectrum are other types of natural hazards that are less geographically predictable, such as tornadoes.

In using hazard zonation data both for understanding the location of risk and for educating the public about this geography, it is important to note the limitations of any map in the representation of boundaries. Most hazard zones are polygons, an area of hazard risk with a boundary that indicates a sharp change from hazard on one side to no hazard on the other side. Maps necessarily generalize reality, and for many types of maps this limitation is understood. However, with spatial data moving from static maps at a fixed scale, to interactive Web maps and Google Earth data, the public can control zooming in and out of these data in the context of their own lives (e.g., where is their home in relation to a hazard zone— on one side of the boundary there appears to be risk, but step just across the boundary and risk apparently disappears).

Whereas the main objective of hazard zonation data is to identify where, based on scientific evidence, hazards exist or are likely to exist, in regard to protecting people, this is only half of the equation. Where hazards exist and where people believe they exist can lead to quite different maps. This difference matters in emergency management as what people perceive to be true will influence their behaviors, regardless of what scientific evidence suggests. Furthermore, most people are not scientists, so detailed knowledge of hazard zonation should not be expected of them. However, understanding their perceptions can be a first step in educating them on the realistic proximity to risk and therefore the preparedness and mitigation activities they should undertake. A number of studies have examined the spatial aspects of perception of hazard

Table 5-1 Example of Resources for Hazard Zonation and Past Events

Data	Resource
Tsunami inundation zones	Oregon Tsunami Clearinghouse: http://www.oregongeology.org/tsuclearinghouse/
Wildfires	Cal Fire (California) FRAP GIS Data including a fire hazard severity zone map: http://frap.fire.ca.gov/data/frapgisdata-subset
Tornadoes	http://www.nws.noaa.gov/gis/

Table 5-2 Examples of Spatial Data on Hazard Zonation Perception

Data	Characteristics/Zonation
Tornado warnings and watches	Rapid onset, dynamic zonation
Flood	Variable onset; variable zonation—dynamic (flash flood) or fixed (flood zones)
Tsunami	Rapid onset, fixed zonation
Landslide and Liquefaction	Rapid onset, fixed zonation
Hurricane	Slow onset, dynamic zonation

zonation (Table 5-2) (Brennan et al., 2016; Cheung et al., 2016; O'Neill et al., 2015, 2016; Ruin et al., 2007).

5.4.3 Our Human–Hazard Interface

Identifying the human–hazard interface, and then using it to guide planning/preparedness, response, recovery, and mitigation activities, is at the heart of where GT should play a central role in emergency management. Traditionally, the techniques for mapping these areas are relatively straightforward and consist of overlay (placing one or more GIS layers with others in the same map and looking for areas where hazard zones, people, and resources coincide) and **buffer** (identifying a set distance of risk and identifying people and resources within this set distance).

With all of the advances in spatial analysis built into GIS, as well as reliance on overlays and buffers, it can be easy to assume that this level of investigation is necessary for any phenomena. However, the best map is the one that meets your needs. Whether this is a choropleth map or the results of spatial modeling, there is no judgment on what is best—as long as it provides realistic decision support to protect people and the environment. Even a poster-size map on a wall with thumb tacks or sticky notes can be effective if it can be used to discern patterns and identify priorities. Of the two common "analysis" techniques, overlay is perhaps the most straightforward approach to enable mapped interpretation of the relationship among different variables. For example, Figure 5-6 shows historical wildfire burn perimeters over current residential parcels in Southern California.

5.4.4 Understanding Overlays and Buffers

While overlay shows spatial coincidence (structures coinciding with a hazard zone), **buffers** are used to show proximity (structured within specified distances of a hazard point, line, or polygon). But we need to know more than what is where. We also need to know the conditions of the physical and built environment. In a GIS, buffers are areas that are designated around a point, line, or polygon based on fixed distances of influence/impact. Buffers are user defined on two aspects: size

Figure 5-6

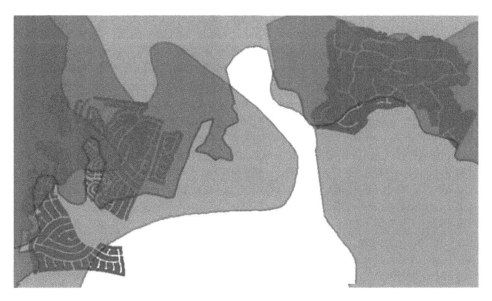

An example of overlay with historical wildfire burn perimeters and current
residential development.

and shape. Users set the distance or distances of interest away from a point, line, or boundary of a polygon. The buffer that results is equidistant around this risk location. Commonly, a circle is drawn around the area of interest at set intervals. This procedure assumes an isotropic plane, where everything is the same in all directions. This is problematic when analyzing exposure to a hazard, but also when access to resources is needed in an event. For example, if we wanted to examine access to a Level 1 Trauma center, one metric may be the number of people within walking distance to this resource, with walking distance often considered as 1600 m. However, a buffer will consider this 1600 m to be equal in all ways, in all directions. Variations in the physical environment (e.g., steep slopes, presence of water bodies), the built environment (e.g., walls, fences), and even the social environment (e.g., gang boundaries) may vary within this buffer, resulting in real differences in access depending on where people are in this zone.

The second aspect of buffers is their shape. Although users can easily generate buffers of any size, they have less choice in its resulting shape in commonly used GIS software. The buffer is usually a circle or it is linear around a specific network (e.g., roads). However, there have been some advances outside of common GIS software packages to more user-defined control on buffer development (e.g., the sausage buffer by Forsyth and colleagues (2012)). For airborne risks, plume models are an advance over the standard concentric circles or other types of buffers to identify areas of potential exposure, though they require training beyond standard GIS operations (e.g., circle or network buffers). In sum, there have been many studies into the development, use, and limitations of buffers, mostly in the field of air pollution or airborne toxic releases or in studies on exposures in the built environment (Chakraborty and Armstrong, 1997; Cova et al., 2005; Crowell et al., 2010; Maantay, 2002; Tate et al., 2010).

Once the buffers are established, a spatial query can be calculated to find out how many of any particular variable (people, structures, etc.) fall within or intersect this buffer. Overlay and buffer are not necessarily separate operations, but may complement one another. For example, Cutter and colleagues (2000) used these approaches in an all-hazards analysis of Georgetown County, South Carolina. Furthermore, in both operations, a spatial join or spatial query can be performed to quantify the number of people or structures, and the number of certain classes of people or structures at risk defined by spatial coincidence or proximity (e.g., number of people under the age of 5, number of structures built on slab foundations). Despite the straightforward procedures of these techniques, they also have limitations which should be considered and acknowledged in such mapping. Some GIS applications have a suite of spatial analysis tools that only require a few clicks of the mouse and then result in buffers on the map. Take caution in using these tools and make sure you understand all of the options and their implications for the results. There are some stand-alone products that offer more transparency, but require some additional training on use (Forsyth et al., 2012).

5.5 Dissemination and Hazard Communication

Using GT to create and analyze spatial data is ineffective unless these results are shared to inform the decision-making process of emergency management practitioners and/or the public (Haynes et al., 2007). Usually, this requires making a map. However, deciding how to make these maps is an art and science unto itself, which is why knowledge of cartography is equally as important as knowledge of GIS. Despite all of the power and potential of GIS, at the end of the day, it is only software. In this sense, it does not do all of the thinking for the user, but rather is directed to do certain operations in certain ways by a person. Think of it like the word processing software you use on a daily basis. Just because you know how to press buttons and you know what the buttons do does not mean you know how to compose a report.

Composition is key to communication. This is true in writing, as well as in making maps. In addition to the need to know how to effectively design maps for emergency management practitioners is the need to provide the maps in ways that will be useful. Sharing GIS data in its native format or even in a GIS viewer are not necessarily going to be useful to the many stakeholders who need these data to inform their decision making. Although certainly there are growing numbers of people with awareness of and comfort in using GIS and related technologies, they are still in the minority. Technology should not be a barrier to communication, but rather should enhance it so that we know more, faster to create quality situation awareness for as many people as possible. Viewing GIS data in a GIS is sometimes the best approach, but often it is not when dealing with nonspecialists or the general public.

Table 5-3 Examples of Hazard Data in Google Earth Formats

Data	Link
National Weather Service	http://www.nws.noaa.gov/gis/kmlpage.htm
USGS	http://earthquake.usgs.gov/learn/kml.php
FEMA National Flood Hazard Layer Web Map Service	https://hazards.fema.gov/femaportal/wps/portal/NFHLWMSkmzdownload

5.5.1 Contribution of Google Earth

In the past decade, the advent of Google Earth has had a monumental impact on public use of geospatial data and comfort in looking at maps and aerial images as a part of everyday life. It has also provided a publicly accessible repository for scientific data on natural hazards that is usable by unprecedented numbers. With the ability to write GIS data out to keyhole markup language (KML)/KMZ (the compressed version of KML) files, people of any background can see what scientists use for hazard zonation and past event data. For example, Table 5-3 provides just a few of the growing numbers of resources created by government agencies to facilitate dissemination of spatial data on hazards in a way that is user-friendly and familiar to the public.

Furthermore, the power and simplicity of repeat imagery should not be overlooked in this discussion of using GIS and GT in emergency management (Figure 5-7). Google Earth often disseminates high-resolution pre- and postevent data collected through a variety of sensors and a variety of sources and the pictures themselves enable observations of spatial and temporal patterns at different scales, from a hazard zone to a neighborhood, and even across a region.

5.6 Summary

Maps and spatial data offer emergency management and the public an opportunity to actively work together in developing disaster resiliency in their communities. Not only are maps a forum upon which to have discussions about planning and mitigation, but they are also a resource to connect with local schools on these issues as well as that of personal safety in emergency events. Use of spatial data and maps on local hazards help teachers meet grade content standards for earth/space science and environmental science on a number of topics from geology to weather (e.g., flood maps, maps of past tornado events). This is just one example of impactful opportunities for use of GT in emergency management to serve our communities.

Indeed, all disasters are local; therefore local level emergency management (e.g., county, city) is critical to success in planning, response, recovery, and mitigation activities. As we have discussed in this chapter, GT plays a central role in effective implementation of such endeavors. However, even having and

Figure 5-7

(a)

8/16/2005

(b)

3/22/2010

Google Earth aerial imagery pre- and post-Katrina for a section of one New Orleans neighborhood. (a) Imagery from August 16, 2005, and (b) imagery from March 22, 2010.

then maintaining sustainable GT operations in local emergency management is a challenge, especially in places throughout the United States with limited resources. Part of the problem is the limited pipeline of students who have the requisite skills and training in both GIS and emergency management. Furthermore, for those that do meet the criteria, they then need to go and stay in the places that are in high need for their services.

What commonly happens is that a young professional with some of these skills goes to work in an emergency management department, they receive training specifically on the use of GIS in emergency management, and then due to the limited pipeline they are highly marketable for a similar job in state or federal government, as well as in the private sector. The local emergency management department can then be left in a cycle of recruiting, training, and then replacing this type of personnel, which results in limited GIS functionality and long-term sustainability.

It is a frustrating cycle and one that is counterproductive to the main objective of protecting our communities. However, this situation can also open up possibilities to be creative in meeting the needs of our communities and in building that pipeline of GIS emergency management professionals, such as developing **Memorandums of Understanding (MOUs)** with local universities that teach GIS. Their faculty, students, and facilities can be used in an event to bolster local government resources, and, indeed, having a backup site for GIS operations is good practice in any case.

Consider developing internship programs for students in GIS at the undergraduate and graduate levels, as many of them are required to engage in a senior project or practicum. Though each individual collaboration would be short term, from one year to one semester, this approach can help accomplish priority GT-related projects in local emergency management, and give the next generation experience with the importance of their work to the lives and well-being of our communities. Hopefully, it makes a lasting mark and influences their future career decisions to go into this area of work.

5.7 Conclusions

Effective use of GT in emergency management can come in a variety of ways, from its complete integration in projects across planning, response, recovery, and mitigation, to good outcomes on individual projects accomplished with even the most limited of technology and personnel. The common thread is creating safer places so that our communities can grow and prosper now and in the long term. Without safety, little else can be sustainably accomplished. Emergency management plays a key role in this outcome and GT provides important tools to help reach this objective.

Spatial data and maps do not make themselves. GT is only as good as the people who use it, and this is a reflection of not only technical skills, but also the thorough knowledge of processes underlying hazards, social/behavioral responses to these phenomena, and the duties of emergency management in connecting them to result in safe, resilient communities.

It can be easy to become overwhelmed with the many different tools, as well as the voluminous number of applications for emergency management. However, effective GT is GT that works for you to improve decision making. This can be a variety of things, from making large wall maps with an overlay of local hazard zones with locations of critical infrastructure to advanced spatial modeling to examine scenarios for evacuation of a major metropolitan area. Regardless of the applications, the key is people, not software.

Having personnel who are committed to the safety of the community and who have experience and skills specifically integrating GT in emergency management is what will lead to effective use of the technology. They should listen to the needs of stakeholders, be flexible in how they make maps in order to serve different constituencies, and always be willing to grow in their technical skills. GT is always growing with new tools; practitioners in this field should engage in professional development so that they are aware of these advances, but then can also make good decisions about whether or even how they might be appropriate for meeting the needs of their community.

KEY TERMS

American Community Survey (ACS)	A nationally ubiquitous data source including a set of observations on the residential locations of a population, as well as social and economic characteristics for a particular time and a particular place.
Buffers	Areas that are designated around a point, line, or polygon based on fixed distances of influence/impact. The areas that are defined by the user in two aspects: size and shape. Users set the distance or distances of interest away from a point, line, or boundary of a polygon. The buffer that results is equidistant around this risk hazardous location.
Geographic Information Systems (GIS)	Software that enables creation and manipulation, analysis, visualization, and dissemination of spatial data.
Geospatial technologies (GT)	A suite of approaches in addition to GIS for data collection, analysis, visualization, and dissemination.
Google Street View	Google Street View is a technology featured in Google Maps and Google Earth that provides panoramic views from positions along many streets in the world.
Hazard zonation	Identification of hazard areas that are at risk, based on scientific evidence, and information used to protect people.

Memorandums of Understanding (MOUs)	A memorandum of understanding is an agreement between two or more parties. It expresses a common intent to act.
Mobile populations	A demographic characteristic of a population that is not linked to an address location where the person is not a homeowner and who might rent or is homeless. When the person is not a homeowner, they are more likely to be mobile, which means that there is a greater likelihood that where their data are placed geographically may not be relevant after the time gap when the data are released. In the case of the homeless, there is an even more basic question of if their data are collected at all, as is true for illegal immigrants.
Socially vulnerable populations	Population groups who face greater vulnerability in disasters such as those who would need preparedness materials in languages other than English or who would need priority assistance in evacuation.
Spatial data	Is any data that is associated with a location and may include, for example, transportation networks, census data, and hazard zones.
Spatial video geonarrative (SVG)	GPS-enriched commentary to capture local knowledge (e.g., institutional or community-based). This approach is especially valuable in dynamic environments, such as places undergoing post-disaster recovery.

ASSESS YOUR UNDERSTANDING

Go to www.wiley.com/go/pine/tech&emergmgmt_2e to evaluate your knowledge of using technology. This website contains MCQ's, self checks, review questions and applying this chapter.

References

Applied Technology Council (ATC). (1988). *Rapid Visual Screening of Buildings for Potential Seismic Hazard: A Handbook.* Earthquake Hazards Reduction Series 41 (p. 154). Washington, DC: Federal Emergency management Agency.

Bhaduri, B., Bright, E., Coleman, P., & Urban, M. L. (2007). LandScan USA: A high-resolution geospatial and temporal modeling approach for population distribution and dynamics. *GeoJournal, 69*(1–2), 103–117.

Borden, K. A., & Cutter, S. L. (2008). Spatial patterns of natural hazards mortality in the United States. *International Journal of Health Geographics*, 7(1), 1.

Brennan, M., O'Neill, E., Brereton, F., Dreoni, I., & Shahumyan, H. (2016). Exploring the spatial dimension of community-level flood risk perception: A cognitive mapping approach. *Environmental Hazards*, 15(4), 1–32.

Chakraborty, J., & Armstrong, M. P. (1997). Exploring the use of buffer analysis for the identification of impacted areas in environmental equity assessment. *Cartography and Geographic Information Systems*, 24(3), 145–157.

Cheung, W., Houston, D., Schubert, J. E., Basolo, V., Feldman, D., Matthew, R., Sanders, B. F., Karlin, B., Goodrich, K. A., Contreras, S. L., & Luke, A. (2016). Integrating resident digital sketch maps with expert knowledge to assess spatial knowledge of flood risk: A case study of participatory mapping in Newport Beach, California. *Applied Geography*, 74, 56–64.

Cova, T. J., Dennison, P. E., Kim, T. H., & Moritz, M. A. (2005). Setting wildfire evacuation trigger points using fire spread modeling and GIS. *Transactions in GIS*, 9(4), 603–617.

Crowell, M., Coulton, K., Johnson, C., Westcott, J., Bellomo, D., Edelman, S., & Hirsch, E. (2010). An estimate of the US population living in 100-year coastal flood hazard areas. *Journal of Coastal Research*, 26, 201–211.

Curtis, A., Mills, J. W., Blackburn, J. K., Pine, J. C., & Kennedy, B. (2006a). Louisiana State University geographic information system support of hurricane Katrina recovery operations. *International Journal of Mass Emergencies and Disasters*, 24(2): 203–221.

Curtis, A., Mills, J. W., & Leitner, M. (2006b). Keeping an eye on privacy issues with geospatial data. *Nature*, 441(7090), 150–150.

Curtis, J. W., Curtis, A., & Upperman, J. (2012). Using a geographic information system (GIS) to assess pediatric surge potential after a disaster. *Disaster Medicine and Public Health Preparedness*, 6, 163–169.

Curtis, J. W., Curtis, A., Mapes, J., Szell, A., & Cinderich, A. (2013). Using Google Street View for systematic observation of the built environment: Analysis of spatio-temporal instability of imagery dates. *International Journal of Health Geographics*, 12(53). https://ij-healthgeographics.biomedcentral.com/articles/10.1186/1476-072X-12-53 (accessed May 10, 2017).

Curtis, A., Curtis, J. W., Shook, E., Smith, S., Jefferis, E., Porter, L., Laura, S., Felix, C., & Kerndt, P. R. (2015). Spatial video geonarratives and health: Case studies in post-disaster recovery, crime, mosquito control and tuberculosis in the homeless. *International Journal of Health Geographics*, 14(1), 1.

Cutter, S. L., Mitchell, J. T., & Scott, M. S. (2000). Revealing the vulnerability of people and places: A case study of Georgetown county, South Carolina. *Annals of the Association of American Geographers*, 90(4), 713–737.

Cutter, S. L., Boruff, B. J., & Shirley, W. L. (2003). Social vulnerability to environmental hazards. *Social Science Quarterly*, 84(2), 242–261.

Forsyth, A., Van Riper, D., Larson, N., Wall, M., & Neumark-Sztainer, D. (2012). Creating a replicable, valid cross-platform buffering technique: The sausage network buffer for measuring food and physical activity built environments. *International Journal of Health Geographics*, 11(1), 1.

Haynes, K., Barclay, J., & Pidgeon, N. (2007). Volcanic hazard communication using maps: An evaluation of their effectiveness. *Bulletin of Volcanology*, *70*(2), 123–138.

Kobayashi, T., Medina, R. M., & Cova, T. J. (2011). Visualizing diurnal population change in urban areas for emergency management. *The Professional Geographer*, *63*(1), 113–130.

Maantay, J. (2002). Mapping environmental injustices: Pitfalls and potential of geographic information systems in assessing environmental health and equity. *Environmental Health Perspectives*, *110*(Suppl. 2), 161.

Mabon, L. (2016). Charting disaster recovery via Google Street View: A social science perspective on challenges raised by the Fukushima nuclear disaster. *International Journal of Disaster Risk Science* [online], *7*(2), 175–185.

Mills, J. W. (2009). Spatial decision support in a post-disaster environment: A community-focused approach. *Cartographica*, *44*(1), 17–31.

Mills, J. W., Curtis, A., Kennedy, B., Kennedy, S. W., & Edwards, J. (2010). Geospatial video for field data collection. *Applied Geography*, *30*(4), 533–547.

O'Neill, E., Brennan, M., Brereton, F., & Shahumyan, H. (2015). Exploring a spatial statistical approach to quantify flood risk perception using cognitive maps. *Natural Hazards*, *76*(3), 1573–1601.

O'Neill, E., Brereton, F., Shahumyan, H., & Peter Clinch, J. (2016). The impact of perceived flood exposure on flood-risk perception: The role of distance. *Risk Analysis*, *36*(11), 2158–2186.

O'Sullivan, T. L., Kuziemsky, C. E., Toal-Sullivan, D., & Corneil, W. (2013). Unraveling the complexities of disaster management: A framework for critical social infrastructure to promote population health and resilience. *Social Science & Medicine*, *93*, 238–246.

Ruin, I., Gaillard, J. C., & Lutoff, C. (2007). How to get there? Assessing motorists' flash flood risk perception on daily itineraries. *Environmental Hazards*, *7*(3), 235–244.

Tate, E., Cutter, S. L., & Berry, M. (2010). Integrated multihazard mapping. *Environment and Planning B: Planning and Design*, *37*(4), 646–663.

Wood, N. J., & Good, J. W. (2004). Vulnerability of port and harbor communities to earthquake and tsunami hazards: The use of GIS in community hazard planning. *Coastal Management*, *32*(3), 243–269.

6

DIRECT AND REMOTE SENSING SYSTEMS: DESCRIBING AND DETECTING HAZARDS

Jessica Mitchell and Burke McDade

Department of Geography and Planning, Appalachian State University, Boone, NC, USA

Starting Point

Go to www.wiley.com/go/pine/tech&emergmgmt_2e to assess your knowledge of operational problems and technology.
Determine where to concentrate your effort.

What You'll Learn in This Chapter

▲ The differences between direct and remote sensing
▲ How data collected using these two approaches are complimentary
▲ How direct and remote sensing can be applied to emergency management tasks
▲ How trends in the field of remote sensing are influencing emergency management and the study of natural hazards

After Studying This Chapter, You'll Be Able To

▲ Use the data gathered from direct and remote sensing to assist in emergency management tasks.
▲ Understand the use of weather stations to track weather patterns and the progress of natural disasters.
▲ Compare and contrast the value of a rain and river gauges.
▲ Examine what hazards can be detected by satellite sensors such as GOES and Landsat.
▲ Analyze what qualities are needed in using direct and remote sensing technologies.
▲ Identify the value of alternative remote sensing technology in disaster response.
▲ Explain the value of spatial resolution of different satellite imagery.

Technology and Emergency Management, Second Edition. John C. Pine.
© 2018 John Wiley & Sons, Inc. Published 2018 by John Wiley & Sons, Inc.
Companion website: www.wiley.com/go/pine/tech&emergmgmt_2e

Goals and Outcomes

▲ Compare and contrast data obtained from direct and remote sensing
▲ Examine the value of weather stations, stream gauges, and rain gauges in emergency planning and response
▲ Evaluate the usefulness of air data sensors in a chemical response
▲ Assess how access to real-time data could influence decision making

INTRODUCTION

Sensors that convert environmental measurements into electronic signals are mounted on a variety of platforms in direct and indirect contact with the Earth. Advances in these direct and remote sensing technologies are used in all phases of emergency management and new applications are rapidly emerging at a time when extreme events are increasing in frequency and severity. While sensors can only record what is happening at a certain time, data can be analyzed to help emergency managers in monitoring, planning, response, and mitigation. Weather station instruments and streams gauges are examples of direct sensors used that can detect hazards by continuously monitoring air, weather, and water conditions. Sensors that are deployed remotely from platforms such as satellites and manned and unmanned aircraft collect imagery and topographical data. Direct sensing is also referred to as in situ data collection and is considered ground reference data when used to validate digital images acquired from remote platforms. Remote sensing datasets are used in a growing number of emergency management applications, such as predicting flood impacts, detecting new wildfire starts, and providing early warnings of landslide danger. In this chapter, you will be introduced to different types of direct and remote sensing systems and learn how different types of data are collected, processed, and served to the public for use in all phases of emergency management, including planning, response, recovery, and mitigation. By the end of the chapter you will be able to explain the differences between direct and remote sensing and discuss how data collected using these two approaches are complementary. Real-world scenarios, applications, and case studies are designed to help you understand how direct and remote sensing can be applied to emergency management tasks. This chapter ends with an examination of how trends in the field of remote sensing are influencing emergency management and the study of natural hazards.

6.1 Data Collection

Vulnerability and resilience to natural hazards vary across communities. Ideally, to prepare for the hazards that threaten a community, managers can assess the conditions that define vulnerability and resilience not only with standardized measurements in the context of the natural world, but at the interface of humans and their interactions with the built and physical environment (Cutter et al., 2008).

Once the greatest threats to a community have been identified, hazards can be monitored using direct and remotely sensed datasets and products that are available from a growing number of public and commercial sources.

Direct and remote sensing data collection is critical to emergency planning, response, recovery, and mitigation efforts. The data that are collected involve measurements and reveal facts that are known at a snapshot in time. These data are typically delivered in raw formats that must be processed and synthesized into higher-level products, often across a series of times, in order to support the calculation of trends, modeling, and decision making. When data is processed or used in some form of analysis, it can be converted into information.

One piece of data might be satellite imagery acquired across a mountainous watershed in West Virginia before a major flood event. Intense or widespread disturbances such as logging and wildfire can increase flood hazards. Therefore, a 20-year archive of time series satellite images for the region can be processed into a single map of time-since-disturbance to locate communities that are most vulnerable to flooding. Specific facts about vegetation changes are assessed in the individual images to determine if the changes were caused by wildfire or deforestation. The identification of communities most vulnerable to flooding is based on processed and synthesized data and therefore falls under the concept of information. Vulnerability and resilience assessments could integrate the "time-since-disturbance" information with slope information derived from Digital Elevation Models (DEMs) as well as summaries of monthly stream-flow and precipitation data directly collected from a network of gauges and weather stations. Collectively, these data sources can depict differential patterns of rainfall and stream levels, as well as locations within the watershed that are expected to be most heavily impacted by flooding.

Direct and remote sensing data that are related to actual or potential disaster provide a synoptic understanding of the hazard. The data also allows managers to determine what, if any, steps can be taken to reduce losses. Data and information like precipitation, stream flow, slope, and "time-since-disturbance" can be treated as variables and also used as model inputs to simulate potential disasters. Common simulations include floods, hurricane storm surges, earthquakes, and wind storms. Collecting and using specific local data on weather, land owner-ship, ecosystem health, and physical structures in disaster models allows for specific hazard conditions or associated risk to be simulated. Some states, such as West Virginia, have developed interactive Web mapping applications related to flood risk using a combination of remote sensing and Geographic Information System (GIS) datasets such as elevation and Digital Flood Insurance Rate Maps (DFIRMs) published by the Federal Emergency Management Agency (FEMA; Figure 6-1).

Data collection methods have rapidly changed in the past few decades because of advances in areas such as sensor technology, remote sensing, large dataset handling, location-based social media, unmanned aerial systems (robotics), Web services, and cloud computing. Today, computerized sensors allow us to see more clearly (at higher resolutions) from ground, aircraft, and satellite platforms. The sensors are engineered to allow us to characterize environmental conditions, including variables such as wind speed, soil drainage and moisture content, water

Figure 6-1

WV flood map

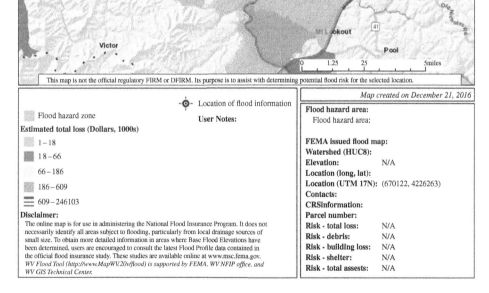

A Flood Risk map generated using the WV Flood Tool (http://www.mapwv.gov/flood/map)
depicts flood risk in terms of economic loss. The basemap is shaded
relief terrain generated from a Digital Elevation Model (DEM)
obtained using remote sensing technology.

flow rates, and vegetation health. You can use the processed information obtained
from direct and remotely sensed datasets for emergency planning, response,
recovery, or mitigation. Here is an explanation of the role data plays in the four
phases of emergency management, along with examples:

Planning: Direct and remotely sensed datasets are used to identify areas that are more vulnerable than others to different types of hazards. Examples include DEMs to delineate floodplain boundaries; a satellite image analyzed for vegetation stress to predict the early onset of drought; and historic stream-flow records to identify stream reaches with the greatest rate of increase during storm events.

Recovery: Direct and remotely sensed datasets provides accurate information on the extent of damage in a disaster. Data collected from real-time satellite imagery, weather stations, chemical sensors, or stream gauge stations identify the high-priority areas affected by a hazardous event. The data collection stations provide a basis for identifying the areas most affected by the event and in directing responders to areas most impacted by the disaster. In the past, response operational decisions were based on emergency management personnel making actual observations in the event. With direct and remote sensing capabilities, response personnel can be directed to critical parts of the disaster without waiting for personal observation of responders.

Response: Direct and remotely sensed datasets provide a basis for decisions involving warning systems for emergencies and the selection of evacuation routes and shelters. Hydrologic modeling of soil moisture is used in landslide threat warning systems. The modeling relies on in situ measurements of soil moisture and digital images of soil moisture obtained from satellites such as NASA's Soil Moisture Active Passive (SMAP) mission, which was designed to combine radar (active) and optical (passive) sensor measurements to provide global estimates of soil moisture in the top 5 cm of soil.

Mitigation: Direct and remotely sensed datasets are used to identify the actual impact of hazardous event damages. The impacts can be reduced or mitigated by, in the case of drinking water contamination, using direct sensing to test water quality and deploying personnel and bottled drinking water to people living in the affected areas.

6.2 Weather Stations

As mentioned earlier, weather stations contain sensors that obtain data by direct contact with the environment. The stations collect data on temperature, precipitation, wind direction and movement, and humidity by way of probing the atmosphere and collecting rainfall or snowfall. In fact, one of the most common applications of direct sensing is the use of weather stations. Weather stations are one of the key elements in predicting weather patterns. Weather stations help us understand hazardous conditions and have been in use in one form or another since the 1800s. In the early 1800s, temperature was the most common data recorded. By the mid-1800s, weather observations included precipitation, temperature, cloud cover, cloud movement, wind direction, barometric pressure, and humidity. This information came from rudimentary gauges and personal observations. These observations were handwritten in logbooks. We now have over 20 000 weather stations that collect, store, and communicate data. Today these stations are instrumented with sophisticated gauges and data loggers that automatically record the information in digital form for use in our computers.

6.2.1 Weather Station Data

Manufacturers who engineer scientific instruments to measure the physical environment produce rugged, small-scale, precision data loggers; data acquisition and control systems; and sensors for environmental measurements that are powered by batteries, solar panels, generators, or other sources of electricity. Many companies manufacture meteorological measurement stations (Figure 6-2). The sensor is the device that measures by direct contact with the environment's air temperature, wind speed, or water level. The reading is then sent to a data logger. The data logger translates the information into a digital form that can be saved in a database format and wirelessly transmitted in near real time. The frequency with which the data logger records sensor measurements is programmable, and can be set to store only necessary information to reduce dataset size. For example, the data logger can be set to not record humidity readings but to record temperature readings every minute, or the maximum every hour. Instrument vendors can help the user choose a system that is customized to provide data used in a given emergency management information system. Many weather station products are operable to –55°C. They have minimal power requirements, which allows for use

Figure 6-2

A weather station manufactured by Measurement Engineering Australia©. Note: These systems use solar energy to operate sensors that directly record atmospheric conditions through a data logger. Recorded data can be transmitted through the Internet.

in inhospitable environments. In addition, data loggers store data in a memory, which provides a reliable backup even if primary power supplies fail. Much of the data used by the National Weather Service (NWS) comes from direct sensors.

Weather stations typically have the following instruments:

▲ Temperature gauge
▲ Barometer gauge for measuring barometric pressure
▲ Hygrometer for measuring humidity
▲ Anemometer for measuring wind speed and direction
▲ Rain gauges for measuring precipitation
▲ Solar radiation sensors

There are additional sensors that can be added:

▲ Snow-depth ultrasonic distance sensors
▲ Soil moisture sensors

Forestry offices, ski areas, public works agencies, and state transportation departments commonly use weather stations equipped with snow-depth sensors for avalanche prediction. Data loggers have also been linked to GPS (Global Positioning System) receivers so that station locations can be accurately mapped to coordinates on the surface of the Earth and integrated into a GIS.

6.2.2 Weather Station Networks

Weather station information can be accessed for hundreds of locations. The National Oceanic and Atmospheric Administration (NOAA) provides weather data and forecasts for locations throughout the United States through an interactive map server hosted by the agency's National Centers for Environmental Information (https://www.ncdc.noaa.gov/cdo-web/datatools/findstation).

Emergency managers may need to track weather patterns in other states. For example, a hurricane can make landfall in several states days apart. The progress of the hurricane needs to be tracked to determine if a community will be affected. Communities across the country send information to the NWS at regular intervals. The NWS collects data in a variety of ways to provide weather, hydrologic forecasts, and warnings. The data are freely available to the public and can be accessed by anyone. The NWS weather storm warnings provide an excellent example of identifying potential hazards, developing a classification system, and implementing a public notification system. The warning system focuses on flood, tornado, earthquake, and hurricane hazards.

The NOAA's Emergency Managers Weather Information Network (EMWIN) is a near-real-time broadcast service that provides forecasts and warnings issued by the NWS. The data stream can be obtained directly from the Geostationary Operational Environmental Satellite (GOES) weather satellite and is primarily used by emergency managers and public safety officials. Specialized hardware and software are needed to receive radio, satellite, or Internet broadcasts (for additional information visit http://www.nws.noaa.gov/emwin/user-intro.htm).

> ## FOR EXAMPLE
>
> ### Remote Automated Weather Stations
>
> The remote automated weather stations (RAWS) is a network of weather stations run by the US Forest Service and Bureau of Land Management and monitored by the National Interagency Fire Center in Boise, Idaho. Most of the RAWS are used to monitor air quality, predict fire behavior, rate fire danger, and monitor fuels. There are approximately 2200 RAWS in the United States, and they are placed in locations where wildland fires often occur. The stations collect and store information on the order of minutes, and the data are usually transmitted every hour from the Interagency Fire Center via the GOES satellite to other computer systems such as the Weather Information Management System and the Western Regional Climate Center in Reno, Nevada. The station data can be searched online through the Western Regional Climate Center (for additional information visit http://raws.fam.nwcg.gov/).

Weather is the most important factor in wildfires. Weather plays a role in the destructive force of the wildfire through wind direction, wind speed, and dryness. It also plays a critical role in firefighter safety. RAWS allow professionals to program parameters for indicators such as wind shifts, humidity changes, or sudden temperature changes. When one of these elements reaches a predetermined threshold, RAWS can send out a tone to alert firefighters.

Once wildfires have caused loss of ground cover and vegetation, that area is more susceptible to landslides. RAWS can then be set up in those areas or reprogrammed to monitor the amount of rainfall in a given period of time. There are also portable RAWS that can be deployed across the country.

6.2.3 Geospatial Multi-agency Coordination Wildfire Application

In many cases, emergency response management tools involve the integration of direct and remote sensing data as well as other geospatial coverages that are combined in an interactive Web-based GIS. One such example is Geospatial Multi-agency Coordination (GeoMAC), which was designed after a devastating fire sear in 2000 to help wildland fire managers rank fires in terms of the risks they pose and decide how to best allocate resources. Under GeoMAC, the US Geological Survey (USGS) develops and hosts wildfire perimeter mapping products that are generated from a combination of (1) GPS mapping on the ground **(direct sensing or in situ data collection),** (2) flights over fire areas to acquire infrared imagery, and (3) fire detection data based on thermal anomalies in satellite imagery obtained from Moderate Resolution Imaging Spectroradiometer (MODIS). The wildfire perimeter maps are evaluated for completeness and accuracy and archived for long-term storage and access to historic fire activity (Walters et al., 2011). The GeoMAC Web viewer is available to resource managers and the public (Figure 6-3) for tracking events in real-time, fire planning, and research purposes (see https://www.geomac.gov/).

Figure 6-3

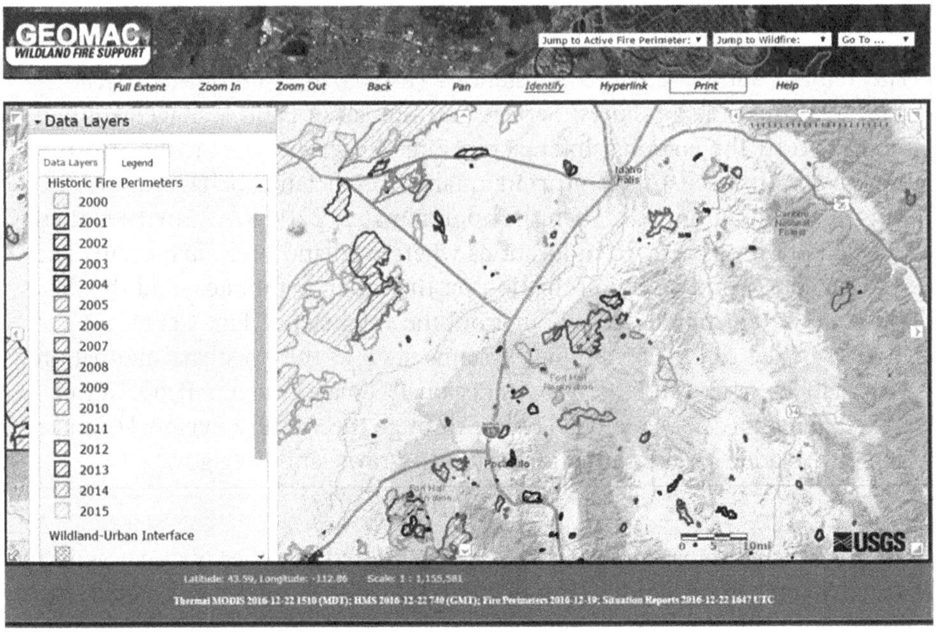

The Geospatial Multi-agency Coordination (GeoMAC) online Web application. Note: GeoMAC can be used to view historic fire perimeters in relation to Wildland–Urban Interface (WUI) boundaries throughout the United States. The map depicted in Figure 6-3 was generated for southeastern Idaho and reveals several fires that occurred in close proximity to or within WUI boundaries.

6.3 Water Data Sensors

According to the NWS, flood damages over the past 30 years average almost $8 billion a year. In 2011, the cost of flood damages surpassed $9 billion because of flooding along the Mississippi River and flood damages associated with the 2012 Atlantic hurricane season, which included Hurricane Sandy, reached over $2 billion. By comparison, in 2005, flooding damage caused by Hurricane Katrina was over $55 billion and in total more than $200 billion was needed to rebuild the affected Gulf Coast areas. As flooding continues to cause damage, communities are constantly looking for ways to mitigate flood losses.

6.3.1 Flood Warning Systems for Local Communities

For communities that have locations subject to flood risk, a local flood warning program can be extremely effective at protecting human lives and property. Guidance, technical support, and outreach are available through the NWS for local communities who want to develop, instrument, and operate a flood warning system. Key components to a flood warning program are (1) the flood warning system, which includes personnel, equipment and warning procedures, (2) a plan of action that is prepared to address measures to take before and during a flood event, and (3) a funding plan for maintaining and updating equipment (for additional details, see http://www.nws.noaa.gov/os/water/resources/Flood_Warning-Systems_Manual.pdf). Flood warning systems are an attractive solution because they are a low-cost and relatively simple way to monitor water levels. Local flood warning systems detect the amount of water in a specific area and then communicate this information with the local emergency management agency. The NWS has taken the lead in the development of these systems in cooperation with state and local disaster and emergency services agencies and the US Army Corps of Engineers and FEMA. Instruments that are strategically located in vulnerable areas can provide the details necessary to more accurately predict floods and implement measures to respond and mitigate flood damage. Automated flood warning systems are recommended and designed to transmit data to a centralized data processing center at the NWS headquarters.

The design of **local flood warning systems** must include instruments that are able to manually or automatically do the following:

- ▲ Measure and detect water levels
- ▲ Transmit data
- ▲ Process and analyze data
- ▲ Forecast preparation
- ▲ Forecast dissemination

When the water in a rain or stream gauge reaches a predetermined level, an alert is sent. Each community may use slightly different equipment. Nevertheless, here is an example of what occurs before an alert is sent out:

1. Emergency managers and local officials determine where to place the rain gauges. Stream gauges are placed in the streams and use a sensor to determine the water depth. Water depth is also referred to as stage. Rain gauges use tipping buckets. The depth of the water is recorded and reported.
2. After the water reaches a predetermined depth, the information is transmitted through communications media to a repeater site. A repeater is a device that receives communications and amplifies them before sending them out.
3. Two base stations receive the information from the repeater. The base station is the final destination for the information from the sensors. The base stations have a decoder to interpret the information. An alert is sent to emergency management and utility personnel. Users can also access the data from Web pages or by using a laptop. The information is also sent to the NWS.

There are many communication systems a local flood warning system can use. Systems can use a number of different communications media, including VHF/UHF, microwave radio, two-way satellite, cellular telephone, and cable/Digital Subscriber Line (DSL). The following are some of the more common communications elements:

Event-reporting sensors: These sensors are programmed with prerecorded measurements. For example, you may want to be alerted only when water depth reaches 2 inches. The sensors then trigger the transmission of signals when the water reaches 2 inches.

Single-frequency repeater: The repeater increases the transmission range of event-reporting sensors. Once the repeater receives an incoming signal, it regenerates, amplifies, and transmits the signal to a base station.

Base station: Data from the repeater is sent to the base station microcomputer. The computer accepts the report, processes it, displays the information, and forwards it to the appropriate computers and personnel. An alert is sent. Users can also access the data from Web pages or by using a laptop and dialing in to their station. The information is also sent to the NWS.

6.3.2 Rain and Stream Gauges

Once funding is secured to instrument a local community with a flood warning system, the next step is to determine where to place the rain and stream gauges. Increasing the number of gauges increases program costs, but also improves the chances of detecting flood-producing rainfall. The minimum number of gauges needed depends on the local area. For example, to accurately measure *rainfall over a basin*, mountainous areas will require more gauges than flat lands.

Rain gauges should be located on ground level and away from obstructions such as trees and buildings. Trees and buildings may cause turbulence and affect the accuracy of the measurements. The gauge should be located in an area where it is protected in all directions.

Stream gauges measure the stream. In small streams, stream-flow observations trigger alarms when flooding is about to happen or is happening. The location of the stream gauges should be based either at the point where flooding would require public notification or where there is information needed for forecast models. Gauges used for alarms should be located at key vulnerable areas that are far enough upstream that you have time to warn downstream inhabitants and locations.

6.3.3 How a USGS Stream Gauge Works

Most USGS stream gauges operate by measuring the elevation of the water in the river or stream and then converting the water elevation (called "stage") to a stream flow ("discharge") by using a curve that relates the elevation to a set of actual discharge measurements. This is done because currently the technology is not available to measure the flow of the water accurately enough directly.

The USGS standard is to measure river stage to 0.01 inches. This is accomplished by the use of floats inside a stilling well, by the use of pressure transducers that measure how much pressure is required to a push a gas bubble through a tube (related to the depth of water), or with radar.

At most USGS stream gauges, the stage is measured every 15 minutes and the data is stored in an electronic data recorder, most often powered by solar energy. At set intervals, usually between every 1 and 4 hours, the data is transmitted to the USGS using satellite, phone, or radio. At the USGS offices, the curves relating stage to stream flow are applied to determine estimates of the stream flow and both the stage and stream-flow data are then displayed on the USGS Web pages.

6.3.4 The USGS Stream Gaging Program

In addition to local communities that have implemented flood warning systems with stream gauges to monitor their water levels, the USGS has a stream gaging program that collects similar data from stream gauges across the country. The first stream gaging station was established in 1889 in New Mexico, and now the USGS collects real-time water data for over 8100 stream gauges in the United States. This data is available in real time for many agencies to conduct water resources projects and for the NWS to forecast floods. Data from the active stations, as well as from discontinued stations, are stored in a computer database that currently holds mean daily discharge data for about 18 500 locations and more than 400 000 station years of record (Wahl et al., 1995). Additional data are added to the database each year. The stream discharge database is used in natural resource planning and design, hydrologic research, and operation of water resources projects.

Funding for technology such as the USGS stream gaging network is expensive. The USGS has effectively established relationships with other governmental and private agencies to fund the gauge stations. By joining USGS in installing a river gauge station, public and private organizations gain access to the desired technology for their operations. Just as the network of stations represents an aggregation, so does the program funding. Operating funds for individual stations in the program may come from a blend of federal funds appropriated to the USGS, funds from state and local agencies, and funds appropriated to other federal agencies. Federal funds are allocated to the USGS for matching state or local agency offerings under the USGS Federal–State Cooperative Program.

More than half of the stations operated by the USGS are funded through the Cooperative Program. Under that program, the USGS provides up to 50% of the funds, and the state or local agency provides the remainder. Currently, more than 600 state and local agencies participate in the stream gaging program. The other stations in the program are operated by the USGS. Federal agencies fund these stations. For example, the US Army Corps of Engineers and the Bureau of Reclamation (BOR) fund the stations. In return, the agencies are provided with the hydrologic data needed for planning and operating water resources projects. Less than 10% of the stations the USGS operates are fully funded by the USGS (Wahl et al., 1995).

The USGS stream gaging program provides hydrologic information needed to help define, use, and manage the nation's water resources. The program provides a continuous, well-archived source of reliable and consistent water data that is integral to emergency and natural hazards management (Wahl, 1995).

6.3.5 Using USGS Stream-flow Data for Emergency Management

As part of its agency mission, the USGS supports water data collection for emergency management. The USGS hosts numerous programs, initiatives, Web site tools, technical support, and resources for monitoring, studying, and communicating flood information. During major floods, the USGS deploys field crews to measure water quality and flood flows at critical locations such as chemical spills and breached levees. If stream gauges are not located in these areas, the USGS can install rapid deployment stream gauges (RGSs) that transmit near-real-time data in support of activities such as flood response operations, road closures, and evacuations (for additional details see http://water.usgs.gov/floods/resources/emgmt/).

The NWS uses data from USGS stations to forecast river stages and flow conditions on large rivers and their associated tributaries. Flood forecasts are issued at about 4000 locations. These locations are strategically located throughout the nation. The reliability of flood forecasts depends on having reliable current data for precipitation and stream flow. The USGS collects the stream-flow data, and the NWS collects the precipitation data and combines both types of data when making the flood forecasts. The USGS stream gaging network is vital to emergency management because it is part of the NWS river forecast and warning program. Without data from this network, our nation would experience increased losses of both life and property.

6.4 Air Sensors

Air sensors can determine the quality of indoor and outdoor air and the amount of pollution in the atmosphere. Sensors can detect a spill of hazardous industrial chemicals in manufacturing plants and alert management and workers. Air sensors can also react to chemical, nuclear, and biological weapons.

6.4.1 Outdoor Air Quality Sensors

Since the Clean Air Act became law in 1970, the Environmental Protection Agency (EPA) has used a coordinated system to monitor outdoor air quality. The system is a network of thousands of individual air monitoring stations located across the United States. There are currently 4000 monitoring stations in the country. These stations collect data on the six common or criteria air pollutants:

- ▲ Lead
- ▲ Carbon monoxide
- ▲ Particles
- ▲ Sulfur dioxide
- ▲ Nitrogen dioxide
- ▲ Ground-level ozone (also known as smog)

The EPA also monitors toxic pollutants that cause cancer in key areas of the country that are most vulnerable to these hazards. Monitoring the air has led to better air quality. For example, monitored levels of lead have dropped 98% over the past 20 years.

The EPA plays a big role during disasters as well. For example, the devastation of Hurricane Katrina also had an impact of the air quality in New Orleans and the surrounding areas. The EPA monitored the air quality to determine how to clean up the sites and when it would be safe for the displaced residents to return home. To do this, the EPA used several different methods of gathering data including:

Fixed site monitors: These are set up in hurricane-impacted areas, and they continuously monitor the levels of fine particulates.

Particle pollution measurements: These are small portable instruments (e.g., DataRAM™ nephelometers) and can be moved daily. They are battery-powered and provide immediate readings. The readouts provide a measure of inhalable particles.

Airborne Spectral Photometric Collection Technology (ASPECT): Remote sensing aircraft known to locate chemical spills that need emergency response. This is done to protect both water and air quality. Data from ASPECT is forwarded to ground-level personnel who evaluate the data and request follow-up monitoring if needed.

Trace Atmospheric Gas Analyzer (TAGA): Mobile labs that are buses. The labs gather samples and analyze them for industrial chemicals, including those commonly found in gasoline, such as benzene, toluene, and xylene.

6.4.2 Chemical Sensors

In addition to pollution that comes from everyday chemicals, toxic chemicals and hazardous materials also pose a threat. Chemical sensors can be installed in manufacturing facilities that detect toxic chemicals. The sensor system can be set up so alarms will go off once chemicals have reached a predetermined level. Sensors can also be handheld and portable. Many of the sensors work by emitting laser beam pulses through the air to detect the chemical signature of the material released. This type of sensor is known as an **active sensor**. There are also **passive sensors** that can pick up a target chemical's unique pattern of radiation emissions without emitting laser pulses. These sensors, however, can only be used when the distance between the sensor and the chemical is short.

Emergency managers work with the business community to determine which industries and facilities produce hazardous chemicals. The types of chemicals produced and the toxicity of the chemicals should be documented. Finally, consideration should be given to which chemical sensors are needed to protect human health and safety as well as potential risks to the surrounding communities should a chemical spill occur.

6.5 Evaluating the Technology

Emergency managers are often faced with choosing technology systems to support operations. A process for evaluating the systems must be in place in order to select the technology or application that is most appropriate for operational needs. The following provides a basis for evaluating the technology. These criteria can be used in evaluating a direct sensing technology such as a portable weather system. However, the criteria offered here fit many different technologies in emergency management.

System flexibility: Once the system is designed, is it possible to make changes in an easy and timely manner? Can changes in the type and nature of data be made without totally replacing the sensor? Can alternative communication technology be used without having to replace the technology when major disasters occur?

Interoperable systems: Most industry efforts are targeted to the commercial market and are focused on providing a communications infrastructure whose underlying organization is static (placement of routers and sites as hosts). Current systems are designed to carry anticipated loads and provide security. Communication patterns in times of crisis may be unpredictable. It may be impossible to establish and maintain a static routing structure since the host and units are inherently unstable. A self-organizing system may need to be designed.

Security: Direct sensing data systems are often in an open environment and subject to tampering by the public. An example is the river gauge system operated by the US Army Corps of Engineers. These units are often found on bridges in public view and easily accessible to anyone. The only security is a simple locking system. Are these direct sensing systems able to communicate data frequently so that if tampering is determined, the data collected is not sacrificed?

Lack of current relevant information on technology: A key factor in selecting a data collection system is the use of current technology. Any system should be evaluated for state-of-the-art communication technology, including digital data transfer technology and wireless communications that avoid having to reenter the data after collecting sensor data.

Financial constraints: The current weather stations are an example of systems that are reasonably priced, easy to install and maintain, and reliable over a long period.

Collaboration with other agencies: Can the system be sponsored by multiple federal, state, and local agencies; educational institutions; and private companies or not-for-profit agencies and therefore be more useful to a wider user group? Many weather stations are located on college campuses and are supported jointly by public agencies and private companies. In some cases, the direct sensing system is collecting information that cannot be shared with other agencies without significant oversight by the sponsoring agency. Collaboration may be inhibited because some state or local agencies may be subject to significant legal and programmatic restrictions and thus unable to share their data with other public bodies.

6.6 Remote Sensing

Now that we are familiar with how sensors in direct contact with Earth's terrestrial and atmospheric resources, such as weather stations and stream gauges, can be used in emergency management, the remainder of this chapter focuses on remote sensing technologies that are relevant to describing and detecting hazards.

Remote sensing data provide critical information that *emergency managers need to make decisions and predictions* about disaster events such as flooding, oil spills, earthquakes, landslides, droughts, heat waves, tornadoes, winter storms, floods, wildfires, and volcanic eruptions.

6.6.1 An Overview of Remote Sensing

While remote sensing is broadly defined as the study of remote objects including Earth, other planetary surfaces, and even the human body, remote sensing of natural hazards is concerned with observations of Earth's land and water surfaces and the atmosphere using reflected or emitted electromagnetic radiation (Figure 6-4). Electromagnetic radiation is all around us and includes ultraviolet, visible, infrared, and radio energy across a spectrum of wavelengths. Sunlight is a form of electromagnetic radiation.

Remote sensors are usually specialized cameras mounted to satellites or aircraft and pointed directly to Earth from a known distance. The cameras are designed to measure electromagnetic energy that is either reflected from or emitted by physical objects on the ground, such as buildings, trees, waters, soil, and rock formations. Sensors that record this upwelling solar energy from targets on the ground are categorized as passive remote sensors. The parts of the electromagnetic spectrum that these sensors use to record images determine the **spectral resolution** of the data. For example, true color aerial photography collects data in three channels of visible light: red, blue, and green. Color infrared aerial photography collects data in four channels: three are visible and the fourth is near infrared. Many satellites are **multispectral** in design and collect imagery in visible, near infrared, shortwave, and thermal infrared channels. A small number of sensors, mainly airborne, are hyperspectral in design and collect data in hundreds of narrow channels from the ultraviolet to the shortwave or thermal infrared. A second aspect of image clarity is **spatial resolution**. Aerial images tend to have finer resolution or smaller pixel size (e.g., 3- to 5-m pixels) than most satellite images (e.g., 30- to 250-m pixels). Satellite imagery is becoming available in increasingly finer resolutions, especially in the commercial market. Imagery acquired by commercial satellite sensors is usually not freely available to the public.

Figure 6-4

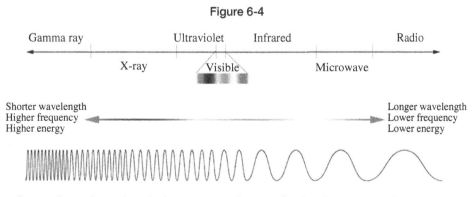

Comparison of wavelength, frequency, and energy for the electromagnetic spectrum.

A second type of technology uses active remote sensors that emit energy from a portion of the electromagnetic spectrum and record information that is reflected back to the sensor from either the landscape or the atmosphere. Two active sensing systems that are widely used in describing and detecting hazards are light detection and ranging, or **lidar** and radio detection and ranging, or **radar**. Lidar emits laser beam pulses and uses the speed of light to calculate the elevation of the bare earth as well as vegetation canopies, building, and other objects on the ground. The further the object is from the laser transmitter, the longer it takes for backscattered light to return to the sensor. The resolution of lidar data is determined by the density of lidar returns, or the number of pulses that cover a specified area. Lidar can also be used to measure atmospheric components that are needed for weather forecasting and environmental monitoring, such as aerosol particles, ice crystals, water vapor, or trace gases such as ozone. Radar devices are active microwave sensors that measure time delay and changes in shape between transmitted and received signals. Radar can penetrate cloud cover and does not depend on solar illumination. Images are formed as the radar moves along a flight path. The area illuminated by the radar, or foot-print, is moved along the surface in a swath, building the image as it does so. The length of the radar antenna determines the clarity of the image. The longer the antenna, the finer the resolution.

Emergency managers who are interested in using remote sensing data (see Table 6-1 for a summary of current programs) to detect and describe hazards should keep in mind that effective use of the data often requires image processing, analysis, and interpretation to convert data to information that can be used to address practical problems. Image analysts are trained to extract information from remote sensing data and techniques can vary depending on the purpose of the analysis. For example, a single Landsat scene can be processed into a vegetation index to reveal plant stress, or it could be classified to detect surface water features. The vegetation stress and surface water products could then be combined with other geospatial data layers in a GIS to address real-world emergency management problems. The remote sensing systems presented in Table 6-1 are not exhaustive and do not include many of the commercial and research airborne platforms that can acquire high-resolution lidar and multispectral or hyperspectral imagery.

6.6.2 Optical Satellite Remote Sensing

Remote sensors on board satellites orbiting hundreds of kilometers above the Earth have made enormous contributions to regional and global geophysical surveys. Satellite remote sensing is the largest single source of digital spatial data. The advantages of satellite remote sensing data include large area coverage; consistent repeat coverage; potential for value-added products that can be calibrated and validated; and compatibility with many databases and statistical, imaging, and GIS programs.

The information that is provided by remote sensing affords opportunities to inventory hazards, visualize hazardous events, assess risks and impacts, and aid in recovery efforts. Imagery from satellites such as the Landsat series (30 m × 30 m pixels) and MODIS (250 m × 250 m pixels) provides a bird's eye view and comprehensive

Table 6-1 A Summary of Current Remote Sensing Programs that Collect Optical, Radar, and Lidar Imagery, Along with Emergency Management Applications

System and Program Duration	Sponsor	Spectral Resolution	Spatial Resolution	Temporal Resolution	Application Areas
National Agricultural Imagery Program (NAIP) (2002–present)	US Department of Agriculture (USDA)	4 bands	0.5–2 m pixels	Every 3 years, during growing season	Evacuation and other response planning
Landsat 8 (1972 to present)	National Aeronautics Space Administration (NASA)	11 bands	15–60 m pixels	16 days	Long-term trend monitoring; land cover, drought, dust storms; coastal storm damage; hydrologic modeling; mitigating fire damage
MODIS (Moderate Resolution Imaging Spectrometer) (1999 to present)	NASA	36 bands	250–1000 m pixels	1–2 days	Real-time monitoring; warning systems Water inundation, flooding in coastal areas, ash plumes, hurricanes, wildfire
Sentinel-2 (2015 to present)	European Space Agency (ESA)	13 bands	10–60 m pixels	5 days with two satellites	Provides land observations similar to Landsat
Hyperion (2000 to present)	NASA	200 bands	30 m pixels	By request	Measures chemical constituents in Earth materials; volcanic activity, oil spills

(Continued)

Table 6-1 (Continued)

System and Program Duration	Sponsor	Spectral Resolution	Spatial Resolution	Temporal Resolution	Application Areas
GOES (Geostationary Operational Environmental Satellite)	NOAA	5 bands	1–4 km	15 minutes; 5 minutes during extreme weather events	Cloud coverage, weather forecasting
GeoEye-1 (2008 to present)	DigitalGlobe 1 (commercial)	5 bands	0.46–1.84 m pixels	Less than 3 days	Terrain elevation for 3D modeling of emergency scenarios; disaster mitigation and risk assessments
Shuttle Radar Topography Mission (SRTM) (February 2000)	NASA, National Geospatial Intelligence Agency, German and Italian Space Agencies	Elevation	30–90 m pixels	Flown in 2000	Global digital elevation model; volcano visualization; hydrologic modeling
RADARSAT (1995 to present)	Canadian Space Agency (CSA)	1 frequency	3–100 m	3 days	Ice monitoring, oil spills, flooding
Lidar 3DEP (3-D Elevation Program) (2013 to present)	USGS partnership funding	Elevation		8 years	Flood and landslide risk assessment, fault detection

understanding of large-scale events. Regular, repeat acquisitions from satellite platforms provide a reliable tool for delineating impacts using scenes acquired before and after an event. Moderate-resolution satellite observations are also highly relevant to mapping inventories of windstorms and wildfires (Van Westen, 2013). Datasets collected in a time series can be used monitor changes on the ground or to provide a historical perspective for emergency planning, recovery, and mitigation. Systematic satellite measurements also provide the capability to quantify the magnitude and impact of disasters through modeling and simulation.

Very high spatial resolution optical remote sensing from commercial satellites such as GeoEye (pixels less than $2\,m \times 2\,m$) are particularly useful for response planning and for detailed risk and impact analysis in urban areas. Individual features such as bridges, buildings, and warehouses are recognizable in very high spatial resolution imagery and can be inventoried for impact assessments (Deichmann, 2011). The downside to very high spatial resolution satellite imagery is that most images are not publically available and there is generally a lag time between when an event occurs and when images are acquired over the area of interest. Rapid response and image processing options may be available to minimize lag time.

The Landsat Satellite Remote Sensing Program

The Landsat satellite remote sensing program developed by NASA is the longest running enterprise for acquisition of digital imagery of Earth from space. The first Landsat satellite (Landsat 1) was launched in 1972 and subsequent satellites have continued through the most, Landsat 8, which was launched on February 11, 2013. The program is expected to continue to provide long-term observations into the future. The USGS provides the full archive of Landsat scenes to the public at no cost. The consistency of sensors on board Landsat satellites has ensured data continuity for tracking not only sudden events, but also disaster indicators that occur slowly over time, such as drought. Landsat makes it possible to check the health of the Earth and plays a critical role in responding to natural disasters and pollution events. The practical applications include, but are not limited to, the following: mitigating damage from wildfire, quantifying flood extents, assessing hurricane and tornado impacts, mapping the movement of volcanic eruptions, observing severe drought, and automatically detecting landslides (for additional details see http://landsat.gsfc.nasa.gov/wp-content/uploads/2013/02/LandsatDisastersFS.pdf).

One approach to mitigating the damage from wildfire using Landsat data is burn severity mapping. Burn severity mapping can help land managers identify and treat areas most severely burned to reduce impacts such as runoff and erosion. The Landsat 8 satellite sensor Operational Land Imager (OLI) was used to create a burn severity map using ratios of near and shortwave infrared bands in prefire and postfire images for the 2013 Table Rock fire in the Linville Gorge Wilderness Area near Boone, NC (Figure 6-5). The US Forest Service Remote Sensing Applications Center maintains a Burn Area Emergency Response (BAER) Imagery Support program in cooperation with the USGS Survey Center for Earth Resources

Figure 6-5

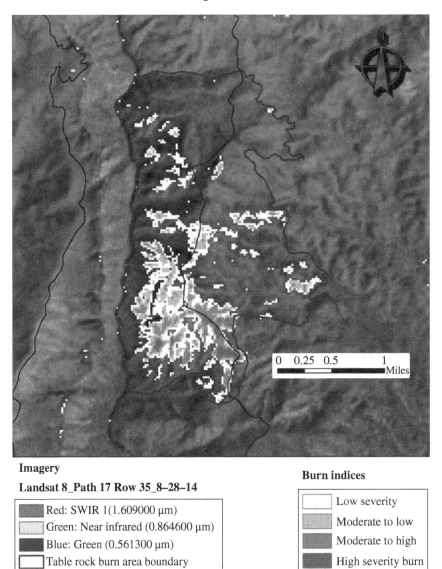

Imagery

Landsat 8_Path 17 Row 35_8–28–14

▨	Red: SWIR 1(1.609000 µm)
▨	Green: Near infrared (0.864600 µm)
■	Blue: Green (0.561300 µm)
☐	Table rock burn area boundary

Burn indices

☐	Low severity
▨	Moderate to low
▨	Moderate to high
■	High severity burn

A burn severity map of the 2013 Table Rock fire in the Linville Gorge Wilderness Area near Boone, NC. Note: It was generated using a combination of multispectral Landsat images acquired prefire and postfire. The mapping reveals how severely soil and vegetation have been burned.

Observation and Science. Members of BAER teams can request imagery, Burned Area Reflectance Classifications, and Soil Burn Severity. The Soil Burn Severity data is currently available for public download (for additional details, see https://fsapps. nwcg.gov/afm/baer/download.php). The Landsat Image Gallery that is available through NASA provides hundreds of Landsat images and visualizations that illustrate applications in detecting and describing natural hazards (see http://landsat. visibleearth.nasa.gov/).

Figure 6-6

Imagery obtained from Landsat 5 Thematic Mapper preflood (left) and postflood (right) show areas inundated by heavy rains near St. Louis Missouri.

"The Great Flood of 1993" impacted over 20 million acres of land along the Upper Mississippi River and was one of the greatest natural disasters in the United States in terms of extent, duration, and intensity (Johnson et al., 2004). Levees, dykes, and other control structures failed during this event. Transportation routes and entire towns were destroyed and human loss and suffering was enormous. Scientists began to turn to satellite imagery to study this event because the extent of flooding was so expansive. Landsat 5 Thematic Mapper images acquired over the St. Louis, Missouri, area before the flood (August 14, 1991) and slightly after peak flooding (August 19, 1993) demonstrate one of the first uses of Landsat for flood mapping (Figure 6-6).

When the images are displayed in false color using infrared, near infrared, and green bands from the Thematic Mapper sensor, healthy vegetation appears green, bare and freshly exposed soil appears pink, concrete is grey, and water is dark blue. Mapping the Great Flood of 1993 with satellite imagery was followed by a NASA-funded project led by Bob Brakenridge to study "extreme hydrological events" with remote sensing. The project, named the Dartmouth Flood Observatory, was designed to provide a global archive of flood information to help future relief efforts and improve flood prediction (for additional details, see http://earthobservatory.nasa.gov/Features/HighWater/printall.php).

The Moderate Resolution Imaging Spectrometer

MODIS collects earth observation data in 36 bands of the electromagnetic spectrum (Figure 6-4) and therefore provides a suite of parameters for terrestrial, ocean, and atmospheric monitoring. The instrumentation is on board two satellites: Aqua and Terra. These satellites operate as a pair. Terra's orbit passes from north to south across the equator in the morning, while that of Aqua passes south to north over the equator

Figure 6-7

A MODIS image acquired from the NASA Terra satellite on January 12, 2017,
depicts dust storms along the West coast of Africa.

in the afternoon. This design ensures that the entire surface of Earth is viewed every
one to two days. While the MODIS coverage area or footprint on the surface of the
Earth is larger than Landsat, the spatial resolution is relatively coarse (250 m × 250 m
pixels). The scientific research community has worked to validate MODIS measurements on the ground. Higher-level value-added products such as burned area and
snow cover have been developed that contain quality assessment values for each pixel.

To address hazards and disasters, near-real-time MODIS data is provided for
applications such as fire detection, smoke tracking, ash and dust plume detection;
aerosol monitoring; and sea ice, snow, and flood delineation (Figure 6-7; for additional details see https://earthdata.nasa.gov/earth-observation-data/near-real-time/
hazards-and-disasters).

Land, Atmosphere Near real-time Capability (LANCE) for Earth Observing
System (EOS) provides data and imagery from NASA satellite sources such as Terra
and Aqua, as well as Aura (atmospheric chemistry) and the Visible and Infrared
Imager/Radiometer Suite (VIIRS) on board Suomi National Polar-orbiting Partnership
(NPP). Data visualization and download is currently available through the system
"Worldview" (see https://worldview.earthdata.nasa.gov/).

The fact that MODIS data can be transmitted on a daily basis in near-real time through designated downlinks has facilitated the development of several early warning systems that generally operate by detecting an anomalous change in the values of a particular pixel across a span of time. This anomaly detection approach tends to pick up moderate- to large-scale disturbances such as fire, weed invasion, overgrazing, insect infestation, vegetation stress, landslides, and flooding. Vegetation anomalies can be determined by calculating changes in the Normalized Difference Vegetation Index (NDVI), which is a relative measure of crops, plants, grasses, shrubs, and trees that are growing and photosynthesizing. The NDVI can be quickly calculated from red and near infrared MODIS bands. Droughts across the globe can be detected by comparing NDVI values in a given year to long-term NDVI averages for the same area (Figure 6-8). Information from MODIS imagery can also be combined with climate data for monitoring phenomena such as droughts, fire activity, and rangeland and forest health. For example, the Famine Early Warning System Network tracks developing droughts using ground reports, weather data from NOAA satellites, and vegetation anomaly data from MODIS (see https://www.fews.net/). The network distributes the information to aid organizations and governments to help them plan responses to food shortages.

Figure 6-8

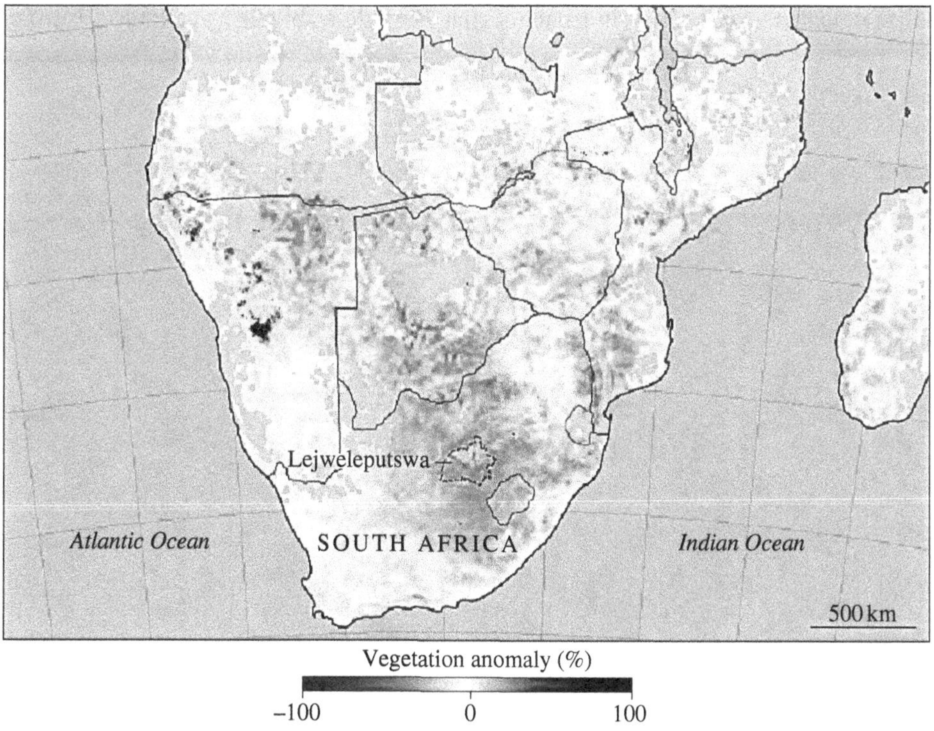

Drought in Southern Africa was detected by comparing a MODIS image acquired by Terra in December 2015 to December averages from 2000 to 2015. Locations are identified where vegetation greenness is less than normal.

As another example, the US Forest Service developed a vegetation monitoring tool, ForWarn, which tracks vegetation changes every 8 days in the United States by calculating departures from average vegetation conditions over time using MODIS NDVI products. Data developed through ForWarn can be accessed through an interactive viewer and products related to themes such as forest disturbance are available for public download (see https://forwarn.forestthreats.org/).

Commercial Very High Spatial Resolution Satellite Imagery

Commercial very high-resolution satellite images are used by emergency responders who need detailed baseline and near-real-time information for developing evacuation routes and prioritizing relief efforts in response to major disasters (e.g., Figure 6-9). The National Geospatial-Intelligence Agency (NGA) currently provides federal, state, and local responders access to nonclassified commercial satellite data. For example, the NGA has provided FEMA with very high-resolution image products used by emergency responders in hurricanes from Katrina in 2005 to Sandy in 2011. The NGA also provided flood and damage assessments in and around impacted cities in South Carolina and Georgia in 2015. In some cases, such as the 2015 earthquake in Nepal, the commercial satellite vendor DigitalGlobe provided unrestricted access to critical imagery. In fact, DigitalGlobe has also begun to use crowdsourcing as a tool where volunteers help tag features of interest in imagery that is made publically available. Human

Figure 6-9

A very high spatial resolution image. Note: It was captured by the commercial satellite Worldview-2, which provides a look at the Zaatari Refugee Camp in Jordan on January 13, 2014. Monitoring the growth of Syrian refugee camps in neighboring countries has helped organize effective aid distributions.

Figure 6-10

A hillshade image created from a 50 cm pixel resolution. DigitalGlobe sample image acquired over Washington, DC.

networks have helped solve real-world problems by joining a system named "tomnod" to identify objects such as tents, shelters, bridges, and damaged buildings (see http://www.tomnod.com/). Recent campaigns include population mapping in the Congo, the earthquake in Nepal, and wildfires in Cape Town, South Africa, and Adelaide, Australia.

In addition to object identification, very high-resolution satellite imagery can also be used to create three-dimensional surface models as illustrated by Figure 6-10 of buildings in Washington DC. This technology shows bare earth terrain or surface elevation, as well as models of the heights of vegetation canopy and buildings and other built infrastructure (Figure 6-10). Elevation and surface height models are generated using pairs of photos taken over the same footprint on the ground, but with cameras that are pointed at oblique angles from the Earth. Usually cameras acquire images that are perpendicular or orthogonal to Earth's surface to minimize distortion, but overlapping stereo pairs can be combined with coincident ground control points with known elevation to geometrically calculate elevation values for locations in the imagery where ground control point data were not collected.

6.6.3 Satellite Remote Sensing of Weather

Weather satellites are routinely used by the NWS to show weather patterns and develop forecasts and storm simulations. Frequently, decisions regarding what communities should be evacuated and routes to be used have to be made. These decisions can be enhanced by the use of high-resolution satellite imagery and topographic mapping.

The Geostationary Operational Environmental Satellite

The **GOES** system provides global weathering monitoring by collecting continuous observations of cloud cover, atmospheric temperature, and moisture. The GOES system is operated and managed by NOAA, which is also responsible for processing and distributing the millions of bits of data and images that are collected. The NWS is NOAA's primary end user and processes the satellite technology for hurricane modeling, weather forecasting, and communication of public weather advisories.

The GOES satellite is designed to collect imagery every 15 minutes under normal weather conditions, and can be switched to a 5-minute collection interval during extreme weather events such as hurricanes. This continuous data collection is possible because the satellite is in a **geostationary orbit** rather than a sun-synchronous orbit, like Landsat, which repeats a collection over the same area every 16 days. *In a geostationary orbit, a high-altitude satellite is set in a motion that is parallel to Earth's rotation. The satellite's velocity matches that of Earth and the system remains in a position that is fixed relative to Earth. Because of this, the satellite can monitor an entire hemisphere all of the time, and provides a constant vigil for the atmospheric conditions that trigger severe weather conditions.* While this type of satellite is especially useful for climatic observations, the resolution of the imagery is coarse since the satellite is at a great distance from the surface of the Earth.

Severe weather conditions that GOES monitors include tornadoes, flash floods, hail storms, and hurricanes. When these conditions develop, the NOAA GOES satellites are able to monitor storm development and track their movements. For example, data from the GOES-East satellite (Figure 6-11), along with weather observations and computer models, were used to provide forecasters with near-real-time movements and developments for a storm system that was generating tornados in Nebraska, Kansas, Iowa, Oklahoma, Arkansas, Louisiana, and Mississippi in spring 2014.

State and local emergency management agencies use images from the GOES satellite to track the paths of hurricanes and assess their potential impacts on local

Figure 6-11

A NOAA GOES-East satellite image of severe weather acquired on April 28, 2014.

communities. Data acquired from GOES can also be analyzed to estimate rainfall during thunderstorms and hurricanes for flash flood warnings and to estimate snowfall accumulations and overall extent of snow cover. Such data help meteorologists issue winter storm warnings and advisories. This weather satellite can also detect ice fields and map the movements of sea and lake ice.

6.6.4 Radar Imaging

An imaging radar works like a flash camera. It provides its own light to illuminate an area on the ground and take a snapshot picture. However, it does this by actively emitting pulses of microwave energy. Instead of a camera lens and film, radar uses an antenna and computer to record its images. In a radar image, one can see only the light that was reflected back toward the radar antenna. In the case of imaging radar, the radar moves along a flight path. The area illuminated by the radar, or footprint, is moved along the surface in a swath as the image is built. The length of the radar antenna determines the clarity of the image. The longer the antenna, the finer the resolution. Radar images are not affected by cloud cover. This allows detailed observations at any time, regardless of weather or sunlight conditions. The data is used to better understand the global environment and how it is changing. This satellite data can be complemented by aircraft and ground studies. This gives scientists clearer insights into which environmental changes are caused by nature and which are induced by human activity.

One satellite radar system frequently used by the disaster management community is **RADARSAT**. The RADARSAT constellation mission was developed by the Canadian Space Agency. The Canadian Space Agency makes radar imagery available to mitigate the effects of natural disaster through its participation in the International Charter, "Space and Major Disasters," which maintains an interactive Web portal of archived imagery of natural disasters (http://cgt.prod.esaportal.eu/). *The archived imagery is organized by events such as oil spills, landslides, oil spills, forest fires, flooding and volcanic eruptions.*

RADARSAT is a valuable technology that can verify flooding areas after a storm, even if there is extensive cloud coverage. Images acquired from RADARSAT-1 following the oil spill along the coast of Louisiana were used by federal and state officials to detect and respond to the spill. A technique for automatically detecting oils spills from RADARSAT-2 was also developed for monitoring this oil spill in the Gulf of Mexico (Marghany, 2015).

6.6.5 Manned and Unmanned Airborne Remote Sensing

During some natural disasters, lidar airborne acquisitions are contracted to provide a detailed model of damaged buildings, roads, trees, and power lines from three-dimensional point cloud data. The three-dimensional point cloud data that is obtained from airborne lidar can be combined with very high-resolution multispectral or hyperspectral imagery that can reveal unique information about conditions on the ground. The detailed height information that is available from lidar data can provide more detailed information about damages caused by earthquakes, tsunamis, tornados, and hurricanes than coarser surface models derived from satellite images (Clasen et al., 2012).

Damage assessments from lidar data can also be obtained from terrestrial platforms, which are especially effective at monitoring changes in dam stability. In addition, optical imagery and lidar are becoming increasingly effective in disaster response when deployed from unmanned aerial platforms. For example, in recent years, the amount and intensity of forest fires in the American West have been unprecedented. These wildfires have destroyed thousands of acres and hundreds of homes. To combat this threat, emerging autonomous remote sensing systems have been tested that could be used in situations to gather vital data that would otherwise be unattainable. The AWARE project used multiple unmanned aerial vehicles (UAVs) to test the platform's ability to be used in disaster management situations. The AWARE project consisted of four main components in the test missions: the UAVs, ground cameras (GCs), Wireless Sensor Networks (WSNs), and a fire truck equipped with an automated water cannon.

Each of the five UAVs was assigned a separate task. This task allocation involved cooperation and coordination between the UAVs. The UAVs were outfitted with both visual and infrared cameras, a Node Deployment Device (NDD), and a Load Transportation Device (LTD). The mounted cameras could be used for both fire identification and personnel surveillance. The NDD is used to drop off WSNs to expand the range of the AWARE network or to replace damaged WSNs due to malfunctioning WSNs. The LTD allows the transportation of different devices by rope. The GCs served to provide information about changing conditions in the field of view from visual and infrared cameras. The WSNs consists of a laptop acting as a gateway connected to the AWARE network through a wireless link. WSNs measure different variables such as temperature, humidity, and CO; WSNs can be autonomously deployed by the UAVs via the NDD. The Fire Truck was equipped with an automated water cannon. Once the AWARE platform has detected fire in a location the water cannon can be commanded to point and deliver water on that location.

This research concluded that the AWARE platform successfully carried out missions involving surveillance, sensor deployment, and fire confirmation and extinguishing. The applications of this system could be applied more widely in challenging scenarios involving disaster management and civil security.

FOR EXAMPLE

Long-Term Monitoring of Environmental Change

The Great Salt Lake is a terminal lake. It does not have any outlet rivers running to the ocean. Water leaves the lake only through evaporation. Water leaves behind its dissolved minerals. This makes the lake up to eight times as salty as seawater. The lack of outlets also means the lake responds dramatically to change in inflow. Rainy weather beginning in 1982 brought the highest levels in recorded history. The water peaked in June 1986 and March–April 1987. The lake is shallow for its size. It is only about 40 feet deep. It is 70 miles long and 30 miles wide. Because the lake basin is so shallowly sloped, extra inflow to the lake makes it rise slowly. However, any rise means a large increase in area. Highways, causeways, and parts of Salt Lake City were flooded or threatened in the 1980s. This cost the city millions of dollars.

In 1902, the Southern Pacific Railroad constructed a rail line directly across the lake. It was constructed so engines would not have to climb over the mountains. In 1959 this route was rebuilt by a causeway. This solid raised roadway divided the lake into two parts. Two 15-foot culverts allowed water to flow under portions of the causeway. The south part of the lake receives most of the lake's inflow from rivers. The south part became higher than the north part. In the 1972 Landsat image of the Great Salt Lake (Figure 6-12a), notice that the northern portion of the lake is slightly lighter than the southern portion of the lake. The color difference is because the northern part is saltier, which causes different types of algae and bacteria to grow.

By July 1984, after 2 years of above-normal precipitation, the south part of the lake was 3.7 feet higher than the north. This is the highest difference it would ever reach. In August of 1984, a 300-foot section of the causeway was replaced by a low bridge, allowing water to flow underneath. Within 2 months, there was no difference between the south and north parts of the lake (Figure 6-12b).

In 1986, Utah began construction of a system to pump excess water west on to the Bonneville Salt Flats. This created the Newfoundland Evaporation Basin. The effects of this effort are shown in Figure 6-12c. Notice the new water body west of the Great Salt Lake.

Figure 6-12

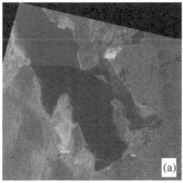
August 07, 1972 (Landsat 4 MSS)

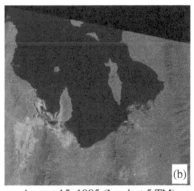
August 15, 1985 (Landsat 5 TM)

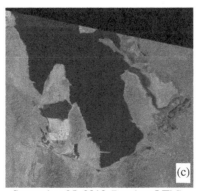
September 05, 2010 (Landsat 5 TM)

Imagery acquired over the Great Salt Lake by Landsat 4 Multispectral Scanner (MSS) and Landsat 5 Thematic Mapper (TM) capture long-term changes associated with causeway construction (a), causeway replacement (b), and water pumping and lake level decline (c).

6.7 Using and Assessing Data

Image analysts can produce remote sensing map products, some of which are straightforward to generate or can be integrated into a larger GIS application for use by emergency managers. Map products can include recognizable landmarks, and can offer a synoptic view of an area. Three- and four-band photography a broad view of an area and provide information on potential losses. The satellites may also provide detailed information on the intensity of storms, including winds, rainfall, and potential storm surge.

Remote imaging data can display data on arid or flooding areas. The images can illustrate before and after characteristics of the area to identify the vulnerability of the site to conditions such as flooding and drought. Remote sensing imagery also provides an excellent background for displaying roads, water features, city boundaries, and flood zones. The viewer can observe the general features of the area and then zoom into the display and examine specific areas of interest.

Remote sensing data can be a valuable tool. However, the data quality, accessibility, and information presentation varies with the type of data. The following provides an evaluation checklist for the many alternative remote sensing providers and the use of the data for emergency management activities.

Data Quality:

- ▲ Accuracy, precision, completeness, age, timeliness, and source
- ▲ Relevance of the data to the user
- ▲ Who collects the data, when, how it is imputed in the system, and how the data will be used
- ▲ Who will use the data and how the data will be used should influence what data is collected, who loads it and how it will be loaded into the system, and who will manipulate the data for users

Accessibility and Cost:

- ▲ Public agencies may restrict access to some remote sensing images because of the sensitivity of work that is done at specific sites
- ▲ Availability and possible access restrictions

Information Presentation:

- ▲ Format of the data may limit the user in presenting information
- ▲ Format for output
- ▲ Data flow diagrams
- ▲ Definition of the data item
- ▲ Name of the file where the data item is stored
- ▲ Abbreviation that can be used as a column heading for reports
- ▲ Range of values

6.8 Trends in Remote and Direct Sensing Technology

The accessibility of critical hazard information from remote and direct sensing sources is rapidly improving through the use of Web-based mapping applications and cloud storage and computing. Data accessibility has also improved as a result of improvements to computer networks, wireless communication, and real-time links to sensors. Images from GOES, Landsat, and MODIS, along with commercial images, including RADARSAT, provide critical information throughout the disaster recovery process. In addition to remote sensing image data, the USGS network of stream monitoring gauges provides timely information on water levels in streams, lakes, and rivers, and on weather variables such as temperature and precipitation. More widespread use of sensors will give you valuable information in a crisis. The growing role of direct and remote sensors in managing hazardous events can have significant impacts, including the following:

Information overload: Our increasing attention to technology may inadvertently result in information overload. If a communication system is highly centralized, even a limited emergency can result in communication bottlenecks. Subnetworks may need to be created to divert communication from the operation center. A planned distributed computing capability can be designed by examining elements of the emergency management system. Who needs to communicate directly and frequently and with whom?

Data integration: Many organizations have been struggling to cope with increasing demands for timely and accurate data to support ongoing decision making. As a result, large centralized systems have been adapted to more distributed databases. Maintaining linkages and integration of the data is critical in times of crisis. In the future, data will include more databases (relational), digital libraries, and multimedia databases maintained in a distributed environment. Distributed datasets also provide an opportunity for agencies that create or obtain data to maintain it as well. Documenting data sources, types, and collection methods using meta-data protocols and standards will be critical to ensure that information is used for its intended purpose.

Real-time response data: In a disaster, complex computing may not be possible for those directly involved in the response. In disasters, a rear support team can be organized to carry out high-performance modeling and analysis. Dependable networks should be designed to allow for detailed analysis to occur even during stressful events. Links between support staff and operations units must be maintained in a secure environment.

SUMMARY

Direct and remote sensing tools are among the most important tools for any emergency manager. **Digital sensors** allow for continuous monitoring of the natural and built environment. Computerized weather stations provide an ongoing means of collecting, recording, and transmitting data for use in emergency planning and response. Direct sensors can be linked to information systems that provide hazard warnings on a local or regional basis. For those areas not covered by direct sensors, field-deployed sensors can provide essential information for areas where data are not available. Remote sensing images are well suited for display and analysis along with road, water feature, railroad, and other layers in a GIS. High-resolution images provided by aircraft or satellites allow emergency responders to see flooded areas and direct rescue efforts.

In this chapter, we assessed how to use weather stations and water and air sensors to protect life and property at the local community scale. We also went through the steps to evaluate and select the most appropriate technology tools for the job. After reading through this chapter and learning about the remote sensing capabilities that are provided by satellites, you should be able to determine how satellite images can be used in all phases of emergency management. Finally, you examined ways to assess the quality and value of the data you receive from these tools. With this knowledge, students and emergency managers should be able to use direct and remote sensing information in all phases of emergency management to protect lives and property.

KEY TERMS

Air sensors
Air sensors are instruments that can determine the quality of indoor and outdoor air and the amount of pollution in the atmosphere. These sensors can detect a spill of hazardous industrial chemicals in manufacturing plants and in a community to alert management, workers, and the public to a chemical, nuclear, or biological exposure.

Active sensor
An active sensor emits pulses of electromagnetic energy at specific wavelengths, and the backscatter that is reflected from targets on the ground is recorded back at the sensor.

Direct sensing
Direct sensing is also referred to as in situ data collection that measures by direct contact with the environment. Weather stations collect direct sensing data on temperature, precipitation, wind direction and movement, and humidity by way of probing the atmosphere and collecting rainfall or snowfall.

GOES
The Geostationary Operational Environmental Satellite system provides global weathering monitoring by collecting continuous observations of cloud cover, and atmospheric temperature and moisture. This continuous data collection is possible because the satellite is in a **geostationary orbit** that is in a position that is fixed relative to Earth, providing a constant vigil for the atmospheric conditions that trigger severe weather conditions.

Lidar	Light detection and ranging uses active remote sensor technology that emits energy from a portion of the electromagnetic spectrum and records information that is reflected back to the sensor from either the landscape or the atmosphere. Lidar emits laser beam pulses and uses the speed of light to calculate the elevation of the bare earth as well as vegetation canopies, building, and other objects on the ground. Lidar can be used to measure atmospheric components that are needed for weather forecasting and environmental monitoring, such as aerosol particles, ice crystals, water vapor, or trace gases such as ozone.
Local Flood Warning Systems	These are automated systems that provide communities with the capacity to measure and detect water levels, transmit data, process and analyze data, forecast preparation, and provide forecast dissemination to the public.
Multispectral	Multispectral resolution remote sensors collect data from more than one channel including imagery in visible, near infrared, shortwave and thermal infrared channels.
Passive remote sensors	Passive remote sensors are instruments that measure and record electromagnetic energy that is either reflected from or emitted by physical objects on the ground, such as buildings, trees, waters, soil, and rock formations. The sensors include specialized cameras mounted to satellites or aircraft and pointed directly to Earth from a known distance and measure upwelling solar energy from targets on the ground.
Passive sensors	Passive sensors record upwelling solar energy from targets on the ground.
Radar	Radar devices are active microwave sensors that measure time delay and changes in shape between transmitted and received signals. Radar can penetrate cloud cover and does not depend on solar illumination. Images are formed as the radar moves along a flight path. The area illuminated by the radar, or footprint, is moved along the surface in a swath, building the image as it does so. The length of the radar antenna determines the clarity of the image.
RADARSAT	RADARSAT is a satellite remote sensing technology that was developed by the Canadian Space Agency and is used to clarify the nature of oil spills, landslides, oil spills, forest fires, flooding, and volcanic eruptions and can be used even if there is extensive cloud coverage.
Rain gauges	Rain gauges are direct sensing systems that collect and measure rainfall at specific locations.

Remote sensors	Systems that are deployed from platforms such as satellites and manned and unmanned aircraft collect imagery and topographical data that are used in predicting flood impacts, detecting new wildfire starts, and providing early warnings of landslide danger.
Digital Sensors	Sensors are instruments that collect and convert environmental measurements into electronic signals and are mounted on a variety of platforms in direct and indirect contact with the Earth. Weather station instruments and stream gauges are examples of direct sensors and are used to detect hazards by continuously monitoring air, weather, and water conditions.
Spatial resolution	Spatial resolution refers to the image clarity such as aircraft aerial images which have finer resolution or smaller pixel size (e.g., 3- to 5-m pixels) than images from satellites (e.g., 30 to 250-m pixels).
Spectral resolution	Refers to the electromagnetic spectrum that sensors use to record images including true color aerial photography that collects data in three channels of visible light: red, blue, and green. Color infrared aerial photography collects data in four channels: three are visible and the fourth is near infrared. Many satellites use multispectral resolution that includes visible, near infrared, short-wave, and thermal infrared channels. A small number of sensors, mainly airborne, are hyperspectral in design and collect data in hundreds of narrow channels from the ultraviolet to the shortwave or thermal infrared.
Stream gauges	Stream gauges are instruments that measure the elevation of the water in a stream (stage) and then convert it to a stream-flow observation (discharge). This information could trigger alarms when flooding is about to happen or is happening.

ONLINE RESOURCES

- ▲ USGS Water Watch
  https://waterwatch.usgs.gov/
- ▲ Landsat's Critical Role in Responding to Natural Disasters
  http://landsat.gsfc.nasa.gov/wp-content/uploads/2013/02/Landsat DisastersFS.pdf
- ▲ Landsat Image Gallery
  http://landsat.visibleearth.nasa.gov/
- ▲ Landsat Soil Burn Severity data
  https://fsapps.nwcg.gov/afm/baer/download.php

▲ Near Real-Time Earth Observation Data (LANCE) for Hazards and Disasters
https://earthdata.nasa.gov/earth-observation-data/near-real-time/
hazards-and-disasters

▲ LANCE Rapid Response MODIS Image Gallery (https://lance.modaps.eosdis.
nasa.gov/gallery/)

▲ "Worldview" for near-real-time data visualization and download
https://worldview.earthdata.nasa.gov/

▲ ForWarn Satellite-Based Change Recognition and Tracking
https://forwarn.forestthreats.org/highlights/137

▲ Famine Early Warning System Network
https://www.fews.net/

▲ Crowdsourcing DigitalGlobe commercial satellite imagery to solve real-world
problems
http://www.tomnod.com/

▲ International Charter Space and Major Disasters—Charter Geographic Tool
http://cgt.prod.esaportal.eu/

ASSESS YOUR UNDERSTANDING

Go to www.wiley.com/go/pine/tech&emergmgmt_2e to evaluate your knowledge of using technology. This website contains MCQ's, self checks, review questions, applying this chapter and you try it.

References

Clasen, C., Kruse, F. A., & Kim, A. (2012). Analysis of LIDAR data for emergency management and disaster response. In *Optical Remote Sensing of the Environment* (paper no. RTu2E-2). Washington, DC: Optical Society of America.

Cutter, S. L., Barnes, L., Berry, M., Burton, C., Evans, E., Tate, E., & Webb, J. (2008). A place-based model for understanding community resilience to natural disasters. *Global Environmental Change*, 18(4), 598–606.

Deichmann, U., Ehrlich, D., Small, C., & Zeug, G. (2011). Using high resolution satellite data for the identification of urban natural disaster risk. European Union and World Bank. http://ccsl.iccip.net/using_high_resolution_data.pdf (accessed May 11, 2017).

Johnson, G. P., Holmes, R. R., & Waite, L. A. (2004). *The Great Flood of 1993 on the Upper Mississippi River: 10 Years Later*. Urbana, IL: US Department of the Interior, US Geological Survey.

Marghany, M. (2015). Automatic detection of oil spills in the Gulf of Mexico from RADARSAT-2 SAR satellite data. *Environmental Earth Sciences*, 74(7), 5935–5947.

Van Westen, C. J. (2013). Remote sensing and GIS for natural hazards assessment and disaster risk management. In J. F. Schroder and M. P. Bishop (Eds.), *Treatise on Geomorphology* (pp. 259–298). San Diego, CA: Academic Press, Elsevier.

Walters, S. P., Schneider, N. J., & Guthrie, J. D. (2011). *Geospatial Multi-Agency Coordination (GeoMAC) Wildland Fire Perimeters, 2008.* U.S. Geological Survey Data Series 612 (6 p.). Urbana, IL: US Department of the Interior, US Geological Survey

Wahl, K. L., Thomas, W. O., & Hirsch, R. M. (1995). *The Stream-Gaging Program of the US Geological Survey* (No. 1123). Reston, VA: US Geological Survey.

7

EMERGENCY MANAGEMENT DECISION SUPPORT SYSTEMS: USING DATA TO MANAGE DISASTERS

Starting Point

Go to www.wiley.com/go/pine/tech&emergmgmt_2e to assess your knowledge of emergency management decision support systems.
Determine where to concentrate your effort.

What You'll Learn in This Chapter

▲ Components of a management decision support information system
▲ Characteristics of a useful decision support information system
▲ Examples of decision support information systems
▲ How data may be organized for emergency management
▲ How to use a hazardous chemical decision support system
▲ Criteria for assessing decision support systems
▲ Useful emergency management datasets
▲ Examples of data sources that are useful to emergency managers

After Studying This Chapter, You'll Be Able To

▲ Use emergency management information systems to make well-informed decisions during a crisis.
▲ Examine the characteristics of a decision support system and its application to emergency management.
▲ Examine how emergency managers can use decision support systems, CAMEO, and agency datasets for managing hazards.
▲ Use meta-data to sort information and support emergency management efforts.
▲ Compare and contrast different datasets on the basis of data quality, accessibility, and information presentation.
▲ Use public data sources to support emergency management efforts.

Technology and Emergency Management, Second Edition. John C. Pine.
© 2018 John Wiley & Sons, Inc. Published 2018 by John Wiley & Sons, Inc.
Companion website: www.wiley.com/go/pine/tech&emergmgmt_2e

Goals and Outcomes

▲ Evaluate management decision support information systems
▲ Assess how to use a decision support system to support emergency management tasks
▲ Evaluate data tables to access and sort information
▲ Evaluate the design of a hazardous chemical dataset
▲ Evaluate a database and its potential use in emergency management
▲ Select data sources to support your daily emergency management tasks

INTRODUCTION

As an emergency manager, you will be asked to make many decisions and to collaborate with many agencies in your community, region, state, and nationally. Some of the decisions will be easy day-to-day decisions while other decisions will be difficult ones made during a crisis. As a decision maker, you need to have data and information available to you and the capacity to work seamlessly with others.

▲ **Data** is a fact or things that are known.
▲ Information is data that is processed or used in some form of analysis.
▲ Functioning organizational systems are essential in ensuring that the right information is shared to support effective response operations.

During this chapter, you will examine how decision support information systems and their databases, if correctly designed, will give you the information you need to make effective decisions. In addition, building a capacity to share information with others will also be examined. You will also determine the characteristics for useful information systems. You will assess public and private decision support information systems. You will then assess the elements of these systems and their quality to support decision making. You will evaluate datasets and distinguish between dynamic collaborative systems from agency established information systems that include public data sources and emergency management databases.

7.1 Emergency Management Information Systems and Networks

You must be able to make quick, well-informed decisions in a crisis. You must also be able to make quality decisions when preparing for emergency situations. Information about community resources, vulnerable populations, as well as the hazards is fundamental to effective response. In the past, managers maintained lists of local and regional contacts, paper maps and layouts of critical resources, and charts showing when to make contacts. Today, we can store this information and much more in a digital format and available in the office and on the move. Further, this information can be made available to agency staff, community partners, and the public. We can also store it in ways that support effective decision making. Records may be maintained in digital formats to ensure that agency activities are effective (Borbinha and Delgado, 1996). Agency digital records are data and may be created, stored, sorted, merged, retrieved, displayed, and used to make decisions or calculations. When data is processed in such a way as to enable the organization to make decisions, it is referred to as a decision support system or a **management information system**. A management information system is a set of digital databases that may be sorted, merged, retrieved, displayed, and used to make decisions or calculations.

Kapucu and Hu (2016) stress that effective emergency management is greatly influenced by collaborative operational networks such as those used today by emergency management agencies. They stress that these networks are both formal and informal and are important for encouraging organizations to be involved in disaster preparedness networks. Yet it is the collaboration ties and friendships during disaster preparedness that influence the formation of collaborations during disaster response. Structural attributes of emergency management systems have impacts on the development of multiplex relationships among organizations within various networks.

Reddick (2011) notes that emergency management decision support systems are critical for emergency management since they enable officials to record, select, sort and save population, chemical, or weather data about their community. Preece et al. (2013) add that in the aftermath of a disaster the rate of information sharing increases dramatically making ineffective information decision support systems critical to organizational success.

A management decision support information system must include the following:

▲ Inputs: data, storage processes, or procedures
▲ Transformation: methods of sorting, merging, accumulating, and retrieving the inputs/data
▲ Outputs: information that allows you to make decisions about evacuations, disaster declarations, and evacuation zones

FOR EXAMPLE

Using a Management Information System

One way to use a decision support management information system is to determine where vulnerable populations are located. For example, if a town is prone to flooding, you could use a management information system to determine who lives in the flood zone as well as what businesses are located in the flood zone. You can then use this information to help residents take mitigation measures, evacuate, or even just to warn them.

The idea behind information systems is that they provide a systematic way to collect, manipulate, maintain, and distribute information throughout an organization. This provides unlimited opportunities to collect, explore, and display information relating to disasters, risks, or the community (Belissent, 2010; Isett et al., 2011).

Computer-based management information systems are critical in emergency management. These systems allow you to record, select, sort, and save population, chemical, or weather data about a community (Gall et al. 2009; Kron et al., 2012). The systems allow you to process the data. You can sort, calculate, or retrieve specific data. Individual facilities with hazardous chemicals and local communities can use an information system to comply with or monitor federal and state requirements. Information systems allow you to access data that will enhance planning, response, recovery, and mitigation efforts (Noble et al., 2014).

A systems view of an organization suggests that it has several elements:

▲ Inputs: information, equipment, and computer programs
▲ Transformation: the manipulation of the data using the program
▲ Outputs: decisions and actions based on lists, messages, reports, or maps from the information system

Decision support information systems have become increasing complex with the introduction of a larger number of users of these systems and their complexity (Cutter et al., 2015). As an example of the increasing complexity and size of information systems, the concept of the Internet of Things (IoT) has evolved and connects small devices such as security video cameras to remote sensing weather systems. The increasing presence of the IoT suggests that our systems allow "network enabled" objects to be connected and extend our sources of information (Gubbi et al., 2013; Zanella et al., 2014).

One of the definitions of the IoT describes it as "a self-configured dynamic network infrastructure with standards and interoperable communication protocols where physical and virtual 'things' have identities, physical attributes, and virtual personalities, and are seamlessly integrated into the information infrastructure." The concept of "things" in the network infrastructure refers to any real or virtual participating actors such as real world objects, human beings, virtual data, and intelligent software agents (Yang et al., 2013). The purpose of the IoT is to create an environment in which the basic information from any one of the networked autonomous actors can be efficiently shared with others in real time. With more powerful and efficient data, collection and sharing ability could support sophisticated decision support systems through more accurate, detailed, and intelligent data.

FOR EXAMPLE

Local Utilities

Many local utilities are taking advantage of the IoT concept by installing connections to homes, office buildings, and commercial enterprises to control information on the use of utilities. Utilities are able to read "meters" remotely and perform system functions such as making system connections, disconnections, or change service to the user. Homeowners, for example, can also use these "digital meters" to monitor their service and control the use of lights and security systems.

System integration and asynchronous control will be needed to allow effective emergency response. Functional separated tasks, such as sensing, storage, computation, and decision making, need to be conducted by independent functional units, so as to facilitate the integration of multiple technologies (Gelenbe and Wu, 2013). To achieve this goal, information systems will need to support emergency response systems that include not only formal units but also elements that are external to their control such as citizens linked to our operations. Consider actions by large numbers of civilians who are making evacuation choices based on information from local traffic operations. One could envision decision support systems that independently tap into weather forecasts and traffic flow.

7.2 Evaluating Information Systems

There have been many cases in recent years where decisions were made with accurate information that was provided by citizens on the disaster scene or remotely by a security camera in a place of business. There has been a debate about when information and what information might be available from security or traffic cameras during a disaster, but accurate and timely information can be critical to effective decision making (Singh et al., 2009).

Your decisions are only effective if you have accurate information. You rely on the advice and counsel of the people you work with. However, you also base decisions by assuming your data is reliable. Your information system must be clear, accurate, reliable, and complete. It must be able to provide you with all the information you need.

7.2.1 Quality

Quality consists of several factors, including, accuracy, clarity, and the medium through which the information is communicated. If the details do not accurately reflect current conditions, then any decision made using the information may be adversely affected. Clarity refers to the meaning and intent of the information and if it is clear to the decision maker. Finally, the information must be presented in a neat and orderly way so that it assists the decision maker. Providing the decision maker with a massive computer printout instead of several pages of summary information could disrupt effective decision making. In addition, the quality of the system could include the cost when compared to other similar systems. As a part of the quality consideration, there are other questions you should ask: Does the system and data conform to any state or national standards? Does the system use custom data format (databases, graphics, maps, or images)? Does the system allow the user to import common format database, spreadsheet, text, image, or map files?

7.2.2 Timeliness

Many day-to-day decisions are time sensitive. Decisions on how to respond to situations must be made quickly. Timely information has several ingredients. First, it should be provided when it is needed to support making a decision.

Another key ingredient of timely information is currency so that information would be provided to decision makers as changes occur. For example, changes in the weather could drastically influence the dispersion of hazardous chemicals.

Information systems should provide for an easy means of updating data, even real-time changes as it occurs. Information should be timely when it is given to the decision maker. And should be provided as often as needed or at an appropriate frequency.

7.2.3 Completeness

Information must be complete to be of value. The data must allow the decision maker to make an accurate assessment of the situation and to arrive at a suitable decision. Where appropriate, decision makers should have access to current information and to past history and future plans. Conciseness and detail are part of completeness. Information should be presented to the decision maker in as concise a form as possible, but there should be sufficient detail to provide the decision maker with enough depth and breadth for the current situation. Finally, only relevant information should be provided so as to avoid information overload.

7.2.4 Performance

Performance of information systems has the following variables:

▲ Capacity: The amount of work that the system can perform or the number of users at the same time.
▲ Productivity: The extent that data input is required and the types and quality of outputs from the system.
▲ Consistency: The number of breakdowns in the operation of the system.
▲ Cycle time: The time it takes the system to perform functions.
▲ Flexibility: How easily is the system able to switch from one process to another, and must the user perform numerous steps to move from one function to another?
▲ Security: What protection does the system provide to restrict unauthorized users?
▲ Responsiveness: Can the system be changed based on user input?
▲ Reliability of the product: Does the system require frequent support?

FOR EXAMPLE

First Reports

During a crisis, first reports may not be complete and may contain inaccurate information. First reports of a school bus accident or a civil unrest may not reflect the true situation that might be reflected in a business video camera. It is important for you to have the most accurate up-to-date information and a strong communication network in place. Without accurate information, you will not be able to make effective decisions.

7.3 Federal, State, and Local Information Systems

Public agencies have been using collaborative information systems to support information gathering and communications. The Federal Emergency Management Agency (FEMA) National Emergency Management Information System (NEMIS) illustrates efforts on a national scale to support information gathering and reporting throughout the national, state, and local emergency management network.

7.3.1 Management Information Systems

The Department of Homeland Security (DHS) noted in its description of the National Incident Management System that management information systems are used to provide decision support information to managers by collecting, updating, and processing data, and tracking resources (DHS, 2008). They enhance resource status information flow and provide real-time data in a fast-paced environment where different jurisdictions, emergency management/response personnel, and their affiliated organizations are managing different aspects of the incident and should coordinate their efforts. Examples of management information systems include resource tracking, transportation tracking, inventory management, reporting, and geographical information mapping systems. The selection and use of systems for resource management should be based on the identification of the information needs within a jurisdiction.

7.3.2 The National Emergency Management Information System

Singh et al. (2009) stressed that sharing information in a disaster is critical to effective operations. Federal, state, and local efforts to ensure ongoing communications and coordination have been in place for many years building on the NEMIS at the federal level and state and local efforts to encourage effective coordination and communication.

The **National emergency Management Information System (NEMIS)** is an information system that was designed to support FEMA and automates vital functions and tasks. These tasks include providing disaster assistance for individual victims; support of infrastructure and mitigation programs for state and local government recovery efforts; and support for direction, control, and administrative activities at both the headquarters and field levels of operations. NEMIS builds on existing FEMA information technology capabilities and drives standardization in FEMA. This system established agency-wide standards for personal computer configurations, operating systems, relational databases, and Geographic Information System (GIS) software. FEMA provides an online system to provide individuals the opportunity to apply for assistance.

> ## FOR EXAMPLE
>
> ### State and local information system: WebEOC
>
> WebEOC (Web-based Emergency Operations Center) is a commercial online tool for information sharing and resource request tracking during emergencies, disasters, significant events, and daily operations. WebEOC provides a comprehensive information system that fits within the requirements of the U.S.

National Incident Management System and includes a common operating framework and real-time situational awareness of events affecting a geographic region. Public agencies and their response partners utilize this program to enhance communication and coordination. It also provides secure real-time information sharing to help managers make sound decisions quickly.

It is currently used by many state and local jurisdictions, federal agencies, nonprofit entities such as faith-based and volunteer response partners, and private business operations. Uses include situational reporting, report summaries, request for resources, damage assessments, and financial summaries and reports. A secure, Internet-based emergency information management application that facilitates real-time information sharing of operational details is included and may be adapted to address specific organizational needs. It is a product of Intermedix which provides data analytics and cloud-based technology to support emergency management and manage risks.

The primary goal of many of these organizational information systems is message routing, resources tracking, and document management for the purpose of achieving situational awareness, demonstrating limited capabilities for automated aggregation, data analysis, and mining (Hristidis et al., 2010).

7.3.3 Computer Aided Management of Emergency Operations

Computer aided management of emergency operations (CAMEO) is computer software for public, private, and nonprofit organizations that are involved in chemical emergencies. It was developed by the Environmental Protection Agency (EPA) and National Oceanic and Atmospheric Administration (NOAA) to help plan for and mitigate chemical accidents as well as to comply with the Emergency Planning and Community Right to Know Act of 1986. CAMEO is a widely used information and decision support system for chemical emergency response, planning and regulatory compliance, planning and response to natural hazards. CAMEO includes the following functions:

▲ Provides safety and emergency response information on 4700 hazardous chemicals
▲ Tracks chemical inventories in the community and on transportation routes
▲ Automates chemical inventory reporting
▲ Provides a basis for conducting hazards analysis and off-site consequences analysis
▲ Included with CAMEO is the Arial Locations of Hazardous Atmosphere (ALOHA) air dispersion model and Mapping Applications for Response, Planning, and Local Operational Tasks (MARPLOT—a GIS program designed for use within CAMEO and provide mapping and data utilities with ALOHA and CAMEO data elements) mapping application
▲ CAMEO is used for Chemical Emergency Response, Planning, and Regulatory Compliance (including substances that might be part of a terrorist incident)

Users of CAMEO include local emergency planning committees (LEPCs), fire departments, state emergency planning commissions (SERCs), emergency planners, chemical facilities, health care facilities, and universities. CAMEO is a suite of separate, integrated software applications: CAMEO, MARPLOT, LandView, and ALOHA. CAMEO also includes many databases and other applications. The purpose of this suite of software is to assist front-line chemical emergency planners and responders in planning for and responding to hazards and disasters. The addition of LandView was to bring extensive data from the Census Bureau. This helps you better understand the characteristics of a community. Although LandView can be run independently from CAMEO, it is linked to each of the CAMEO components.

A key component of CAMEO is ALOHA, which is an atmospheric dispersion model and supports the assessment of actual or potential releases of hazardous chemical vapors. MARPLOT is the mapping application component of the CAMEO suite of software allowing users to see their data (e.g., roads, schools, factories), display this information on computer maps, and print this information on area maps. The areas contaminated can be overlaid on these maps to determine potential impacts and define hazard areas.

CAMEO includes a chemical database which contains information on more than 4700 chemicals, 70 000 synonyms, trade names, and other labeling conventions. It provides a powerful search engine that allows users to find chemicals instantly. Each chemical is linked to a response information data sheet (RIDS) that details the chemical-specific information on fire and explosive hazards, health hazards, firefighting techniques, cleanup procedures, and protective clothing.

Local governments use CAMEO to track the location of hazardous chemicals in their community and maintain detailed information of the on-site location of each of the chemicals, contacts at each site, and records on any chemical accidents. Each of the datasets is associated with a reporting facility and thus considered a "relational database."

7.4 Using Data

Decision support systems such as CAMEO and WebEOC provide a means for the emergency manager to get correct information quickly. Information and decision support systems are based on data. As an emergency manager, you have to make many decisions. Some are daily decisions such as who to meet with and what supplies you need. Some decisions affect many people and businesses, such as when to evacuate or how to enforce building codes. You cannot make these decisions in a vacuum. You make these decisions, however, based on data. Data is a fact that is known. Data is something that is used as a basis for discussion, decision making, calculating, or measuring.

For example, data might be the number of hours it takes to drive from point A to point B at 60 miles per hour, or the elevation of a school that is used as a shelter in a community subjected to frequent heavy rains. When data is processed or used in some form of analysis, it can be converted into information. For example, a small community might have six schools constructed or remodeled in the last 5 years. When new shelters are being identified, each school is assessed as to factors affecting shelter location. Only four schools may be suitable as a shelter in a storm. Specific facts or data about each school are assessed to determine if they are suitable as a disaster shelter. The suitable shelters are thus the result of processed data and therefore fall into the concept of information.

7.4.1 Databases

We organize data and store it in a database. For example, the CAMEO system described earlier combines data relating to facilities with hazardous chemicals. The database includes separate sets of information about hazardous chemicals, facilities, and their organizational contacts as well as a list of accidental releases from each facility. Each type of information is linked to create a related dataset or a database. A database is thus a collection of related information that is organized so that it provides a foundation for procedures and making decisions.

Databases include tables, fields, and records. A table is a set of data arranged in rows and columns reflecting individual records and fields. A record is a collection of fields or a row of a table representing one record entry. A field is a subdivision or a record; it contains a single piece of data. For example, you might have a table of hazardous chemicals that your city produces. A record details the chemicals and related information on the chemicals that a particular company in your city produces. A field could be the amount of chemicals the facility produces in a year.

In this example, we are describing a relational database that uses a particular field as an index and links the separate data tables of information. Each table is made up of rows of data (records), and each record contains information organized into columns (fields). When tables are related, they contain a common element or field. The common fields allow for matching of information between tables. Within CAMEO you can look up chemicals by their name and determine who uses or stores the substance, the amount at the facility, and if any accidents had involved this substance.

7.4.2 Data Dictionary (Meta-data)

The most costly and time-consuming part of developing a useful information system is the design of the data tables. The system should allow the user to sort or find information quickly and accurately with ease of effort. After systems are designed, support staff often tell the manager that the information system cannot provide the requested need. Planning can prevent this problem and ensure that the system is responsive to the user's needs. Time should be taken in setting up the database to identify how and by whom the system will be used. The types of data should be outlined before a system is selected. In addition, the system should be easily adapted to reflect the special needs of the user. A critical part of any database is documentation or creating a data dictionary.

For the information in a database to be useful to the manager, users must have confidence in the quality of the data. A data dictionary or (**meta-data**) should be developed and maintained for each dataset used. Meta-data can broadly be defined as data about data. It refers to searchable definitions used to locate existing information. Meta-data has become a crucial concern as the Web has emerged as a major research tool. Meta-data may determine how accessible a particular Web site is to researchers. Every Web site is indexed based on meta-data tags.

For example, if you wanted to look up information on a business, you could look it up under "Name." The record should have an address that reflects its location in the community. Unfortunately for many datasets, the location of a business might be the main headquarters of a site rather than the location of the site you are seeking. The data dictionary includes information as to where the data was obtained, when, how the data was formatted, and if the data has been altered. The meta-data could clearly state that each site is the actual access rather than a corporate headquarters and thus allow the user of the data to understand where a site is located. The following are common elements of a data dictionary:

▲ Name of each table and fields in a table
▲ Definition of each field
▲ Name of the file where the data item is stored
▲ Typical format for output
▲ Range or type of values for a record
▲ Description of data flow
▲ Identification of user input screens

Many GIS datasets include meta-data that reflects the content and development of specific map layers such as streets, water features, public entity boundaries. Many of the layers include information such as coordinate points, geographic codes, census feature class codes, address ranges, zip codes, legal entities, statistical entities, landmarks, and other features. Each map layer has a database file associated with the map feature.

FOR EXAMPLE

GIS road and street files

The street layer shown in Figure 7-1 includes meta-data files describing the characteristics of the map layer, the developer, contact, and key information such as the scale of accuracy of the layer. A data table is also part of the GIS files and includes road features such as the road name, a road classification code, local zip code, and county code information and many more details about local roads throughout the United States. The meta-data file is provided to users of the map files to ensure that the mapping files are used correctly and with an understanding of the quality of the road data. A good example of why meta-data is important is that when one places the road files over a high-resolution photo image, roads and streets may not appear in the proper location. The street files shown in Figure 7-1 was designed using a resolutions (scale) of $1:24000$. Today, many high-resolution photos are used by local governments and may be $1:10000$ or less. When you place the road/street layer that was developed at a $1:24000$ scale over a high-resolution photo reflecting a $1:10000$ scale, the roads may not lay in the proper place. The roads in Figure 7-1 are almost in the correct place but not exact. The high-resolution image reveals errors in the road/street lines that just do not fit exactly over the streets in the image. Many organizations use road and street GIS files and display them over high-resolution images of a jurisdiction. Consulting the meta-data information for a map layer allows the user to fully understand the limitations that come with the map data.

Figure 7-1

GIS road files shown on a high-resolution image of Baton Rouge, Louisiana.

7.5 Evaluating Databases

Databases and information systems are not all the same. Some are limited in the scope of the information reflected in the dataset and in some cases the information could be old and out of date. The accuracy of the data could be very questionable. You have probably had the experience of looking for something in a database and not being able to find it. It can be a frustrating experience when you cannot find the information you need. For many information systems, it is very difficult to get the data that you need. Others are well designed, user-friendly, and provide the needed information and details on the source of the information.

If you are involved in the input of data into a database, there are several things to keep in mind. You will need to understand:

▲ What data will be collected
▲ The purpose of the data
▲ Who will collect the data
▲ Who will input the data
▲ How the data will be used
▲ Who created the data
▲ How the data will be placed into the system
▲ Who will manipulate the data for users

FOR EXAMPLE

Community Water Sources

The Safe Drinking Water Information System (SDWIS) contains information about public water systems and their violations of EPA's drinking water regulations. These statutes and accompanying regulations establish maximum contaminant levels, treatment techniques, and monitoring and reporting requirements to ensure that water provided to customers is safe for human consumption. You can search for this information within the US EPA and it can also be found at https://www.epa.gov/enviro/sdwis-search.

The report generated from the US Environmental Protection Agency (EPA) SDWIS database lists the public drinking systems in Chattanooga, TN, and notes the source of water (Table 7-1). Systems that obtain water from surface sources are noted and could reveal potential vulnerability to contamination. Those systems that use surface sources of water might be asked to examine security measures that are in place to protect from water contamination.

7.6 Using Emergency Management Databases

National databases and information systems are available from many federal, state, and local public agencies for public access, use, and dissemination. These databases provide essential information on local communities. The information is useful in risk assessment and hazards analysis. Envirofacts provides an excellent illustration of a national database. It has extremely useful hazardous chemical information for local communities in the United States. Envirofacts includes several environmental datasets available to you from the EPA on a national basis. It provides public access to sets of related databases. The system allows the user to select records by geographic area, by EPA program, or by chemical. Take a look at the Envirofacts site maintained by the US EPA (https://www3.epa.gov/enviro/). What data might be useful to a local community from this set of environmental data?

Table 7-1 EPA Public Water System (SDWIS) Report for Chattanooga, TN

Water System Name	County(s) Served	City(s) Served	Population Served	Primary Water Source Type	Public Water System (PWS) Activity	Water System ID
Eastside Utility District	Hamilton	Chattanooga	50 253	Surface water	Active	TN0000219
Hixson Utility District	Hamilton	Hixson	58 420	Ground water	Active	TN0000303
Northwest Utility District	Hamilton	Soddy-Daisy	17 899	Surface water	Active	TN0000169
Savannah Valley Utility District	Hamilton	Georgetown	22 452	Surface water purchased	Active	TN0000613
Signal Mountain Water System	Hamilton	Not reported	8 130	Surface water purchased	Active	TN0000634
Tennessee American Water	Hamilton	Chattanooga	195 491	Surface water	Active	TN0000107
Union Fork-Bakewell Utility District	Hamilton	Bakewell	4 767	Purchased ground water under influence of surface water source	Active	TN0000037
Walden's Ridge Utility District	Hamilton	Signal Mountain	7 926	Surface water purchased	Active	TN0000635
Showing 1–8 of eight entries		Show 10	Entries	Search:		

7.6.1 HAZUS-MH Datasets

Databases within HAZUS-MH (Hazards United States) may be useful to local communities. The HAZUS-MH program was developed by FEMA and was intended to be used as a comprehensive hazard modeling and vulnerability assessment tool for many natural hazards. Today, the model has expanded. It now provides for modeling of floods, wind, and coastal hazards in the United States. An examination of the HAZUS-MH Flood model is included in Chapter 9 of this text.

Within the HAZUS-MH program are extensive databases that provide the location of police and fire stations, emergency medical services (EMS), schools, and hospitals. In addition, it provides a comprehensive count of buildings for commercial, industry, educational, governmental, and residential property. The database provides the count of buildings by type of property, type of construction, value of the property, as well as the value of the contents. The building inventory database is summarized by block. It provides a good basis for examining the impact of hazards on a community. FEMA recognized that this national database would need updating and provided tools for editing and updating all the data in HAZUS-MH. Emergency managers from small to large communities should examine this resource. They should ensure that the data accurately reflects the local community. Accurate building inventory data in HAZUS-MH will enable you to accurately determine the potential impacts of disasters on their community.

The following list is a sample of one data table from HAZUS-MH for schools. Note what information is included in the database. Think about how you could use this information in different emergency management tasks.

- ▲ Name of school
- ▲ Identification number
- ▲ Address (city, state zip code, and county)
- ▲ Contact name and phone number
- ▲ School type and description (primary school)
- ▲ Year built, cost, number of stories, building type (masonry)
- ▲ Design level, foundation type, and first-floor height
- ▲ Generator (yes/no)
- ▲ Number of students and shelter capacity
- ▲ Kitchen (yes/no)
- ▲ Latitude and longitude
- ▲ Comment field

FEMA designed the database as a resource to emergency managers.

7.7 Management Roles in Decision Support Systems

Van de Walle and Turoff (2008) note that emergency management operations face many challenges for individual or group decision support systems in emergency situations. They examined large-scale disasters and concluded that there were specific roles for those engaged in decision making in a disaster. It is critical that everyone involved appreciate their role throughout the emergency management process. The fundamental role functions include:

▲ Requesting: Specifically the acquisition of resources.
▲ Observing or Reporting: Information generated about the situation by observers and reporting that information.
▲ Allocating: Individuals allocating resources that respond to the requests being made.
▲ Local Oversight: Individuals who have information about the situation who can share potential conflicts with an effective response operation.
▲ Maintaining and Servicing: Ensuring that resources are resupplied including people and supplies.
▲ Situation Analysis and Awareness: Those who are monitoring the situation to see if resources might be increased or if there are threats to resources.
▲ Global Resupply: Ensuring that resources are maintained and continue to be available.

These functions and roles need to be explicitly known to everyone involved as the response take place.

7.8 Obtaining Data from Public Federal Data Sources

You can obtain useful data from many federal agencies. The following federal agencies collect, store, use, and provide access to datasets that are useful to the emergency management community. Take a look at the type of information that is available from these agencies and assess the data using the evaluation criteria previously noted.

▲ US Department of Agriculture. Includes information on agricultural statistics and reflects the volume and value of agricultural products at the county and state level. See https://www.nass.usda.gov/Statistics_by_State/ For information on timber values and production in a state or local area see: https://www.fia.fs.fed.us/.
Many states in the United States experience frequent droughts that have a significant impact on communities. Outdoor activities may be restricted and thus reduce recreation opportunities. In extreme circumstances, droughts may result in forest fires. States maintain information on timber value and production which could be used to understand the vulnerability of communities to severe droughts.
▲ National Centers for Environmental Information within NOAA and the Department of Commerce provides information on severe weather in the United States (https://www.ncdc.noaa.gov/stormevents/; take a look at their site and explore how information from NOAA might identify vulnerabilities to extreme weather at the county or regional level).
▲ Department of Energy (https://www.eia.gov/tools/faqs/faq.cfm?id=207&t=3). See the Department of Energy for information on the location of nuclear power plants and other energy-related locations throughout the United States.

▲ Emergency Managers Weather Information Network (EMWIN) radio broad-cast is one method used by the National Weather Service (NWS) and other public and private agencies for disseminating the EMWIN data stream (http://www.nws.noaa.gov/emwin/index.htm). The NWS broadcasts the EMWIN data stream by radio only in the Washington, DC, and Norman, Oklahoma, areas. Elsewhere, other public and private agencies downlink from a satellite and then retransmit by radio or other means. To receive an EMWIN radio broadcast, hardware and software is needed.

▲ US Geological Survey (USGS; www.usgs.gov). The USGS is the nation's larg-est earth science research and information agency. Access is provided to USGS fact sheets, general information and contacts, public issues, education, grant information, and Internet resources. See the type of hazards that are monitored by the USGS in the Emergency Management–related datasets. https://www2.usgs.gov/natural_hazards/emergencymanagement/.

FOR EXAMPLE

Understanding your Watershed

You can use the EPA site (www.epa.gov/surf) to search and determine the watershed in your region. Search for "Surf your watershed" to find data from many databases concerning water quality in your community. This is an excel-lent source of information associated with water resources in your region. Find your watershed and explore the resources for your area. Note a key part of the information available includes stream flow stations. These stations are managed by the USGS and provide real-time information on stream flow rates and levels along with historical information on flowing in the region.

7.9 The Future of Decision Support Systems: The Intelligent Community

Sánchez et al. (2013) note that in an intelligent community, energy, water, transpor-tation, waste management, and other key services are managed by different utilities that manage their own infrastructure. Significant levels of automation, commu-nications, and information technology are linking these systems in a manner to support integrated decision support systems by emergency management and public safety. There is a clear movement toward driving more intelligence into field equipment to make faster decisions on fault isolation, location and restoration, reconfiguration, and management of the complex system these utilities control (Ward and Wamsley, 2007; Wirtz et al., 2014).

Critical issues related to the growth of information systems in local utilities and public agencies are the collaboration and integration between entities in disaster response. Lee et al. (2011) explain that response to disasters, whether natural (e.g., floods, earthquakes) or human induced (e.g., terrorist attacks), is a complex process that involves severe time pressure, high uncertainty, and many stakeholders, which results in unpredictable information needs. These support operational decision support systems and are information-intensive activities. They point out that most disaster responders have to cope with incomplete, unavailable, and/or outdated information when a disaster strikes.

Access to quality information is essential for agencies to decide and act under demanding conditions since poor information quality can be lethal for both emergency responders and victims (Alcántara-Ayala et al., 2015). Determining how to integrate local information systems to support effective decision making will be critical in ensuring effective emergency response and recovery activities (Pelling and Blackburn, 2013).

SUMMARY

As you have learned, it is critical for you to have up-to-date and accurate information to plan, mitigate, and respond to disasters. In obtaining accurate information, you will need to use and rely on databases. Before you use databases to make important decisions, you will also need to evaluate them. In addition, there are many federal and state databases that are available to you to help you make well-informed decisions. The idea behind management information systems is that they provide a systematic way to collect, manipulate, maintain, and distribute information throughout an organization. Management information systems provide a way for you to get the right information quickly and thus support decision making.

KEY TERMS

Data	A fact or things that are known.
Management information system	A set of digital databases that may be sorted, merged, retrieved, displayed, and used to make decisions or calculations.
Meta-data	Data about data, and includes information on where the data was obtained, when, how it was formatted or altered, geospatial references if available, purpose of the data, and ownership.
National Emergency Management Information System (NEMIS)	An information system that was designed; Management Information to automate and support vital emergency System (NEMIS) response and recovery operations by the federal government.

ASSESS YOUR UNDERSTANDING

Go to www.wiley.com/go/pine/tech&emergmgmt_2e to evaluate your knowledge of using technology. This website contains MCQ's, self checks, review questions, applying this chapter and you try it.

References

Alcántara-Ayala, I., Altan, O., Baker, D., Briceno, S., Cutter, S., Gupta, H., Holloway, A., Ismail-Zadeh, A., Jimenez Diaz, V., Johnston, D., & McBean, G. (2015). Disaster risks research and assessment to promote risk reduction and management. In *ICSU*, Paris, France, March 2015, p. 49.

Belissent, J. (2010). *Getting Clever About Smart Cities: New Opportunities Require New Business Models*. Cambridge, MA: Forrester Research.

Borbinha, J. L. B., & Delgado, J. C. M.. (1996). Networked digital libraries. *Microcomputers for Information Management: Global Internetworking for Libraries*, *13*(3–4), 195–216.

Cutter, S. L., Ismail-Zadeh, A., Alcántara-Ayala, I., Altan, O., Baker, D. N., Briceno, S., Gupta, H., Holloway, A., Johnston, D., McBean, G.A., Ogawa, Y., Paton, D., Porio, E., Silbereisen, R.K., Takeuchi, K., Valsecchi, G.B., Vogel, C., & Wu, G. (2015). Global risks: Pool knowledge to stem losses from disasters. *Nature*, *522*, 277–279.

Department of Homeland Security (DHS). (2008). *National Incident Management System*. Retrieved from http://www.fema.gov/pdf/emergency/nims/NIMS_core. pdf (accessed April 24, 2017).

Gall, M., Borden, K., and Cutter, S. L. (2009). When do losses count? Six fallacies of natural hazards loss data. *Bulletin of the American Meteorological Society*, *90*(6), 799–809.

Gelenbe, E., & Wu, F. J. (2013). Future research on cyber-physical emergency management systems. *Future Internet*, *5*(3), 336–354.

Gubbi, J., Buyya, R., Marusic, S., & Palaniswami, M. (2013). Internet of Things (IoT): A vision, architectural elements, and future directions. *Future Generation Computer Systems*, *29*(7), 1645–1660.

Hristidis, V., Chen, S. C., Li, T., Luis, S., & Deng, Y. (2010). Survey of data management and analysis in disaster situations. *Journal of Systems and Software*, *83*(10), 1701–1714.

Isett, K. R., Mergel, I. A., LeRoux, K., & Mischen, P. A. (2011). Networks in public administration scholarship: Understanding where we are and where we need to go. *Journal of Public Administration Research and Theory*, *21*, 157–173.

Kapucu, N., & Hu, Q. (2016). Understanding multiplexity of collaborative emergency management networks. *The American Review of Public Administration*, *46*(4), 399–417.

Kron, W., Steuer, M., Löw, P., & Wirtz, A. (2012). How to deal properly with a natural catastrophe database—analysis of flood losses. *Natural Hazards and Earth System Sciences*, *12*, 535–550.

Lee, J., Bharosa, N., Yang, J., Janssen, M., & Rao, H. R. (2011). Group value and intention to use: A study of multi-agency disaster management information systems for public safety. *Decision Support Systems*, *50*(2), 404–414.

Noble, K. T., White, C., & Turoff, M. (2014). Emergency management information system support rectifying first responder role abandonment during extreme events. *International Journal of Information Systems for Crisis Response and Management (IJISCRAM)*, *6*(1), 65–78.

Pelling, M., & Blackburn, S. (Eds.). (2013). *Megacities and the Coast: Risk, Resilience and Transformation*. London: Earthscan.

Preece, G., Shaw, D., & Hayashi, H. (2013). Using the Viable System Model (VSM) to structure information processing complexity in disaster response. *European Journal of Operational Research*, 224(1), 209–218.

Reddick, C. (2011). Information technology and emergency management: Preparedness and planning in US states. *Disasters*, 35(1), 45–61.

Sánchez, L., Elicegui, I., Cuesta, J., Muñoz, L., & Lanza, J. (2013). Integration of utilities infrastructures in a future internet enabled smart city framework. *Sensors*, 13(11), 14438–14465.

Singh, P., Singh, P., Park, I., Lee, J., & Rao, H. R. (2009). Information sharing: A study of information attributes and their relative significance during catastrophic events. In K. J. Knapp (Ed.), *Cyber-Security and Global Information Assurance: Threat Analysis and Response Solutions*. Hershey, PA: IGI Publishers.

Van de Walle, B., & Turoff, M. (2008). Decision support for emergency situations. *Information Systems and e-Business Management*, 6(3), 295–316.

Ward, R., & Wamsley, G. (2007). From a painful past to uncertain future. In C. B. Rubin (Ed.), *Emergency Management: The American Experience 1900–2005* (pp. 207–242). Fairfax, VA: Public Entity Risk Institute.

Wirtz, A., Kron, W., Löw, P., & Steuer, M. (2014). The need for data: Natural disasters and the challenges of database management. *Natural Hazards*, 70, 135–157.

Yang, L., Yang, S. H., & Plotnick, L. (2013). How the internet of things technology enhances emergency response operations. *Technological Forecasting and Social Change*, 80(9), 1854–1867.

Zanella, A., Bui, N., Castellani, A., Vangelista, L., & Zorzi, M. (2014). Internet of Things for smart cities. *Internet of Things Journal, IEEE*, 1(1), 22–32.

8

WARNING SYSTEMS: ALERTING THE PUBLIC TO DANGER

John J. Walsh, Jr.[1] and John C. Pine[2]

[1] Program in Disaster Research and Training, Vanderbilt University Medical Center, Nashville, TN, USA
[2] Department of Geography and Planning, Appalachian State University, Boone, NC, USA

Starting Point

What You'll Learn in This Chapter

▲ Different components of warning systems
▲ Different ways to detect disasters
▲ Issues to consider when issuing warnings
▲ Types of warning systems
▲ Factors associated with public response to warnings

After Studying This Chapter, You'll Be Able To

▲ Examine the composition of warning systems and their subsystems.
▲ Examine different ways to detect and manage disasters.
▲ Assess how organizational issues affect the process of issuing warnings.
▲ Examine the advantages and disadvantages of each type of warning system.
▲ Analyze the factors of public response to warning systems.

Goals and Outcomes

▲ Evaluate the organizational and technical obstacles to implementing a warning system
▲ Evaluate the role of detection, management, and response in warning systems
▲ Evaluate the potential public response to warnings
▲ Select national and local resources to help monitor disasters
▲ Select the types of warning systems that best serve your community

Technology and Emergency Management, Second Edition. John C. Pine.
© 2018 John Wiley & Sons, Inc. Published 2018 by John Wiley & Sons, Inc.
Companion website: www.wiley.com/go/pine/tech&emergmgmt_2e

INTRODUCTION

Warning the public of a disaster is one of your most critical functions as an emergency manager. Warning, however, is a complex function. In this chapter, you will examine the qualities of warning systems. You will then examine ways disasters are detected and managed. After a disaster has been detected, you must decide what criteria to use to warn others. You must decide what warning system to use. You will examine different types of warning systems and analyze the advantages and disadvantages of each. You will end the chapter by examining the myths of public response to warnings and how to ensure that the public has all the information it needs to respond appropriately to a warning.

8.1 Warning Systems

Issuing warnings is one of the most important tasks you have. Warnings allow people to take appropriate actions to protect themselves, their families, and their property. If a warning is issued early enough, people will also have time to prepare for a disaster. The warning process includes disaster assessment and dissemination (Quarantelli, 1990).

▲ *Assessment*: This is the phase when information is gathered, decisions are made, and the message is formulated.
▲ *Dissemination*: This is the phase when information is relayed to those who will assist with the issuance of the warning. Information is relayed to and received by the public, which then hopefully acts in accordance with the warning.

8.1.1 Key Information

Warnings provide three pieces of key information:

1. When a disaster may occur
2. How long a disaster could last
3. What the impacts of the disaster could be

A **warning system** is a means of getting information about an impending emergency, communicating that information to those who need it, and facilitating good decisions and timely response by people in danger (Mileti and Sorensen, 1990). The most effective structure for a warning system is that of an integrated system. This includes the integration of the physical and meteorological sciences with the behavioral and social sciences.

8.1.2 Key Components of Warning Systems

Today's integrated warning system incorporates three components:

1. The technology associated with detection of the hazard (Dean et al., 2006; Jiren and Yesou, 2006).
2. Warning message development and dissemination (Lindell and Perry, 2004; Mileti and Sorensen, 1990).
3. Receiver response and protective behaviors related to hazard warnings (Balluz et al., 2000; Golden and Adams, 2000).

FOR EXAMPLE

Warning Times

The ability to give people enough time to respond to a warning varies widely depending on the type of hazard, the technology used to detect the hazard, and the circumstances surrounding the hazard. For example, earthquake and tsunami warnings can be issued only minutes before impact. Hurricane warnings, on the other hand, can be issued days before impact, although there is always a chance that the storm will weaken or change course between the time the warning is issued and impact. Warning time impacts are being further studied as a result of the 2010 Joplin, MO, tornado where adequate warning was given but individuals failed to act appropriately (NOAA, 2011).

8.1.3 Warning Subsystems

The warning system is composed of three separate subsystems: the detection, management, and response subsystems.

▲ *Detection*: Detection includes the monitoring, prediction, and forecasting of the natural, technological, and civil environments. Detection includes collecting information for analysis. The National Weather Service (NWS) has many detection systems for different hazards. The collection of this weather data would be viewed as the "inputs" for the warning system.

▲ *Management*: Management integrates the information from the detection subsystem. Examples include the federal NWS Severe Weather Warning systems. Local and regional weather centers analyze the information. They determine if a warning is justified. This is the transformation part of the warning system. They then disseminate this information to emergency management officials and to the general public.

▲ *Response*: Individuals respond to a warning message. They bring their own interpretations of the warning and determine what appropriate action is required. The warning message and the individual response are both outputs of the warning system.

We will now further examine detection, management, and response.

8.2 Detection and Management

Effective response to a disaster includes the timely warning of the local community and the region of a potential hazard. Detecting hazards or potential disasters is a difficult process. It cannot always be done accurately. For example, alerts about terrorist activities are based on human intelligence that may or may not be accurate. Industrial accidents resulting from mechanical or human error are difficult to predict. We can, however, predict and forecast severe weather. We can predict and forecast floods, hurricanes, tsunamis, and other types of severe weather. Once a disaster is set in motion, we can detect it. We can then warn the population to take protective action. There are several hazard-appropriate technologies we can use to monitor, forecast, predict, and detect hazards. Let's first examine how detection works at a local level before we look at what is in place at the national level.

8.2.1 Case Study: Detection at a Local Level

In 1997, Fort Collins, Colorado, had several days of heavy thunderstorms. As a result, sections of Fort Collins flooded. The flooding caused a freight train to derail and crash into two residential trailer parks. Five people were killed. Colorado State University sustained extensive damage. The flooding had a huge financial impact on all of Fort Collins.

After this experience, the emergency manager wanted to install a flood warning system. After being awarded a $250 000 grant from Federal Emergency Management Agency (FEMA), the city developed and installed a complete system. The system provides real-time information on rain, storm water runoff, and weather conditions. The NWS uses the data and other information to issue flash flood and severe weather advisories.

The flood warning system consists of 54 gauge sites, 38 automatic rain gauges, 35 water level gauges, and 5 automatic weather stations. These stations report information to radio and computer base stations. The software program that the emergency managers use is DIADvisor. This program determines when gauges exceed a predetermined level and automatically sends a notification to emergency management personnel. Figure 8-1 shows a smaller flood warning system from another Fort Collins that is prone to flooding—Fort Collins, Texas.

Prior to initiating a notification, emergency managers and local officials determine where to place the rain gauges. The location of these gauges depends on local weather patterns, potential for flooding, city projects, environmental factors, land availability, and the proximity of other gauges. Stream gauges are placed in the streams and use a sensor to determine the water depth. Water depth is also referred to as *stage*. Rain gauges use tipping buckets. The depth of the water is recorded and reported.

1. A solar-powered 12 V battery powers this particular system.
2. The tipping bucket rain gauge is on top of a 12-foot-tall pipe.
3. A conduit runs from both gauges through a conduit to a sitting well.

Figure 8-1

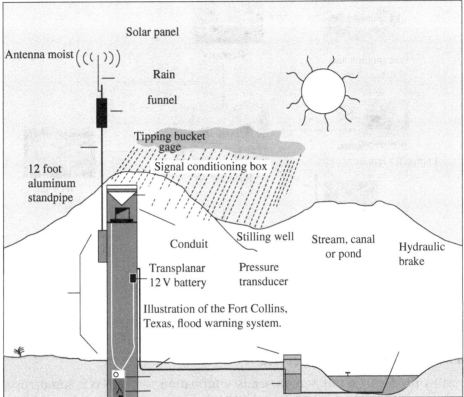

Rain and stream gaging diagram.

4. After the water reaches a predetermined depth, the information is transmitted through a very high frequency (VHF) radio signal to a repeater site on top of a tall grain tower. A repeater is a device that receives communications and amplifies them before sending them out.
5. Two base stations receive the information from the repeater. The base stations have a decoder to interpret the information. A page is sent to emergency management and utility personnel. Users can also access the data from Web pages or by using a laptop and dialing in to their station. The information is also sent to the NWS. See Figure 8-2 for an illustration of the process.

The Fort Collins flood warning system is an example of ALERT (automated local evaluation in real time). As you can see, it uses remote sensors strategically placed in different locations to transmit data to a central computer in real time. ALERT was developed by the NWS in the 1970s and is used by many federal and local agencies. There are many manufacturers of ALERT software and hardware. All hardware and software is designed to meet the same end result, so they are all interchangeable regardless of the manufacturer. Competition helps keep costs low.

Figure 8-2

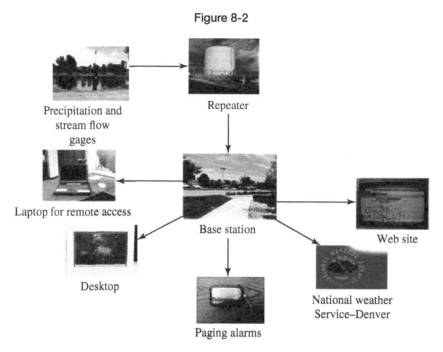

The Fort Collins ALERT system.

8.2.2 National Weather Service

Just as the Fort Collins station sends information to the NWS, hundreds of locations also send information to the NWS at regular intervals (NOAA, 2011). The NWS has 5000 employees at 122 weather forecast offices. In addition, the NWS has 13 river forecast centers and 10 national centers and 21 Aviation Center Weather Services Units. It issues approximately 1.5 million forecasts and 50 000 warnings yearly and collects 76 billion observations of data. The NWS has other support offices around the country. The NWS provides weather and hydrologic forecasts and warnings. On a daily basis, it issues public, aviation, marine, fire weather, climate, space weather, and river and flood forecasts and warnings. With a 2016 $1.1 billion annual budget, the NWS collects data in a variety of ways. The data can be used by anyone. Their weather storm warnings provide an excellent example of identifying potential hazards, developing a classification system, and implementing a public notification system. The warning system focuses on flood, tornado, earthquake, and hurricane hazards. It provided an excellent model for state and local governments. It is also a model for nonprofits and the private sector. Complementing this system is the Emergency Alert System (EAS). Backing up this warning system is a set of sensors that monitor weather patterns. These sensors include National Oceanic and Atmospheric Administration (NOAA) satellites, local airport radar, US Geologic Survey (USGS) river gauge and weather sensors, and offshore weather monitoring stations. In addition, NWS uses trained volunteers to collect weather data information.

The NWS provides current hourly reports for weather conditions for each state. State forecasts are provided twice daily for each state. Other forecasts include the following:

▲ Local forecasts: City specific and covers 1–3 days; not all sites issue this.
▲ Zone forecasts: Twice daily for individual county/zones in every state.
▲ Information reports: Past and current record reports, public information statements, recreational reports, and additional state information reports.
▲ Climate data: Historical comparisons, running totals for precipitation, and so on. Issued daily for each state.
▲ Coastal, river, and hydrologic information: Various hydrologic reports. Select water-related recreation reports.
▲ Other weather statements: Additional details on current conditions. Can give more detailed information on any current severe weather in each state.
▲ Watches, warnings, and advisories: For tornados, severe thunderstorms, floods, flash floods, winter storms, marine warnings, and severe weather incidents.

Extreme weather and water events cost billions of dollars annually. In 2005, the damage skyrocketed due to hurricanes. The services provided by the NWS help you predict and track severe weather patterns (U.S. Congress, 2006).

NWS—NOAA Weather Radio Network

The NWS Weather Radio Network provides an excellent example of a well-designed warning system. This network provides ongoing communication with public agencies, the public, and private businesses. The means of communication is adapted to suit the target audience.

The NWS was an early contributor to the emergency warning system. Today the NWS receives weather data from ground-based weather sensors and remote sensing data systems. The data is assessed and distributed to a broad group of users, including the public, public agencies, and private organizations. The NWS broadcasts warning and postevent information of multiple types of hazards:

▲ Natural and weather-related hazards (hurricanes and tropical storms, tsunamis, floods and tornadoes; local marine forecasts)
▲ Technological (chemical and radiological releases and oil spills)
▲ Public safety announcements including Amber alerts

The NWS also has the Emergency Management Weather Information Network (EMWIN). The EMWIN supplements other NWS dissemination services. It provides a low-cost method for receiving NWS information on a wireless data system. EMWIN presents the information directly on your computer in a user-friendly graphic display. Simple mouse clicks retrieve the latest weather and flood warnings, watches, forecasts, statements, observations, and other data in text format, along with a subset of weather graphics, including the national radar summary and some satellite imagery. Users set alarms to be alerted to particular information, whether for their local area or adjacent areas.

8.2.3 Case Study: Detection at a National Level

The United States is served by two tsunami warning centers: the Pacific Tsunami Warning Center and the West Coast/Alaska Warning Center. The Pacific Tsunami Warning Center is also an international warning system, and 26 nations are participating members. The West Coast/Alaska Warning Center is a regional warning center. NOAA and the NWS operate both centers.

A tsunami may originate from two sources: a distant source or a local source. If the source is local, there is little time to prepare. If an earthquake occurs along a coastal region and lasts for several minutes, the earthquake is the warning. If a tsunami originates from a distant source, the Pacific Tsunami Warning Center and the West Coast/Alaska Warning Center can detect a tsunami hours before it reaches land. When a tsunami is detected, tsunami watches and warnings are issued. When a tsunami watch or warning is received, coastal offices of the NWS activate the EAS. All broadcasters receive the tsunami EAS message at the same time. NOAA's Weather Radio also activates the All-Hazard Alert Broadcast units.

FOR EXAMPLE

Working with the NWS

If your community is under threat from severe weather, the NWS will warn you. One of the first people to convey the seriousness of Hurricane Katrina to New Orleans Mayor Ray Nagin was Max Mayfield of the National Hurricane Center, which is run by the NWS (Colten et al., 2008).

This system alerts people living in isolated areas. Warnings to the general public can be issued in less than 15 minutes.

The warning systems designed to detect tsunamis and save lives and property have three components:

1. The equipment to detect earthquakes and ocean wave activity and scientists to analyze data
2. Communications equipment to issue warnings
3. Local emergency response teams to mobilize quick evacuations

Another key element in reducing losses is education. Many coastal areas have marked evacuation routes to guide people to higher ground. Local officials conduct community meetings and workshops, and distribute tsunami education information. The NWS has a community program called Tsunami Ready. Through this program, the NWS recognizes communities that have put extra effort into enhancing their tsunami warning system. Communities do this through awareness activities and widespread use of weather radio receivers.

8.3 Issuing Warnings

Before your organization is faced with the need to issue warnings, you must make some decisions. It is critical to coordinate with other organizations to ensure that warnings have the desired individual and organizational actions. To do this, you must do the following:

▲ Understand the roles and responsibilities of other organizations.
▲ Establish clear lines of authority.
▲ Identify procedures that will be followed in a crisis.

Coordination with others might present other issues, including technical, organizational, and societal issues.

8.3.1 Technical Issues

With a warning system, you must become technically and scientifically informed in order to make sound warning decisions. As an example, you must understand the differences between tropical depression and a hurricane. It is critical that you build technical competence in warning systems so as to understand what actions should be taken in an emergency. You can take other actions to ensure that effective decisions are made from the scientific information received, including the following:

▲ Identify local experts who can provide advice and consultation on a disaster and appropriate actions for warnings for various hazards. Members of the local emergency preparedness committee often include those with knowledge of chemical and natural hazards as well as terrorism. Identify volunteers who can provide advice on the disaster.
▲ Contact the nearby NWS office for detailed and up-to-date information.
▲ Contract for expertise from a private company, government agency, and university.
▲ Examine monitoring and detection issues. Is the entire community covered by a warning system, or are there gaps in coverage in the community? For example, if you are using sirens, you may not have sirens placed in rural areas of your community. Sounds produced by sirens do not follow jurisdictional boundaries, so siren activation protocols should be consistent and integrated between adjoining jurisdictional boundaries.
▲ Examine communication hardware issues. Does the system require specialized technology that may not be present in some homes or businesses? For example, if a weather radio is the only way someone may receive a warning, then most people will not hear it. This is especially relevant for individuals with special needs such as those with hearing loss.

8.3.2 Organizational Issues

Warning systems are perceived from different points of view. The detecting organization such as the NWS, the community emergency manager, and the public may all have different perceptions. How they perceive the effectiveness of the system affects their role. Many organizational issues impact the operational success of a warning system (Mileti and Sorensen, 1990). Each issue varies based on the scope of the system and if it has a national, regional, state, or local focus. The first question you have to ask is how the warning system is activated. You need to know what rules govern the process. In determining the rules, the following list of questions needs to be considered:

▲ Interpretation dilemmas. How do organizations ensure that the correct information is not distorted or lost in the system.
▲ Recognition of the event, the hazard, and the magnitude of the event. How do you verify that an incident is an emergency and avoid unnecessary false alarms? This is important, as a series of false alarms will lead people to ignore the real alarm.
▲ Sorting of relevant information in an event. For example, if there is a terrorist attack 100 miles away and another one 200 miles away, what is the relevant information to give to people quickly?
▲ Clarification of authority of organizations involved in the warning system.

This is part of the reason the EAS was not activated on September 11, 2001. There was confusion as to who had the power to activate it—EAS officials, the president of the United States, the mayor of New York, or the governor of New York.

▲ Lack of clarity on whom to notify. If there is a hurricane heading toward the state, do you notify everyone or just those in the affected regions? You will have to determine what criteria to use.
▲ Physical ability to communicate. Is the communication equipment up-to-date and working?
▲ Conflicting information. During a disaster, information comes in quickly and a portion of it is usually inaccurate or conflicting with other information. You will need to choose an information source prior to disasters, if possible, and rely on it.
▲ Liabilities. What are the liabilities in terms of death, damage, and lawsuits if the warning is issued or not issued?
▲ Cost. What is the cost of protective action? Many organizations initiate emergency procedures when a "warning" is issued by the local emergency management agency. The cost of protective actions taken by local businesses, schools, agencies, and the public must be taken into consideration in issuing a warning.
▲ Feasibility. Is it possible to carry out an effective warning? There may be times when an effective warning is difficult to deliver because there is not any advanced indication that a disaster would occur. For example, if there is a chemical explosion at a warehouse and several people are killed instantly, there would not be a need for a warning. What factors increase the possibly of warnings being heeded and properly acted upon by the public?
▲ Timing. When do you issue a warning? For example, do you issue a warning when there is a threat of a tornado or do you wait for it to touch down?

> **FOR EXAMPLE**
>
> ### Chemical Processing Facilities and Warnings
>
> The Mississippi River corridor between Baton Rouge and the city of New Orleans has many chemical processing facilities. Chemical facility representatives established a warning system for the metropolitan Baton Rouge area utilizing real-time Internet communications. The system was designed to provide immediate notification and warning of a chemical release from a facility in the Baton Rouge area. The system was designed by a company in Baton Rouge. It links chemical facilities and local emergency management operations. The system can send an electronic message to selected users or to all users on the system and activates an alarm on the receiving end of the electronic (e-mail) communication. The receiving units must respond manually to confirm receipt of the "emergency warning message." This secure system provides real-time warning to the emergency management agencies in the Baton Rouge area. The City of Baton Rouge and other local entities can then determine if further warning is required for the chemical release. (See www.i-notification.net/ for more details on this use of technology.)

8.3.3 Societal Issues

You have to consider the cost/benefit of issuing a warning on society as well. The societal issues to consider are as follows:

▲ What are the costs and benefits of the warning system?
▲ Under what conditions should the warning system not be activated?

8.4 Types of Warning Systems

Warning systems have been a part of the US emergency management system for years. Initial efforts centered on radio broadcast warning systems. Today, warning systems include a variety of methods to warn the public.

Many communities have established ways of communicating with the public in the event of a disaster. Some of these systems are completely within the local emergency management agency. Others utilize commercial warning systems such as cable providers, radio stations, and companies that use Internet communications or a mass phone dialing capacity. Each system has the ability to quickly relay information to the public. Each system is different. For example, some allow you to identify and send a warning message to a specific part of the community in the case of a chemical incident. Each system has its pros and cons. Also keep in mind that the local media (radio, TV, cable, and cellular phone) all work closely with the emergency management community. You often see closed-captioned emergency warnings scrolling along the bottom of the screen on the TV. This is separate from the national emergency warning system currently in place.

8.4.1 Sirens

Many communities use sirens in a wide variety of disasters, including tornadoes, fires, and chemical accidents. Outdoor mechanical and electronic sirens are often used for tornadoes. Although the sirens can warn a large number of people at once, people must be close to the siren to hear it. Often, they must also be outside to hear the siren. Electronic sirens also have the capability of allowing voice warnings that are good for people who do not understand what a siren means. People must be close to hear electronic sirens as well and both types of sirens are not usually heard by people inside the building. In metropolitan and urban areas, coordination of siren activation protocols between jurisdictions is required.

8.4.2 The Emergency Alert System

Warnings from the NWS are often broadcast over the **EAS**. The EAS is a national initiative of over 13 000 radio, television, cable systems, wireless cable systems, satellite digital audio radio service providers, and direct broadcast satellite providers that voluntarily organize and plan for warning of local communities. The EAS was established in 1994 by the Federal Communications Commission (FCC). The EAS replaced the EBS, or the Emergency Broadcasting System. This system has many benefits that include the following:

▲ Any transmission means can be used to send and receive EAS alerts and tests (telephones, radios, pagers, cell phones, etc.). Hospitals, chemical processing operations, emergency responders, and medical personnel frequently have pagers that can be activated by their sponsoring organizations. In an emergency situation, the "hospital" or other sponsor can activate a pager. This is done with either a message or a call back code or number alerting the person of an emergency. The person receiving the message then contacts the organization or takes other appropriate prearranged actions.

▲ EAS equipment can be programmed for very unique events and specific areas.

▲ These are simple designations for EAS communications facilities.

▲ Automatic visual and audio messages can appear on broadcast stations and cable systems.

▲ The system can interface with computers.

▲ Time comparison of EAS messages to avoid duplicate or outdated messages.

▲ There is multiple monitoring of sources for EAS messages.

▲ Digital storage and retrieval of messages is possible.

▲ There are weekly tests at any time and monthly on-air tests for all EAS communications facilities in state or EAS local areas.

▲ Incoming EAS messages are displayed on EAS equipment.

▲ Any FM, TV, or cellular subcarriers can be used for transmitting EAS messages.

▲ There is interoperability with future NWS and FEMA warning systems.

▲ Equipment is automatically operated.

Figure 8-3

The Emergency Alert System (EAS) was not activated during the
September 11, 2001, terrorist attacks.

The EAS undergoes ongoing changes, but the system continues to face significant challenges in reaching the handicapped or impaired citizens or in providing detailed information on threats. The EAS was not enacted on September 11, 2001, due to internal confusion as to who had the authority to send out the warnings (Figure 8-3).

Due to these criticisms, a bill was passed in Congress in 2005 that appropriates money to replace and/or upgrade the current EAS system. The legislative proposal specifies that technologies would be considered such as "telephone, wireless communications, and other existing communication networks" (Moore, 2006). Many of these technology requirements and upgrades have been implemented and are ongoing.

In 2011 the Department of Homeland Security's (DHS) FEMA initiated the first nationwide test by delivering an emergency alert notification (EAN) to the EAS Primary Entry Point (PEP) stations which initiated the EAN distribution throughout the nation. A report on the nationwide EAS test in 2013 stated that the national EAS distribution process was fundamentally sound (Public Safety and Homeland Security Bureau, 2013). The report also pointed out three areas of concern:

▲ Consumer confusion caused by the discrepancies between the audio and video portions of the test;
▲ Public confusion and equipment errors caused by the use of the Washington, DC, location code issues; and
▲ Public confusion caused by the manner in which some EAS equipment displayed the visual portion of the warning.

8.4.3 Phone Alert Systems: Reverse 911

Reverse 911 is a call issued from one site that is transmitted by computer to homes and businesses. The message can be short or detailed. A phone notification system provides the following advantages in an emergency:

▲ Quick notification of an incident can be provided to a controlled geographic area.
▲ Limited notification of an incident can be provided to individuals affected—the activities of the larger population are not affected.
▲ The message can be customized for the event and even to specific neighborhoods.
▲ The technology is not complex and is easy to customize for a jurisdiction.
▲ Contractors are available to run this function. Not many jurisdictions would be capable of including this activity in their operations.
▲ The receipt of the message by a household can be verified.

8.4.4 Disadvantages of Phone Notification Systems

A phone notification system also has the following disadvantages:

▲ Despite the large number of lines that a company may have, it does take time to make individual calls to those affected by an incident. Remember, once the call is made, the receiver must listen to the message. The message could last 30 seconds or more.
▲ The cost of the service can be significant. Many jurisdictions cannot afford this notification system without private organizations underwriting the cost of the service. Expect ongoing operational charges.
▲ The biggest limitation of this system is the accuracy of the phone records. In many jurisdictions, local phone companies do not make resident and business numbers available. The directory database is often out of date. The reduction in the number of landlines and the increase in cellular phone usage as the primary communication mode is also a factor.

8.4.5 Communicating with Those with Disabilities

Intercoms, teletype writers, telephone devices, strobe lights, and vibration systems warn the deaf and hard of hearing and people in large buildings. However, they have limited use and do not warn a large number of people.

Loud Speakers, Door-to-Door Notification, and Weather Radio Police can drive through neighborhoods and use bullhorns and speakers to broadcast warnings. However, they have the same drawback as sirens in that they warn a limited number of people, and people inside may not hear the warnings.

Before hurricanes Andrew and Katrina, local officials went door to door, urging people to evacuate (U.S. Congress, 2006). This is an effective way of issuing warnings as long as the people delivering the warnings are considered credible. The major drawback of this is that it requires an incredible amount of manpower. Door-to-door warnings are also very time-consuming. Few communities have the resources to spare, especially when they are preparing for a disaster.

The NWS broadcasts weather information and warnings to weather radios. Weather radios are becoming a more popular mode for receiving alerts and warnings, especially for severe weather-related events. Weather radios can now be programmed for more geographically defined areas such as a city or county jurisdiction.

8.4.6 Barriers to Warnings

You must anticipate problems with warning systems. Develop a flexible system that can address the technical, organizational, and social issues that arise. Efforts must be taken to design a system that can respond effectively. Effectiveness is measured in terms of issuing warnings that are directed to the target population. A number of factors contribute to the complex relationship of message structure. These factors commonly address consistency and specificity; sender and receiver perspectives addressing understanding, comprehension, credibility, and believability; and a host of intervening factors affecting warning response related to socioeconomic levels, ethnicity, gender perceptions, hazard experience, knowledge, and age (Drabek, 2010; Hammer and Schmidlin, 2002; Peguero, 2006; Perry and Godchaux, 2005).

A primary goal of any warning system is to alert the public of a potential disaster. But the public could perceive warning systems as inadequate. Mileti and Sorensen (1990) note that warning systems encounter many barriers. The disadvantages of the warning systems we just discussed fall into one of these four categories:

▲ *Geographic barriers*: A warning system may not reach the entire community. Some neighborhoods are outside the range of sirens.
▲ *Language barriers*: In some cases, a warning is provided in written or spoken form and may not be understood by some residents. Many communities have a broad ethnic base. Some residents may not speak English.
▲ *Technical barriers*: Some warning systems are transmitted over radio, cable, or television. Members of the community may not have these communications systems.
▲ *Personal barriers*: Many communities use a telephone alert system to notify the public of an emergency. Unlisted phone numbers or cellular phone numbers may not be included in the notification system group to be called.

8.4.7 Case Example: A Nuclear Disaster

Let's examine what the procedure is for warning the public of a nuclear disaster. Two significant events—the Three Mile Island incident in 1979 and the terrorist attack on September 11, 2001—are partially responsible for a reevaluation of and improvements in the safeguards at our nation's nuclear facilities. The Nuclear Regulatory Commission (NRC), which oversees our nuclear facilities, shares emergency planning and preparedness for potential nuclear accidents or terrorist's attacks with FEMA (Figure 8-4).

FOR EXAMPLE

9/11 Warnings

Prior to 9/11, there was no warning that the World Trade Center and the Pentagon would be attacked by terrorists who hijacked airplanes. The first Americans heard about the events was on the morning news when the events were already unfolding. Even if the EAS had been activated, it is unclear what protective actions New Yorkers could have taken. Congress, however, did evacuate after the Pentagon was struck, and there were reports that a plane was headed for the Capitol. The plane never reached the Capitol, as the passengers fought the hijackers on board and the plane crashed in Shanksville, Pennsylvania.

In the United States, there are 66 pressurized water reactors (PWRs) and 34 boiling water reactors (BWRs) are in commercial operation in the United States. Each site must have emergency plans in place. These plans are approved by FEMA and the NRC. These plans must provide adequate protective measures should there be a nuclear emergency. State and local officials are required to have emergency systems that can alert the public in approximately 15 minutes after learning that a situation requires public action.

There are four categories of nuclear power plant emergencies: notification of an unusual event, alert, site area emergency, and general emergency. In case of an unusual event or an alert, local officials would be notified, but not the general public. In these two cases, the problems can be resolved at the plant. In the case of a site area emergency or a general emergency, the public will be notified through the Alert and Notification System. Information will be available through radio and television. There are two emergency planning zones around each nuclear plant. The first planning zone extends about 10 miles in radius around a plant, and the second planning zone extends to a radius of about 50 miles. Residents within the first planning zone are regularly given emergency information materials. These publications include information on radiation, evacuation, and sheltering arrangements for people with disabilities, and so on. Evacuation routes and shelters have been preplanned, and the public will be asked to follow these routes and use designated shelters.

Figure 8-4

Warnings are a critical first step in the evacuation of areas around nuclear power plants.

8.5 Response

Disaster research over the past 70 years clearly indicates that there are many factors that affect human response. Many situations where disasters occur are contextual in nature and, depending on the circumstances, individual response behavior will vary. Often times response actions are based on hazard knowledge, experience with the specific hazard, motivation for personal safety, and perception of risk. All these **response factors** impact how an individual will respond. Combined with effective warning messaging development, dissemination source credibility and believability, and the decision to respond proactively, all contribute to if, and how well, a person will heed the warning. Mileti and Sorensen (1990), along with many others, have examined the research and explain just how people will behave in a crisis or disaster. The following principles provide a sound basis for the design of warning systems and their operational use:

▲ The public react to warnings rationally when given accurate and specific information regarding the hazard threat.
▲ The public rarely, if ever, gets too much emergency information in an official warning. The initial warning gets one's attention; more information is desired.
▲ Response to warnings is not diminished by what has come to be labeled the "cry wolf" syndrome. This is true as long as the public has been informed of the reasons for previous misses.
▲ People want information from a variety of sources.

▲ Most people do not respond with protective actions to warning messages as soon as they hear their first warning. There generally is an individual assessment process that takes place.

▲ Most people will not blindly follow instructions in a warning unless the basis for the instructions is given in the message. People also examine if the basis of the warning makes common sense.

▲ People do not remember the meanings of various siren signal patterns. However, they do try to find out the reason for the siren.

8.5.1 Case Study: Response to Hurricane Katrina

Emergency management officials in Louisiana, Alabama, and Mississippi used many different warning systems to warn residents about Hurricane Katrina. In Louisiana alone, the governor declared a state emergency on August 26, President George W. Bush declared Louisiana a disaster area on August 27, and Mayor Ray Nagin ordered a mandatory evacuation of New Orleans on August 28. Hurricane Katrina made landfall on August 29. Media reports discussed the damage that could occur. Evacuation orders were given by all three states, although at different times (U.S. Congress, 2006). Local officials and law enforcement went door to door in the most vulnerable areas asking people to leave. The EAS was used, and warnings were issued in different languages. Louisiana governor Blanco noted in congressional testimony that 1.2 million people had evacuated from Louisiana without delay prior to the landfall of Hurricane Katrina. For those who could not evacuate, they went to shelters. Despite the problems in the aftermath of Hurricane Katrina and the large death toll (1400+), it was still one of the most successful evacuations in the nation's history.

FOR EXAMPLE

Once evacuation orders are given, you must do everything you can to facilitate evacuation. Special populations that are not mobile will need help evacuating. Schools, nursing homes, and hospitals may have to be evacuated with school buses. Traffic jams are often a problem as well. During Hurricane Rita, all interstate lanes were open to outflowing traffic, and traffic trying to get into the city was rerouted (U.S. Congress, 2006).

SUMMARY

Issuing warnings is one of the most critical job responsibilities for any emergency manager. In this chapter, you examined the warning process. You assessed the technical and organizational difficulties in issuing warnings. You compared and contrasted the different types of warning systems while examining the disadvantages and advantages of each. You then examined the factors behind the public response to warnings. By examining these factors, you discovered what actions you can take to ensure the public responds appropriately to all warnings.

KEY TERMS

Emergency Alert System (EAS)	EAS is a national initiative of over 13 000 radio, television, and cable systems that voluntarily organize and plan for warning of local communities. It is a system of getting information about an impending emergency, communicating that information to those who need it, and facilitating good decisions and timely response by people in danger.
Response factors	Human characteristics and situational environments affecting why individuals do or do not heed warnings.
Warning system	Warning system is a means of getting information about an impending emergency, communicating that information to those who need it, and facilitating good decisions and timely response by people in danger.

ASSESS YOUR UNDERSTANDING

Go to www.wiley.com/go/pine/tech&emergmgmt_2e to evaluate your knowledge of using technology. This website contains MCQ's, self checks, review questions, applying this chapter and you try it.

References

Balluz, L., Schieve, L., Holmes, T., Kiezak, S., & Malilay, J. (2000). Predictors for people's response to a tornado warning: Arkansas, 1 March 1997. *Disasters*, 24(1), 71–77.

Colten, C. E., Kates, R. W., & Laska, S. B. (2008). *Community Resilience: Lessons from New Orleans and Hurricane Katrina*. Oak Ridge, TN: Oak Ridge National Laboratory, Community and Regional Resilience Initiative.

Dean, A. R., Schneider, R. S., & Schaefer, J. T. (2006). Development of a comprehensive severe weather forecast verification system at the storm prediction center. Preprints. In *23rd Conference Severe Local Storms*, St. Louis, MO, November 6–10, 2006.

Drabek, T. E. (2010). *The Human Side of Disaster* (2nd ed.). Boca Raton, FL: CRC Press.

Golden, J. H., & Adams, C. R. (2000). The tornado problem: Forecast, warning, and response. *Natural Hazards Review*, 1(2), 107–118.

Hammer, B., & Schmidlin, T. W. (2002). Response to warnings during the 3 May 1999 Oklahoma City tornado: Reasons and relative injury rates. *Weather and Forecasting*, 17, 577–581.

Jiren, L., & Yesou, H. (2006). Use of radar remote sensing on flood monitoring and impact evaluation. In *Lijiang Symposium Programme*, Lijiang, China, July 10–14, 2006.

Lindell, M. K., & Perry, R. W. (2004). *Communicating Effectively in Multicultural Contexts: Communicating Environmental Risk in Multiethnic Communities*. Thousand Oaks, CA: SAGE Publications.

Mileti, D. S., & Sorensen, J. H. (1990). *Communication of Emergency Public Warnings: A Social Science Perspective and State of the Art Assessment*. Oak Ridge, TN: Oak Ridge National Laboratory for FEMA.

Moore, L. K. (2006, September). *Emergency Communications: The Emergency Alert System (EAS) and All-Hazard Warnings*. Washington, DC: Congressional Research Service, Library of Congress.

National Oceanic and Atmospheric Administration (NOAA), Central Region Headquarters, National Weather Service. (2011). *NWS Central Region Service Assessment: Joplin, Missouri, Tornado-May 22, 2011*. Kansas City, MO: National Oceanic and Atmospheric Administration (NOAA), Central Region Headquarters, National Weather Service.

Peguero A. A. (2006). Latino disaster vulnerability: The dissemination of hurricane mitigation information among Florida's homeowners. *Hispanic Journal of Behavioral Sciences, 28*(1), 5–22.

Perry, R., & Godchaux, J. D. (2005). Volcano hazard management strategies: Fitting policy to patterned human responses. *Disaster Prevention and Management, 14*(2), 183–195.

Public Safety and Homeland Security Bureau. (2013). *Strengthening the Emergency Alert System (EAS): Lessons Learned from the Nationwide EAS Test*. Washington, DC: Federal Communications Commission.

Quarantelli, E. L. (1990). *The Warning Process and Evacuation Behaviour: The Research Evidence*. Newark, DE: University of Delaware.

U.S. Congress. (2006). *House Select Bipartisan Committee to Investigate the Preparation for and Response to Hurricane Katrina, A Failure of Initiative*, 109th Congress, 2nd session, House Report 109–377. Washington, DC: GPO.

9

HAZARDS ANALYSIS AND MODELING: PREDICTING THE IMPACT OF DISASTERS

Starting Point

Go to www.wiley.com/go/pine/tech&emergmgmt_2e to assess your knowledge of hazards analysis and modeling. Determine where to concentrate your effort.

What You'll Learn in This Chapter

▲ How to use hazard modeling to simulate real disasters
▲ Different components of the SLOSH model
▲ How to read the output of the ALOHA chemical dispersion model
▲ Types of models for evacuations, fires, and drought
▲ Characteristics to consider when evaluating hazard models

After Studying This Chapter, You'll Be Able To

▲ Examine ways to use the results of modeling.
▲ Examine the strengths and limitations of the SLOSH model.
▲ Examine the conditions that make ALOHA chemical dispersion model results unreliable.
▲ Compare and contrast the analysis Levels 1, 2, and 3 of HAZUS-MH.
▲ Analyze what hazard models your office needs based on a careful evaluation of the strengths and disadvantages of each model.

Goals and Outcomes

▲ Evaluate the output of hazard models and how to use the output results to prepare for potential disasters
▲ Evaluate how to use the SLOSH model for planning, response, recovery, and mitigation efforts
▲ Select the optimal conditions for using the ALOHA chemical dispersion model
▲ Evaluate how to mitigate disasters using HAZUS-MH
▲ Compare and contrast the models for fires, evacuations, and drought
▲ Select which hazard models to use based on your community's hazard vulnerability analysis and the quality, cost, usability, completeness, and timeliness of the models

INTRODUCTION

You may not be able to predict the future, but with the help of computer modeling programs, you can predict how a hazard will affect your community. In this chapter, you will examine the strengths and limitations of hurricane predictions in terms of planning, response, recovery, and mitigation efforts. You will also examine the use of a chemical dispersion model that is used by public, private, and nonprofit entities in the United States and internationally for emergency planning and response. You will assess the strengths and limitations of a multihazard modeling tool set, Hazards United States—Multi Hazard Model (**HAZUS-MH**), to understand the impacts from wind, flood, and earthquake hazards. You will also assess when to use additional models for other disasters such as fires and drought. You will then evaluate each model. You will consider how you can use these programs to mitigate disasters, prepare for disasters, and enhance your response to disasters.

9.1 Modeling and Emergency Management

What if you could predict the future? What if you knew a hurricane was coming and would cause thousands of people to be displaced, lose their homes, and be in danger of losing their lives? Would you try to save them? Would you warn them? Would you evacuate? Answering these questions is the purpose of hazard modeling. **Hazard modeling** is a simulation of a real system or replication of a potential hazard event. Before you can determine how a disaster will affect your community, you must first determine what hazards your community is vulnerable to (Pine, 2014). Modeling as a part of the hazards analysis process provides a means of simulating the nature and extent of a disaster. With modeling, you can simulate a disaster using computers and graphics. This lets you see how a specific storm, chemical incident, fire, landslide, or tornado could affect the community. Because modeling is associated with complex mathematical formulas, assumptions, and high-powered computers, it is often left to the experts. Today with advancements in computer technology, you can provide the data inputs for the models, run the model, and interpret the output of the models (Akbar et al., 2013). The key is for you to understand what is needed in the hazard model, what the limitations of the model are, and how to use the results in emergency management activities.

Many hazard models are currently being adapted to run on fast computers, including laptops, that are available in emergency management offices. Further, the Internet allows us access to hazard model predictions that show risk zones on a national, regional, and state level and are run on super computers. Emergency management staff and managers can thus utilize model results to understand local risks from wildland fires, drought, flooding, hurricane storm surge and wind, and earthquakes. The risks described by the hazard models may be run quickly on a laptop computer or the risks posed by an oncoming hurricane may be clarified.

Emergency managers from local communities, state operations centers, and federal agencies utilize large-scale hurricane models to understand the potential impacts of storms. A model such as SLOSH (sea, lake, and overland surges from hurricanes) requires extensive computing capacity and highly trained staff to run and explain the models. Fast fiber optic Internet connections allow access to the high-performing computer model outputs. In addition, robust communication tools allow users access to experts to clarify how the model outputs might be used.

Models are intended to provide an accurate representation of a hazard event. For example, **ALOHA (aerial locations of hazardous atmospheres)** is widely used in both planning and response efforts on a laptop because it provides a very accurate representation of a chemical spill and can be run in a short time period. As with any model, it does require training and practice, but many local emergency responders find this model a great asset in both planning and response to hazardous chemicals. Many local hazardous materials teams are well trained in planning for and responding to hazardous chemical spills; the ALOHA chemical dispersion model is often used by these teams to prepare for and respond to spills in their community. It shows the size of the area in which chemicals will be dispersed during a hazardous materials chemical incident.

9.1.1 The Technology behind Modeling

A model of a natural or technological hazard is a simulation or replication of a potential event. It is a "simplified representation of the real system" (Drager et al., 1993). Voinov and Gaddis (2008) note that models are generally single purpose and represent a single risk; the model can come in a variety of forms and implementations, including mental, verbal, graphical, mathematical, logical, or physical.

In the real world, a disaster is very complex. There are many factors involved. Wind velocity, the surface roughness, air temperature, and surface features all contribute to the effects of natural events such as hurricanes. These factors also affect man-made disasters such as chemical accidents. You can build these factors into a hazard model as data inputs, although the model itself is a set of mathematical equations and formulas (Greenway, 1998).

With this inherent complexity, all models must make simplifying assumptions. Therefore, the attempt to exactly model a disaster is only an approximation. The accuracy of the model's estimation of an event is determined by the assumptions contained within the model along with the data and specifications made by the user. The user thus could provide key inputs based on weather conditions, local geography, and, in a chemical spill, data concerning the chemical and incident scenario. All these factors are used in chemical dispersion modeling. The key is to provide accurate data inputs. For example, if you enter a population of one million for your city when the population is only half a million, your results will be inaccurate. Or, you may enter information into the computer indicating that most people live in low-lying areas when they do not. In this case, the model for a hurricane will simulate a worse disaster than you will have in reality.

Goodchild et al. (1993) explain that computer models that simulate disasters require a variety of datasets. As an example, flood-modeling programs require information on the type of soil, land use characteristics, and elevation points in the study area. These models also require weather information, such as precipitation readings. In many cases, the data is very accurate and meets engineering quality standards. However, some datasets may be less accurate, thus affecting the accuracy of the model output. Complete sets of data that are used in a model are very difficult to obtain. They may require extensive time and expense to prepare.

Real-time access to hazard data is ideal for understanding current and potential impacts. Current data is a critical element of any modeling effort as is input data associated with the hazard. The EPA (Environmental Protection Agency) ALOHA chemical dispersion model is set up to use remote sensing weather data as input into the model. Hurricane storm surge, wind, and flood models also allow the user to utilize real-time data as an input into a hazard model.

A great example of accurate, timely, and dependable data is provided by the United States Geological Survey (USGS) through their Water Watch Program (http://waterwatch.usgs.gov) (Figure 9-1). Water Watch displays by way of the Internet, maps, graphs, and tables describing real-time and past stream flow conditions for the United States. The information from Water Watch is not a hazard model but information about the current situation. The real-time information is

Figure 9-1

Monday, February 06, 2017 11:30ET

Explanation–Percentile classes						
●	●	●			●	●
Low	<10	10–24	25–75	76–90	>90	High
	Much below normal	Below normal	Normal	Above normal	Much above normal	

US Geologic Survey WaterWatch Stream Flow Map of monthly stream flow compared to historical stream flow for the month of the year (United States) http://waterwatch.usgs.gov/index.php?id=mv01d. The Web site allows the user to select a location on the map and produce a list of all stations in the state or stations near the point selected.

generally updated on an hourly basis. The program is based on USGS stream gages and shows the location of more than 3000 long-term (30 years or more) USGS direct sensing stream flow gages. The maps show flow conditions in real-time, average daily, and 7-day average. The real-time maps highlight flood and high flow conditions. The 7-day average maps highlight below-normal and drought conditions. A key feature of this dataset is a display of water flow maps by hydrologic unit code (HUC) maps. These maps show average water conditions for 1-, 7-, 14-, and 28-day periods, and for monthly average. The maps show low flow (hydrologic drought), and provide historic conditions beginning in 1901. This USGS program is critical to almost any effort to model flood conditions in the United States and provides a comprehensive geographic distributed set of data points for an accurate input into flood models.

If an organization is willing to put in the time and expense, hazard models are able to replicate a specific disaster event. Fortunately, regional and national efforts may be established to allocate resources to these modeling efforts on a regional or national scale. Federal agencies such as the National Oceanic and Atmospheric Administration (NOAA) or colleges and universities may have the expertise and resources to assist in using models to support local or state emergency operations.

Even with the limits of our current technology, modeling still provides the best working estimate of the potential impact of a disaster. The outputs from models may provide the basis for determining vulnerability zones to floods or chemical releases. They can be used in response plans and procedures. Modeling also provides a critical tool to help establish priorities for evacuation plans or land use planning.

Drager et al. (1993) noted that modeling attempts to quantify elements of the real world. For example, they looked at models for the evacuation of a building. They determined that with all the assumptions, the best route for a person from a building will depend on the time when he or she starts to escape. The models are usually based on assumptions such as that a person will behave rationally and follow the best route. When modeling human behavior, most models seriously underestimate total evacuation time. This is because the last people who leave the building seldom followed predefined evacuation plans (Drager et al., 1993). An understanding of the assumptions used and how these assumptions were made is critical. You must have this understanding to be able to use the model as a managerial tool. Drager et al. (1993) stress that "the primary condition for performing an evacuation analysis is that the critical questions with respect to the system to be analyzed are raised. This process requires skill of the analyst as well as suitable calculation tools."

9.1.2 Mathematical Models

In addition to the need to understand the assumptions made in a model, it is also helpful to know which type of model was used. The mathematical models used at the National Hurricane Center include statistical, dynamic, and combination (statistical and dynamic together) models.

▲ Statistical models forecast the future by using current information about a hurricane and comparing it to historical knowledge about the behavior of similar storms. The historical record for storms over the North Atlantic begins in 1871, while the record for storms for the East Pacific extends back to 1945.

▲ Dynamic models are designed to use the results of global atmospheric model forecasts in different ways to forecast storm motion and intensity. Global models take current wind, temperature, pressure, and humidity observations and make forecasts of the actual atmosphere in which a storm exists. Because of their mathematical simplicity, dynamic models ignore the behavior of historical storms.

▲ Combination models can be constructed to capitalize on the strengths of each. Because of their simplicity, statistical models were designed first for storm forecasting. Combination models were developed as global models and were used in making forecasts in tropical regions.

9.1.3 Understanding the Results of Modeling

Detailed scientific results from complex models are often not understood by the public (Kirkwood, 1994). Kirkwood states that in many cases the public does not understand or have sufficient scientific knowledge to evaluate risks from hazards. He further explains that new technology is very often presented as being too complex for those outside the scientific community to understand. The fact is that the public cannot know what it cannot understand. There are two implications to Kirkwood's observations. First, you must communicate with the public in direct, nontechnical language. You must take into account the public's lack of technical knowledge. Attempts to gain public acceptance of risks and hazards could be aimed at increasing the level of technical knowledge of the public. Local news outlets can also partner with local officials to inform the public of hazards and risks. Storm warnings that may be based on complex models can also be expressed in graphical form to illustrate the technical basis of the weather model outputs.

Kirkwood also believes that the public has a simplistic view of risk and that decisions are based on a "rule of thumb." The key for you is to provide enough information to the public so that each person can weigh the risks and make decisions. Public education and partnering with the local media are long-term investments in community education. Both the emergency management community and the media have an interest in understanding the science behind the hazard models. An increased understanding of hazards by the public can lead to more informed decisions concerning sheltering, evacuations, and long-term actions to reduce vulnerability. A word of caution here: You cannot assume that simply modeling a disaster will make your community better prepared. You must take the lessons you learned from the simulation and apply them in planning and mitigation. You must also have the support of government officials in order for your efforts to be effective. You must also have the budget needed to take the necessary preparation measures.

9.1.4 Fast Exchange of Model Results to Users

Leskens et al. (2014) stress that despite the advantages that flood simulation modeling may provide, experiences have proven that these models are of limited use to decision makers. This study examined how model information is exchanged among participants in flood disaster organizations and how this exchange affects the use of modeling information. They determined that the extent to which a model is useful depends not only on the type and quality of its output, but also on how fast and flexible a model can be. They stressed that a model's use requires a fast exchange of information between participants in the flood disaster organization.

Stedinger and Griffis (2008) note that a large portion of the US population, infrastructure, and industry is located in flood-prone areas. As a result, floods cause an average of nearly 140 deaths and cost roughly $6 billion annually excluding flooding caused by Hurricane Katrina, which cost $200 billion alone. The 1993 Midwest flooding along the Mississippi and Missouri rivers caused $20 billion in damages. Furthermore, these estimates neglect the real costs associated with loss of personal possessions and shattered lives and communities.

9.2 Using a Hurricane Model (SLOSH)

Different types of disasters are modeled with different programs. One of the models used for hurricanes is called **SLOSH (sea, lake, and overland surges from hurricanes)**. The SLOSH model is used by the National Weather Service (NWS) to calculate potential surge heights from hurricanes. SLOSH was developed for real-time forecasting of surges from actual hurricanes and as a planning tool for evacuation and shelter decisions by state and local entities.

The SLOSH model is used to examine the impact of hurricanes along the Gulf and Atlantic coasts. It is based on information from past storms and is used to determine the effect of a storm as it reaches land. Outputs show the inundation area of a storm as it reaches land and the depth of the water in these areas.

The SLOSH model is based on generalized assumptions and data to model all storms within all basins. The model has been adjusted based on comparisons of computed and observed meteorological and surge-height data for numerous historical hurricanes. It is based on information about many storms rather than a single storm event within a basin.

The model is designed for different Atlantic and Gulf Coast basins. It includes the topography of the following:

▲ Inland areas
▲ River basins and waterways
▲ Bays and large inland water bodies
▲ Significant natural and man-made barriers, such as barrier islands, dunes, roadbeds, floodwalls, levees, and so on
▲ A segment of the continental shelf

The SLOSH model simulates inland flooding from storm surge and permits overtopping of barriers and flow through barrier gaps.

FOR EXAMPLE

Decision support for local emergency managers using HURRE-VAC (short for Hurricane Evacuation):

HURREVAC is a storm tracking and decision support tool that is supported by the Federal Emergency Management Agency (FEMA) and NOAA's NWS. The program combines live feeds of tropical cyclone forecast information from the NWS with data from various state Hurricane Evacuation Studies (HES) to assist the local emergency manager in determining the most prudent evacuation decision time and the potential for significant storm effects such as wind and storm surge.

Program access is restricted to officials in government emergency management. As a general rule, if you are the emergency manager for a county in the hurricane-prone states (Texas to Maine), Puerto Rico, or the Virgin Islands, state Emergency Management Agency (EMA), a FEMA office, Corps of Engineers office, or the NWS office, you are eligible to use the HURREVAC program (Figure 9-2).

HURREVAC tracks hurricanes using the National Hurricane Center's Forecast Advisories. The software translates forecast track and wind extent information from the NHC's (National Hurricane Center) text-based products into interactive maps and reports that are used to chart the progress of an advancing storm. The program also assembles rainfall, flood, tide, and river forecast information from various sources to assist users in evaluating inland flooding threats.

The most key feature of HURREVAC, however, is its ability to keep the local emergency manager apprised of how many hours (or days) a community has for preparation and planning in advance of a threatening storm. As new forecast information becomes available, HURREVAC continually updates and reports on the community's Evacuation Start Time, or last possible time by which an evacuation could be initiated if it is to be completed before the arrival of the storm hazards.

The decision to evacuate a community is not always an easy or obvious one and the advantage of fine-tuning your Evacuation Start Time in HURREVAC is that you can base decisions upon the closest (and therefore most accurate) projections for the storm track, intensity, and size.

HURREVAC cannot make the evacuation decision for you. It is merely one tool that you may elect to use to help you in the hurricane decision-making process. Evacuation decisions are very complex and should only be made after consultation with all officials involved in the process, from NHC and the Weather Service, to state and local emergency management officials.

To determine the arrival time of tropical storm force winds, the program takes a worst case scenario of a direct hit in which the movement speed and wind extents of the official forecast are retained, but the track is straightened and redirected to the county of interest.

Figure 9-2

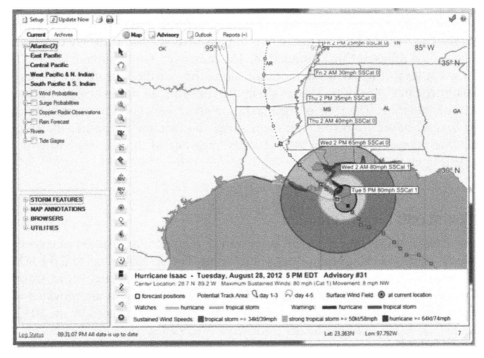

HURREVAC Decision Support Tool. See http://b29b4ca90ed6e8cc2b38-
bda0e469385589e4e71d5c43df4e22e8.r24.cf1.rackcdn.com/HURREVAC_Users_
Manual_2016.pdf for more details on HURREVAC.

9.2.1 SLOSH for Planning, Response, Recovery, and Mitigation

The SLOSH output footprint, wind calculations, and water depth can be used to examine the vulnerability zones to hurricanes. Variables used in the model include the direction, severity of the winds, and the speed of the storm. As a result of the use of the model, you should be able to determine the areas that may be affected by specific types of storms. As a planning tool, it presents a realistic description of the results of an event and provides the basis for conducting drills or capability assessment efforts in the community.

When SLOSH is used in a planning mode for a specific basin, as many as 1500 simulated hurricanes may be computed. As many as 150 storm tracks are modeled for a specific basin. These tracks represent the five categories of hurricane intensity, as described by the **Saffir–Simpson Hurricane Scale**; different paths of the storm track (west, west-northwest, northwest, north-northwest, north, north-northeast, northeast, east-northeast, and east); forward speeds of 5 and 15 miles per hour; and numerous landfall locations.

The characteristics of the simulated hurricanes are determined from an analysis of historical hurricanes that have occurred within the basin. The parameters selected for the modeled storms are the intensities, forward speeds, directions of motion, and radius of maximum winds.

The SLOSH output for a modeled storm consists of a tabulated storm history containing hourly values of storm position, speed, direction of motion, pressure, and radius of maximum winds, a surface envelope of the highest surge. The model also provides a two-dimensional snapshot display of surges at specified times during a simulation. The maximum storm surge is the highest water level reached at each location along the coastline during the passage of a hurricane. Maximum surges along the coastline do not necessarily occur at the same time. The time of the maximum surge for one location may differ by several hours from the maximum surge that occurs at another location. SLOSH basins are being updated at an average rate of three to six basins per year (Figure 9-3).

9.2.2 SLOSH Display Program

The SLOSH Display Program (SDP) is software developed as a tool to aid emergency managers in visualizing storm surge vulnerability. The SLOSH model and the SDP are two different tools. The SLOSH model is used by the NHC to forecast storm surge and model storm surge vulnerability; the SDP is the software provided to emergency managers and other users to visualize the data produced by the NHC. Graphical output from the model displays color-coded storm surge heights for a particular area in either feet above ground level or feet above a specific reference level (Jelesnianski et al., 1992) (Figure 9-4).

Verification of SLOSH is performed in a "hind-cast" mode, using the real-time operational model code and storm parameters and an initial observed sea surface height occurring approximately 48 hours before the storm landfalls.

9.2.3 Strengths of SLOSH

SLOSH is run by experts from the National Hurricane Center and provided to the public and public officials on a timely basis prior to a storm making landfall. With SLOSH, you can receive graphic displays that show the path of the storm and that show coastal areas that could be impacted by the impending storm. Also, public officials and the public can use the outputs to help make decisions concerning when to evacuate and what routes to take.

9.2.4 Limitations of SLOSH

SLOSH requires considerable expertise usually limited to staff from the National Hurricane Center and the NWS. When this model is run for evacuation planning, the Army Corps of Engineers and the National Hurricane Center run many hurricane scenarios. As a result, the process takes extensive planning and a great deal of time. SLOSH can also be used in an operational mode or real time. The National Hurricane Center uses the latest weather data from a specific storm and provides the outputs as part of their public information.

Figure 9-3

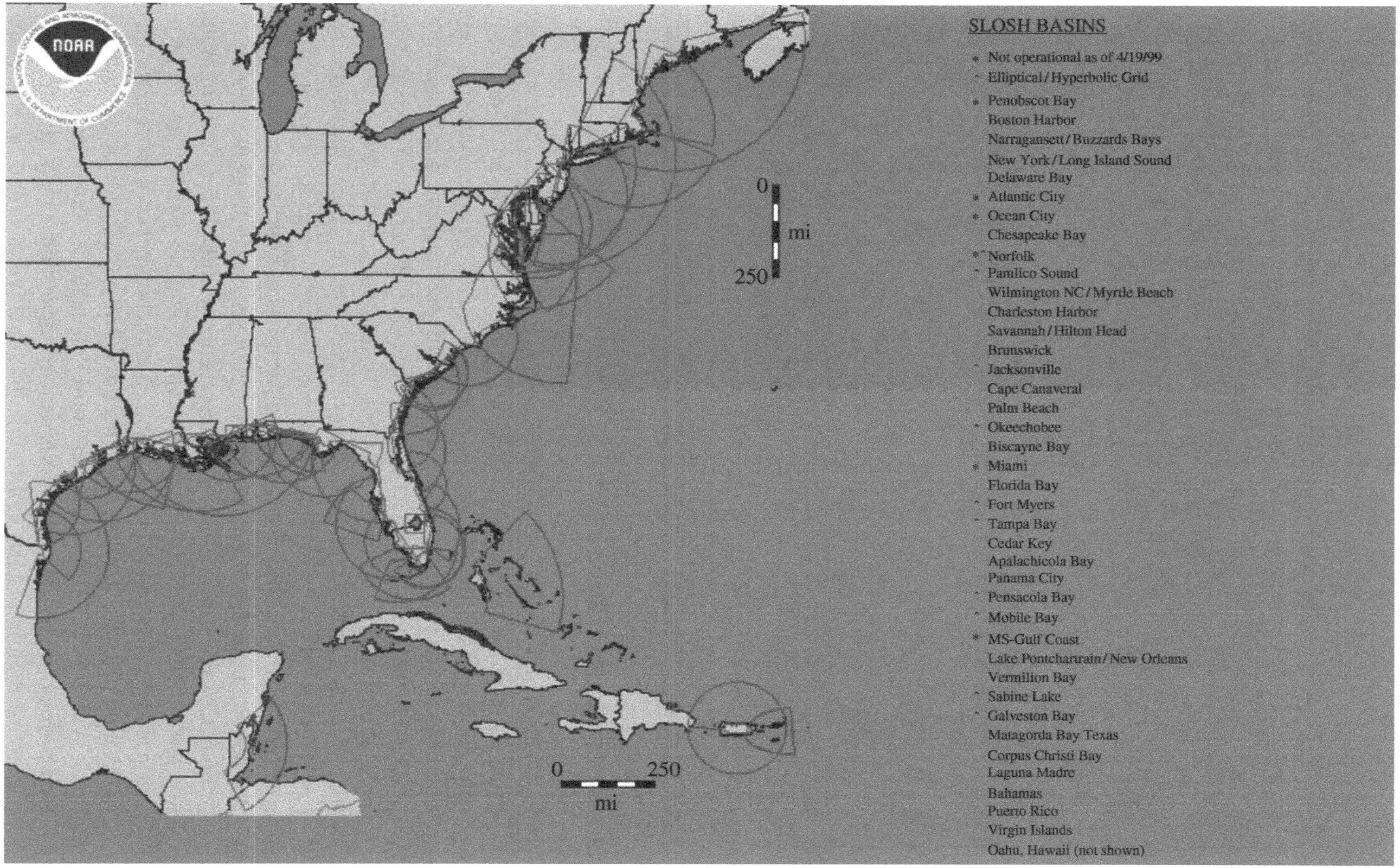

SLOSH storm surge basins. See http://slosh.nws.noaa.gov/slosh/ for more information on SLOSH.

SLOSH BASINS

* Not operational as of 4/19/99
¯ Elliptical/Hyperbolic Grid
* Penobscot Bay
¯ Boston Harbor
¯ Narragansett/Buzzards Bays
¯ New York/Long Island Sound
¯ Delaware Bay
* Atlantic City
* Ocean City
¯ Chesapeake Bay
* Norfolk
¯ Pamlico Sound
¯ Wilmington NC/Myrtle Beach
¯ Charleston Harbor
¯ Savannah/Hilton Head
¯ Brunswick
¯ Jacksonville
¯ Cape Canaveral
¯ Palm Beach
¯ Okeechobee
¯ Biscayne Bay
* Miami
¯ Florida Bay
¯ Fort Myers
¯ Tampa Bay
¯ Cedar Key
¯ Apalachicola Bay
¯ Panama City
¯ Pensacola Bay
* Mobile Bay
* MS-Gulf Coast
¯ Lake Pontchartrain/New Orleans
¯ Vermilion Bay
¯ Sabine Lake
¯ Galveston Bay
¯ Matagorda Bay Texas
¯ Corpus Christi Bay
¯ Laguna Madre
¯ Bahamas
¯ Puerto Rico
¯ Virgin Islands
¯ Oahu, Hawaii (not shown)

Figure 9-4

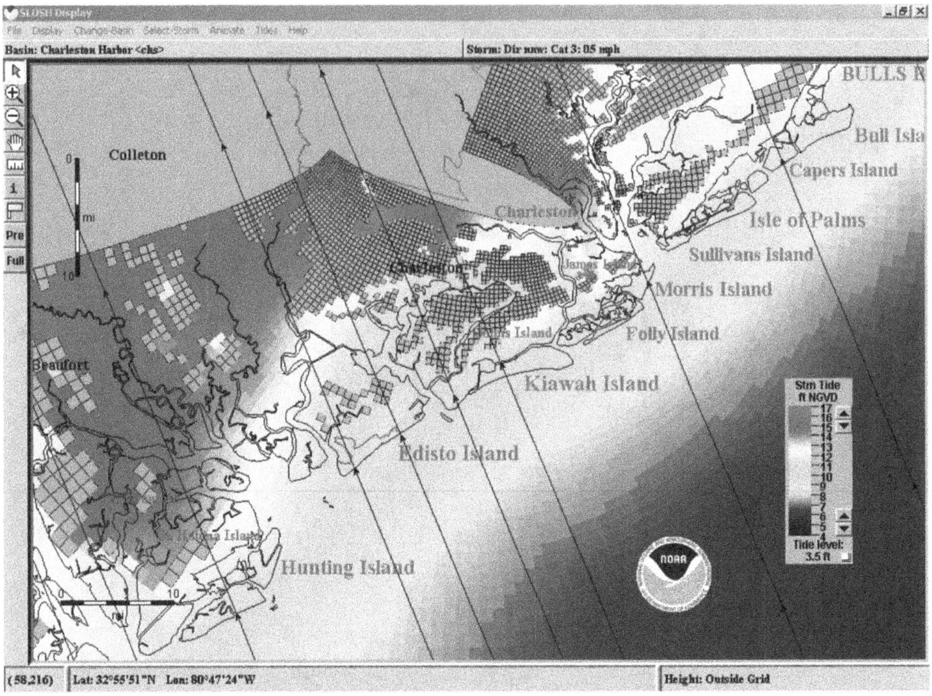

Sample output of the SLOSH model for Hurricane Ike.

9.2.5 Saffir–Simpson Scale

Category 1: Winds of 74–95 miles per hour. Very dangerous winds will produce some damage: Well-constructed frame homes could have damage to roof, shingles, vinyl siding, and gutters. Large branches of trees will snap and shallowly rooted trees may be toppled. Extensive damage to power lines and poles likely will result in power outages that could last a few to several days.

Category 2: Winds of 96–110 miles per hour. Considerable damage may occur to shrubbery and tree foliage. Some trees may be blown down. Major damage can be expected to exposed mobile homes. Extensive damage to poorly constructed signs. Some damage to roofing materials of buildings; some window and door damage. No major damage to buildings. Storm surge 6–8 feet above normal. Coastal roads and low-lying escape routes inland cut by rising water 2–4 hours before arrival of hurricane center. Considerable damage to piers. Marinas flooded. Small craft in unprotected anchorages torn from moorings. Evacuation of some shoreline residences and low-lying inland areas required.

Category 3: Winds of 111–130 miles per hour. Foliage torn from trees; large trees blown down. Practically all poorly constructed signs blown down. Some damage to roofing materials of buildings; some window and door damage. Some structural damage to small buildings. Mobile homes destroyed. Storm surge 9–12 feet above normal. Serious flooding at coast, and many smaller structures near coast destroyed; larger structures near coast damaged by battering waves and floating debris. Low-lying escape routes inland cut by rising water 3–5 hours before hurricane center arrives.

Category 4: Winds of 131–155 miles per hour. Shrubs and trees blown down; all signs down. Extensive damage to roofing materials, windows, and doors. Complete failure of roofs on many small residences. Complete destruction of mobile homes. Storm surge 13–18 feet above normal. Major damage to lower floors of structures near shore due to flooding and battering waves and floating debris. Low-lying escape routes inland are cut by rising water 3 hours before hurricane center arrives. Major erosion of beaches.

Category 5: Winds greater than 155 miles per hour. Shrubs and trees blown down; considerable damage to roofs of buildings; all signs are blown down. Very severe and extensive damage to windows and doors. Complete failure of roofs on many residences and industrial buildings. Extensive shattering of glass in windows and doors. Some complete building failures. Small buildings overturned or blown away. Complete destruction of mobile homes. Storm surge possibly greater than 18 feet above normal. Major damage to lower floors of all structures less than 15 feet above sea level. Low-lying escape routes inland cut by rising water 3–5 hours before hurricane center arrives.

9.3 Using the ALOHA Chemical Dispersion Model

Chemical storage facilities have always posed a security and emergency response challenge for governmental agencies. An accidental release of chemicals from a storage facility or a railway car transporting waste would require you to track the chemical's gas cloud, or plume. You would need to track the plume to determine its potential impact on the nearby population. In light of the terrorist attacks of September 11, you should also be prepared for an intentional release with the potential for a big impact (Tomaszewski, 2005). The tool that you have to help you predict the potential impact of such an event is ALOHA.

ALOHA stands for aerial locations of hazardous atmospheres. It was developed by the EPA and the NOAA. Its purpose is to simulate airborne releases of hazardous chemicals. The National Safety Council distributes ALOHA and provides technical support. The ALOHA plots a "footprint." The footprint represents the area within which the ground-level concentration of a pollutant gas is predicted to exceed individual exposure levels. Several exposure levels are provided by EPA and used in ALOHA. These allow the user to determine the area at which the modeled airborne pollutant could become hazardous to people. ALOHA plots a footprint that represents the zone where the ground-level pollutant concentration is predicted to exceed permitted or recommended exposure levels. ALOHA allows the user to specify different exposure levels, such as levels for children, older adults, and adult male workers.

ALOHA uses the Gaussian model, which is a computer model that was developed to calculate air pollution concentrations. The model assumes that a cloud of pollutants or chemicals is carried downwind from its emission source. The model also assumes that concentrations in the cloud, or plume, can be approximated by assuming that the highest concentration occurs on the horizontal and vertical midlines of the plume. The distribution has Gaussian or bell-shaped concentration profiles in the vertical and horizontal planes. ALOHA uses the Gaussian model to predict how gases that are about as buoyant as air will disperse in the atmosphere. According to this model, wind and atmospheric turbulence are the forces that move the molecules of a released gas through the air, so that an escaped cloud is blown downwind; "turbulent mixing" causes it to spread out in the crosswind and upward directions. According to the Gaussian model, any crosswind slice of a moving pollutant cloud looks like a bell-shaped curve, high in the center and lower on the sides.

▲ Generates a variety of scenario-specific output, including threat zone pictures, threats at specific locations, and source strength graphs.
▲ Calculates how quickly chemicals are escaping from tanks, puddles, and gas pipelines—and predicts how those release rates change over time.
▲ Models many release scenarios: toxic gas clouds, BLEVEs (Boiling Liquid Expanding Vapor Explosions), jet fires, vapor cloud explosions, and pool fires.
▲ Evaluates different types of hazard (depending on the release scenario): toxicity, flammability, thermal radiation, and overpressure.
▲ Models the atmospheric dispersion of chemical spills on water.

9.3.1 How ALOHA Works

ALOHA is designed to be easy to use so that responders can use it during high-pressure situations. A series of dialog boxes prompt users to enter information about a scenario including weather conditions, geographic features, and chemicals and their containers. Detailed help is provided with each dialog box. The scenario information and calculation results are summarized in text and graphic form.

9.3.2 Model Outputs

ALOHA plots a footprint that may be automatically scaled and displayed on a grid or scaled to a user-selected scale in ALOHA's footprint window. On ALOHA's footprint plot, the shaded area represents the footprint itself (see Figure 9-5). The lines along both sides of the footprint represent uncertainty in the wind direction.

9.3.3 Threat Zone Estimates and Threat at a Point

A threat zone is an area where a hazard (such as toxicity or thermal radiation) has exceeded a user-specified Level of Concern (LOC). ALOHA will display up to three threat zones overlaid on a single picture. The red threat zone represents the worst hazard.

Figure 9-5

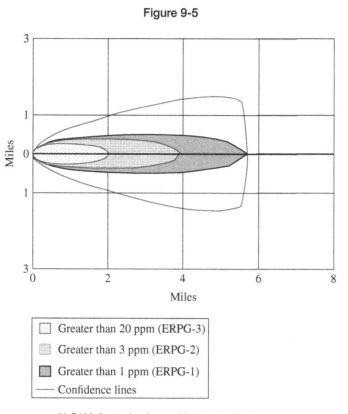

▦	Greater than 20 ppm (ERPG-3)
▨	Greater than 3 ppm (ERPG-2)
▨	Greater than 1 ppm (ERPG-1)
——	Confidence lines

ALOHA footprint for a chlorine tank release.

The Threat at a Point feature displays specific information about hazards at locations.

The wind rarely blows constantly from any one direction. As it shifts direction, it blows a pollutant cloud in a new direction. The "uncertainty lines" around the footprint enclose the region within which the gas cloud is expected to remain about 19 out of 20 times.

The lower the wind speed, the more the wind changes direction. So as wind speed decreases, the uncertainty lines become farther apart. They form a circle when wind speed is very low. A curved, dashed line leads from the end of one uncertainty line, across the tip of the footprint, to the end of the other uncertainty line. This line represents the farthest downwind extent of the footprint, if the wind were to shift to rotate the footprint toward either uncertainty line.

9.3.4 Strengths of ALOHA

ALOHA has several strengths, is available without cost, and is easy to use. The following are also features of ALOHA:

▲ It may be used with heavy gases or neutrally buoyant gases.
▲ It provides easy-to-understand estimates of the source strength.
▲ It can simulate releases from tanks, puddles, and pipes.

▲ It can calculate indoor air infiltration.

▲ It contains an extensive chemical library that is user expandable.

▲ It estimates gas cloud area and concentration over time under varying environmental conditions.

▲ It can be used with real-time input of weather data provided by the user or directly from a meteorological station.

▲ It plots toxic cloud footprints onto area maps.

▲ It has an easy-to-use graphic interface and display.

▲ It includes mapping program, called MARPLOT (Mapping Application for Response, Planning and Local Operational Tasks) that uses digitized mapping data or other mapping images. It also enables customized overlays showing area facilities and vulnerable populations.

▲ It is available for Windows or Macintosh platforms.

9.3.5 Limitations of ALOHA

ALOHA's accuracy is dependent on the quality of the information used. Outputs from a model may not be accurate even when you provide the best input values. ALOHA has limitations and is unreliable in certain situations.

When making concentration estimates, ALOHA assumes that the chemical is released into the atmosphere and immediately becomes mixed so that the concentration looks like a bell-shaped curve throughout the cloud (the highest concentration is downwind along the centerline). Even though that is not exactly what happens in a chemical release, this "Gaussian" assumption is fairly typical and provides reasonable concentration estimates in most cases.

However, ALOHA's concentration estimates can be less accurate when any condition exists that reduces mixing in the atmosphere. For example:

▲ *Very low wind speeds.* At very low wind speeds (less than 3 miles per hour) the pollutant cloud does not mix quickly with the surrounding air. The concentration of the gas in the chemical cloud may remain higher than ALOHA predicts, especially near the source.

▲ *Very stable atmospheric conditions.* Very stable atmospheric conditions (**stability classes** E and F) generally occur at night or in the early morning, and may be indicated by conditions such as low-lying fog. Under these atmospheric conditions, gas concentrations within a pollutant cloud can remain high far from the source.

▲ Concentration Patchiness, Particularly Near the Source

When using ALOHA, keep in mind that the program doesn't account for the effects of:

▲ *By-products from fires, explosions, or chemical reactions.* ALOHA doesn't account for the by-products of combustion (such as smoke) or chemical reactions. The smoke from a fire, because it is has been heated, rises before it moves downwind. ALOHA doesn't account for this initial rise. ALOHA assumes that a dispersing cloud does not react with the gases that make up the atmosphere, such as oxygen and water vapor. However, many chemicals react with dry or humid air, water, other chemicals, or even themselves. Because of these chemical reactions, the chemical that disperses downwind might be very different from the chemical that originally escaped from containment. In some cases, this difference may be enough to make ALOHA's dispersion predictions inaccurate.

▲ *Particulates.* ALOHA does not account for the processes that affect dispersion of particulates (including radioactive particles).

▲ *Chemical mixtures.* ALOHA is designed to model the release and dispersion of pure chemicals and a few select solutions; the property information in its chemical library is not valid for mixtures of chemicals.

▲ *Wind shifts and terrain steering effects.* ALOHA assumes that wind speed and direction are constant throughout the area downwind of a chemical release. ALOHA also expects the ground below a dispersing cloud to be flat. In reality, though, the wind typically shifts speed and direction as it flows up or down slopes, between hills or down into valleys, turning where terrain features turn. In urban areas, wind flowing around large buildings forms eddies and changes direction and speed, significantly altering a cloud's shape and movement. ALOHA ignores these effects when it produces a threat zone estimate.

▲ *Terrain.* ALOHA assumes the ground is flat, which has different implications depending on the release scenario. For liquid releases, ALOHA does not account for pooling within depressions or the flow of liquid across sloping ground. ALOHA assumes that the liquid spreads out evenly in all directions, which may cause the puddle size and release rate to be overestimated when the ground is not flat. For gas releases, ALOHA does not account for changes in wind flow that can occur as the cloud is diverted by tall buildings and mountains.

▲ *Hazardous fragments.* If a chemical release involves an explosion, there will be flying debris from the container and the surrounding area. ALOHA does not model the trajectories of the hazardous fragments.

9.3.6 Terms Used in ALOHA

The following are some important terms and phrases used in the ALOHA model:

LOC or Output Concentration: In ALOHA, an LOC is a threshold value of a hazard (toxicity, flammability, thermal radiation, or overpressure); the LOC is usually the value above which a threat to people or property may exist.

Whenever you use ALOHA to analyze a chemical release scenario, you must choose one or more LOCs. ALOHA will provide you with common default values, or you may choose up to three of your own LOCs. For each LOC you choose, ALOHA estimates a threat zone where the hazard is predicted to exceed that LOC at some time after a release begins. These zones are displayed on a single image. Whenever you use ALOHA to analyze a chemical release scenario, you must choose one or more LOCs. ALOHA will provide you with common default values, or you may choose up to three of your own LOCs. For each LOC you choose, ALOHA estimates a threat zone where the hazard is predicted to exceed that LOC at some time after a release begins. ALOHA includes the following LOCs to model different hazards: toxic LOCs, flammable LOCs, thermal radiation LOCs, and overpressure LOCs.

Immediately Dangerous to Life or Health (IDLH) level: This is the default LOC in ALOHA. An IDLH has been established for about one-third of the chemicals in ALOHA. You may choose to use the IDLH, when a value is available, as your LOC. You can also choose another threshold concentration.

Threshold Limits: The American Conference of Governmental Industrial Hygienists (ACGIH) publishes recommended occupational exposure limits for hazardous chemicals. The TLV, or threshold limit value, is the maximum airborne concentration of a given hazardous chemical to which nearly all workers can be exposed during normal 8-hour workdays and 40-hour workweeks for an indefinite number of weeks without adverse effects.

TLV-TWA: The maximum allowable time weighted average concentration for an 8-hour day and 40-hour work week. TLV-TWA values are obtained from industrial experience, from experimental human and animal studies, or from a combination of both. If a TLV-TWA level has been established for a chemical that you select, this value will be displayed on ALOHA's text summary window.

Stability Class: The atmosphere may be more or less turbulent at any given time. It depends on the amount of incoming solar radiation as well as other factors. Meteorologists have defined six "atmospheric stability classes," each representing a different degree of turbulence in the atmosphere. When moderate to strong incoming solar radiation heats air near the ground, causing it to rise and generating large eddies, the atmosphere is considered "unstable," or relatively turbulent. Unstable conditions are associated with atmospheric stability classes A and B. When solar radiation is relatively weak, air near the surface has less of a tendency to rise and less turbulence develops. In this case, the atmosphere is considered "stable," or less turbulent. The wind is weak. The stability class would be E or F. Stability classes D and C represent conditions of more neutral stability, or moderate turbulence. Neutral conditions are associated with relatively strong wind speeds and moderate solar radiation.

FOR EXAMPLE

Summary of Release Scenario for Figure 9-5

SITE DATA:
Location: BATON ROUGE, LOUISIANA
Building Air Exchanges per Hour: 0.79 (unsheltered single storied)
Time: November 16, 2016 and 1205 hours CST (using computer's clock)

CHEMICAL DATA:
Chemical Name: CHLORINE Molecular Weight: 70.91 g/mol
AEGL-1 (60 minutes): 0.5 ppm AEGL-2 (60 minutes): 2 ppm AEGL-3 (60 minutes): 20 ppm

IDLH: 10 ppm
Ambient Boiling Point: –29.3°F
Vapor Pressure at Ambient Temperature: greater than 1 atm
Ambient Saturation Concentration: 1 000 000 ppm or 100.0%

ATMOSPHERIC DATA: (MANUAL INPUT OF DATA)
Wind: 8 miles/hour from w at 3 m
Ground Roughness: open country Cloud Cover: 0 tenths
Air Temperature: 78°F Stability Class: C
No Inversion Height Relative Humidity: 50%

SOURCE STRENGTH:
Leak from hole in horizontal cylindrical tank
Non-flammable chemical is escaping from tank
Tank Diameter: 4 feet Tank Length: 10 feet
Tank Volume: 940 gallons
Tank contains liquid Internal Temperature: 78°F
Chemical Mass in Tank: 4.35 tons Tank is 79% full
Circular Opening Diameter: 4 inches
Opening is 0.68 feet from tank bottom
Release Duration: 1 minute
Max Average Sustained Release Rate: 136 pounds/second
(averaged over a minute or more)
Total Amount Released: 8178 pounds
Note: The chemical escaped as a mixture of gas and aerosol (two phase flow).

THREAT ZONE:
Model Run: Heavy Gas
Red: 2.0 miles—(20 ppm = AEGL-3 [60 minutes])
Orange: 4.5 miles—(2 ppm = AEGL-2 [60 minutes])
Yellow: greater than 6 miles— (0.5 ppm = AEGL-1 [60 minutes])

9.3.7 Concentration Patchiness, Particularly Near the Source

No one can predict gas concentrations at any particular instant downwind of a release. This is because concentrations result partly from random chance. Concentration patchiness is the term used for situations where the gas concentration cannot be described as a bell-shaped curve. Concentration patchiness occurs in every dispersing cloud, particularly very near the source. Rather than showing exact concentrations, ALOHA shows you concentrations that represent averages for time periods of several minutes. It uses the laws of probability as well as meteorologists' knowledge of the atmosphere to do this.

Near the source, ALOHA's concentration estimates may overestimate or underestimate concentrations, because ALOHA uses concentration averages. For the average concentration to be valid, the cloud must travel downwind to the point where enough eddies have mixed the air and the gas. This distance varies depending on the stability, wind speed, and release details. If the maximum distance to the toxic LOC concentration is less than 50 m, ALOHA will not show the threat zone, because concentration patchiness makes the estimate unreliable near the source of the release (where patchiness is most pronounced).

Avoid using ALOHA's Gaussian model to predict how a large heavy gas cloud will disperse. Large gas clouds that are denser than air ("heavy gases") are not buoyant and disperse in a very different way. They are affected by gravity and other forces besides wind and turbulence. As they move downwind, they remain much lower to the ground than neutrally buoyant clouds and flow like water. Also, be aware that ALOHA cannot take into its modeling processes fires, chemical reactions or solutions, particulates, and terrain.

9.4 Hazards United States—Multi Hazard Model

In addition to programs that model chemical releases and hurricanes, we also have a software program that models potential losses from earthquakes, floods, wind, and hurricane risks (FEMA, 1997). It is HAZUS-MH (Hazards United States—Multi Hazard). It is an emergency planning and response software package. Officials at all levels of government have long recognized the need to more accurately estimate the escalating costs associated with natural hazards (FEMA, 1997). HAZUS-MH was developed as a set of geospatial tools to allow communities to understand the potential impacts of hazards on the community. It serves as a base to identify broad-based hazard mitigation strategies for a community (Schneider and Schauer, 2006). The primary focus of HAZUS-MH is to clarify the direct and indirect economic impacts of riverine flooding events in a geographic region including the depreciated values of structures (Scawthorn et al., 2006).

HAZUS-MH enhances our capacity to determine the potential damage from inland and coastal flooding, hurricane winds, earthquakes, and chemical hazard events (FEMA, 2003). Local, state, and federal officials can improve community emergency preparedness, response, recovery, and mitigation activities by enhancing their ability to characterize the economic and social consequences of flood, wind, and coastal hazards. For modeling flood hazards, HAZUS-MH provides three levels of analysis.

Level 1 Analysis: This can be thought of as an initial screen that identifies areas and communities that are most at risk. A Level 1 analysis uses national average data to produce approximate results. This is also referred to as an "out of the box" estimate or a "default" estimate.

Level 2 Analysis: This requires work on your part. You must enter additional data and hazard maps. You may also work with GIS (Geographic Information System) professionals and urban and regional planners to do this. The system then produces more accurate risk and loss estimates.

Level 3 Analysis: This the most accurate estimate of loss. It usually requires the involvement of experts such as structural and geotechnical engineers.

FEMA designed HAZUS-MH so that it could be used by communities, regardless of the expertise of staff and outside resources. A Level 1 analysis requires no adaptation of the program and makes use of data provided by FEMA. Despite the limitations of a Level 1 analysis, the program outputs provide local communities with a general assessment of flood risks in the community. For communities with internal or external expertise, the Level 2 analysis provides information that is well suited for many hazard mitigation strategies. For communities with a broad experience in flood modeling and use of GIS- spatial analysis tools, a Level 3 assessment is quite possible. HAZUS-MH, thus, can fit with the capabilities and resources of many different communities.

A *Level 1* risk analysis is the simplest type of analysis requiring minimum effort by the user as it is based mostly on input provided with the methodology (e.g., census information, broad regional patterns of floodplain code adoption). The user is not expected to have extensive technical knowledge. Documentation of each data layer is complete and available on a national basis within the United States. While the methods require some user-supplied input to run, the type of input required could be gathered by contacting government agencies or by referring to published information. At this level, estimates are generalized and not suitable for use of property buyouts, nor changes to a flood insurance rate map (FIRM) prepared by the Federal Emergency Management Agency (FEMA). It is suitable as a tool to determine where more intensive flood studies might be initiated. Given that the loss estimates are generalized and not based on specific flood studies in a community, outputs are appropriate only as initial loss estimates to determine where more detailed analyses are warranted.

A Level 2 analysis is intended to improve the results from Level 1 by considering additional data that may be available in a community. Data from a hydrologic modeling program may be available in a community and easily imported into HAZUS-MH Flood. HEC2 studies meet the methodological requirements of HAZUS-MH analysis and are part of the overall Flood Insurance Administration flood assessment efforts. In Level 2, the user may need to determine parameters from published reports or maps as input to the model. The Level 2 analysis may also include more extensive property and infrastructure inventory data and used to enhance damage assessments. The inventory data may reflect a more accurate count of building types, numbers of structures, contents, and age of construction. Many local communities have accurate records of the base first floor elevation of the structure.

A Level 3 analysis allows the user to edit depth-damage curves and curves for general building stock. Engineers and building scientists can provide suggestions on editing the damage curves used by in the HAZUS-MH analysis processes. These changes incorporate results from engineering and economic studies carried out using methods and software associated with the HAZUS-MH methodology. At this level, one or more technical consultants may be needed to recommend the changes, perform analyses, assess damage/loss, and assist in a discussion of the results of the damage assessment. It is anticipated that at this level there will be extensive participation by local utilities, special facilities, and businesses.

Figure 9-6

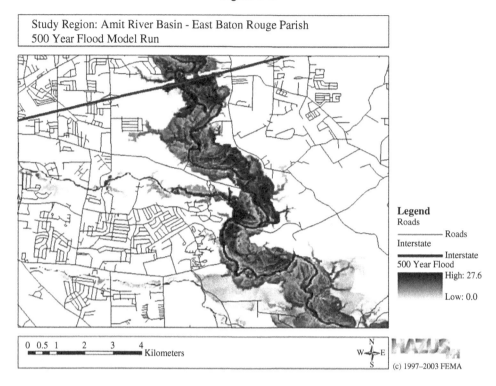

East Baton Rouge Parish with HAZUS-MH flood risk zones.

Once vulnerability zones are created for the hazard, HAZUS-MH calculates damage estimates. It creates a total damage estimate by occupancy for residential, commercial, industrial, agricultural, religious buildings, education buildings, and government buildings for the hazard zone. These calculations include damage to buildings and building contents possibly impacted by the hazard.

Damage calculations in HAZUS-MH are determined from databases included in the software. The building inventory databases were created from information provided by the Census Bureau and business information sources. Figure 9-6 provides an example of the type of building inventory database and shows the total number of buildings as well as the number of buildings by census block for the following categories:

▲ Residential buildings
▲ Commercial buildings
▲ Industrial buildings
▲ Agricultural buildings
▲ Governmental buildings

Additional databases in HAZUS-MH provide information on the value of buildings and their contents by census block as well as the number of structures by the type of construction (wood, steel reinforced, brick, concrete, and manufactured housing) and the square footage of the structures by type of occupancy (residential, commercial, etc.).

HAZUS-MH can be used to determine the structures or critical infrastructure in a risk zone that could be damaged by the hazard and the degree that the structures may be impacted by flood hazards (Assaf, 2011; Remo et al., 2012). As a result, HAZUS-MH is an excellent planning tool that allows a local community to determine the potential damage throughout the area and the differential impacts that may result from flood hazards.

It is important that many local offices and units understand the nature and extent of earthquake, flooding, wind, and coastal hazards. HAZUS-MH increases understanding by providing a tool to share map layers with anyone interested in viewing the HAZUS-MH study results. HAZUS-MH thus provides information to increase understanding of risks associated with disasters and lead to the adoption of community hazard mitigation strategies.

Each year floods worldwide cause severe damages, claim about 20 000 lives, and adversely affect at least 20 million people. It has been proven impossible over the past years to provide 100% security against flood damages despite significant efforts of flood protection activities within the EU (Mostert and Junier, 2009). For this reason the focus of mitigation strategies in Europe has shifted in the past decade from complete protection against flood damages to managing flood risks. One of the significant outcomes of this paradigm was the passing of the European Flood Directive (EFD) and its legal acceptance by all 27 EU Member States. This directive aims to reduce the adverse consequences associated with floods on human health, environment, cultural heritage, and economic activity in the community by performing flood hazard and flood risk assessment actions.

HAZUS-MH represents an extensively applied and well-documented GIS-based framework in the United States for estimation of risk and potential losses from natural hazards like floods, hurricane winds, and earthquakes. HAZUS-MH has been developed and maintained since 1993 by the FEMA (2003).

One big advantage of HAZUS-MH is the centralized inventory data storage, where all the information about assets is stored. The inventory can be stored on an external or a network drive and accessed by multiple HAZUS-MH users.

9.4.1 Strengths of HAZUS-MH

HAZUS-MH is a robust program with many capabilities and strengths. HAZUS-MH provides local government jurisdictions with an exceptional tool in preparedness, response, and the hazard mitigation process. The ease of use and the quality of the data provided with the program enable the user to generate information on where to expect losses in the community and considerable information on the nature of these losses.

FEMA has created a powerful tool for the assessment of hazard-related losses. The tool allows the user to execute a local analysis in a reasonable period of time and estimate losses to the jurisdiction. It provides a basis for examining the economic impact of flooding and using loss estimates in establishing hazard mitigation priorities at the local level. By allowing users to establish a regional study area, the program facilitates a broader examination of hazard mitigation. Counties can work together to examine risks and concentrate more local analysis in HAZUS-MH to specific geographic areas. As the program gains broad use, local jurisdictions will find help and overcome many technical problems that users are encountering today. HAZUS-MH is thus a powerful hazard mitigation tool. It is a tool that makes a significant contribution in informing local decision makers as to the impacts of hazards in their community.

HAZUS-MH is an example of an integrated environmental decision-making tool. It uses an integrated approach for evaluating a highly complex environmental problem holistically by integrating resources and analyses to address the problems as they occur in the real world; including input from appropriate stakeholders (EPA, 2000).

9.4.2 Limitations of HAZUS-MH

As with all robust programs, using HAZUS-MH effectively requires training. You will also need to work with experts to produce accurate estimates of losses in your community. Difficulties in using HAZUS-MH will be overcome as local officials become more skilled in utilizing the power of GIS and the HAZUS-MH hazard models. Training scenarios will likely be prepared to help users anticipate common problems in using the models. Feedback to FEMA on difficulties in using the program will also result in system changes.

One of the biggest concerns raised by local users is the quality of data in HAZUS-MH, especially for building counts and their characteristics. Studies to demonstrate the validity of building counts and the economic values associated with the structures have helped in assuring local officials of the validity of the data. For jurisdictions where major population shifts have not occurred since 2000, local officials can be more confident in the economic loss analysis for residential properties provided by HAZUS-MH.

9.4.3 Multirisk Assessment

Many areas are subject to many hazards including flooding, earthquakes, fires, or chemical accidents. The areas may also have numerous geographic differences from coastal zones and mountains and have significant climate differences (Kaveckis et al., 2012). Kappes et al. (2012) note that HAZUS-MH has the capacity to model very different hazards but only links the analysis of one set of risks in a single modeling effort. They note that the hurricane module allows for an assessment of both wind and flood hazards at the same time.

9.5 Evacuation Modeling

Murray-Tuite and Wolshon (2013) provide an excellent summary of highway-based evacuation modeling and simulation. Their analysis includes major components of roadway transportation planning and operations, forecasting of evacuation travel demand, distribution and assignment of evacuation demand to regional road networks to reach destinations, assignment of evacuees to various modes of transportation, and evaluation and testing of alternative management strategies to increase capacity of evacuation networks or manage demand.

They note that evacuations are quite common based on efforts from the Sandia National Laboratory for the US Nuclear Regulatory Commission (NRC). This study showed that, on average, an evacuation of 1000 or more people occurs about once every 2–3 weeks in the United States (Sandia National Laboratories, 2004). They stress that these trends have led to an increased level of involvement from transportation professionals in emergency planning and response. The roles and responsibilities of transportation during emergencies have been formalized in the National Response Framework (Department of Homeland Security, 2016).

Murray-Tuite and Wolshon (2013) provide a concise review of evacuation strategies including supply side, contraflow, crossing elimination, special signal timings, transit, and the use of highway shoulders. Their discussion also examines modeling hospitals and special facilities, gasoline and other supplies, elderly and homebound populations, pets, and traffic incidents. They note that technology offers new tools for evacuation. They provide a description of how social media can be used to spread information associated with a disaster.

9.6 Centralized Hazard Modeling Initiatives

Many of the models that have been examined in this text are run locally to support emergency planning, mitigation, and response efforts. Efforts to describe hazards such as hurricanes are part of federal agency efforts and are run on a regional basis such as in the Gulf of Mexico or Atlantic regions. Some federal agencies provide information on the current status of drought, rain, and fire risks. Fire modeling is used to describe the threats imposed by wildfires in the United States.

9.6.1 Fire Potential Modeling

The National Interagency Coordination Center (NICC) provides information on fire risks and fires within the United States. The primary focus of this agency is wildfire suppression and is built on a three-tiered system of support—the local area, one of the 11 geographic areas, and, finally, the national level. When a fire is reported, the local agency and its firefighting partners respond. If the fire continues to grow, the agency can ask for help from its geographic area. When a geographic area has exhausted all its resources, it can turn to NICC at the National Interagency Fire Center (NIFC) for help in locating what is needed, from air tankers to radios to firefighting crews to incident management teams.

The agency provides information on current conditions from weather, fuels and fire danger, and outlooks on a regional and national level. The National Significant Wildland Fire Potential Outlook uses information on a national scale to forecast potential wildland fires on a monthly basis.

The NIFC provides a monthly outlook of fire on a regional basis in the United States (National Interagency Fire Center, 2016). This report, as shown in Figure 9-7,

Figure 9-7

Significant Wildland Fire Potential Outlook
October 2016

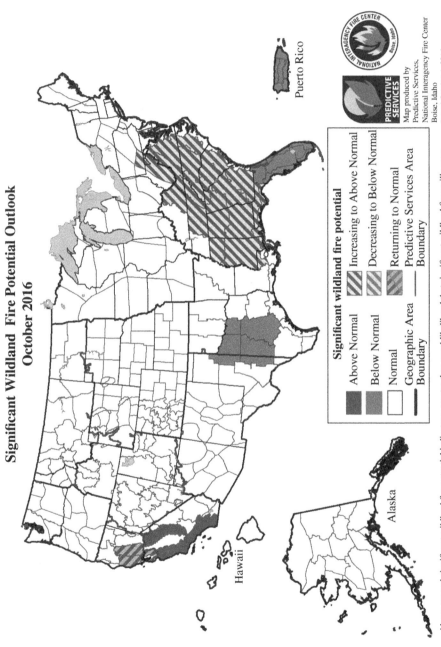

Significant wildland fire potential for October 2016 (http://www.predictiveservices.nifc.gov/outlooks/month1_outlook.png).

highlights recent weather conditions nationally and regionally and especially any drought conditions within the United States. Weather and climate outlook reports are included in each monthly report and provide any updates on fuel conditions that might impact potential fires. Geographic forecasts are provided for regions in the United States. The National Significant Wildland Fire Potential Outlook is intended as a decision support tool for wildland fire and emergency managers at the state or local level, providing an assessment of current weather and fuels conditions and how these will evolve in the next 4 months. The objective is to assist fire managers in making proactive decisions that will improve protection of life, property, and natural resources, increase fire fighter safety and effectiveness, and reduce firefighting costs.

The NIFC is an example of national modeling efforts which support state and local interest in understanding the potential for wildland fires in their geographic region. These national efforts provide critical information on a hazard that confronts all regions of the United States. They also take advantage of complex hazard modeling on a centralized scale. As a result, local governments can obtain the critical information about a significant hazard without investing in the complex computer models and mapping systems.

For many years, the USDA (US Department of Agriculture) Forest Service has been active in forest fire, smoke modeling, and emission tracking. Their intent is to understand the impact of fire on air quality and visibility and support efforts to understand current and future fire risks to communities and natural areas throughout the United States. The National Fire Plan, which was developed in 2000 after a dry season with many forest fires, requires the enhancement of fire behavior models. Fire planners use these models to increase the effectiveness and safety of fire operations.

Four regional fire, weather, and smoke modeling centers have been established. These provide weather and smoke modeling support to forest service, state, and other partners. Weather models and fire behavior models are used together to provide greater detail of anticipated fire spread, better planning for the response and safety of firefighters and the public, and a better allocation of fire-suppression resources. These centers have high-speed computing capabilities.

9.6.2 Drought Modeling

In the last few decades, interest in drought planning has increased. In 1980, only three states had drought plans. Today, 38 states either have drought plans or are in the process of developing plans. The National Drought Mitigation Center at the University of Nebraska, Lincoln, is sponsored by the US Bureau of Reclamation. It was established in 1995. Its activities include the following:

▲ Maintaining an information clearinghouse
▲ Drought monitoring
▲ Drought planning and mitigation
▲ Advising policymakers

▲ Research
▲ Conducting educational workshops for the United States, foreign, and international organizations

This center helps people and organizations plan for droughts. This planning is based on three components: monitoring and early warning, risk assessment, and mitigation and response.

These components complement one another and create an integrated institutional approach. This approach addresses both short- and long-term drought management issues.

9.7 Evaluating Hazard Models

As with any technology or tool, you have to evaluate the pros and cons of using a hazard model and investing and allocating resources for it. When deciding what model(s) to use, you will want to evaluate the models. You can use the following as a framework for identifying the critical elements of a hazard model.

Quality
  ▲ Do the results accurately reflect the event simulated under specified conditions?
  ▲ Do the damage assessments accurately reflect the residential, commercial, industrial, agricultural, government, and educational structures in the community?

Usability
  ▲ Does the model require extensive training to use?
  ▲ Does the model require expertise that is readily available at the local level?
  ▲ Are limitations of the model stated in a clear, straightforward manner?
  ▲ Are results expressed in an easy-to-understand manner?
  ▲ Will you have to format the results before you can use them?
  ▲ Are results outlined to easily understand the intended use?
  ▲ Is the information presented in an orderly arrangement and in a form that assists you?

Timeliness: Many day-to-day decisions are time sensitive. Decisions on how to respond to situations must be made quickly. Timely information has several ingredients:
  ▲ Is the information provided when it is needed for making preparedness, mitigation, and response or recovery decisions?
  ▲ Is the information resulting from the model output current? Information should be up-to-date when it is provided to the decision maker.
  ▲ Is the information from the model updated as needed? When conditions change, is information provided as often as needed or at an appropriate frequency?

Completeness: The results of the model must be complete to be of value to decision makers. Conciseness and detail are two additional aspects of completeness.

▲ Does the model give you enough information to make an accurate assessment of the situation and to arrive at a suitable decision?

▲ Do you have access not only to current information, but also to past history?

▲ Are the results of the model presented to you in a concise form but with sufficient detail to provide you with enough depth and breadth for the current situation?

▲ Is sufficient relevant information provided to you without information overload?

SUMMARY

Understanding the impact different hazards could have on your community is essential in forming your planning and mitigation efforts. In this chapter, you evaluated the strengths and limitations of different hazard models. Specifically, you evaluated the SLOSH hurricane model. You also examined the ALOHA chemical dispersion model. In addition, you assessed what qualities you should consider when you evaluate hazard models. These qualities will guide you in selecting the models you will implement in your community.

KEY TERMS

Aerial locations of hazardous atmospheres (ALOHA)	A chemical dispersion model developed by the US Environmental Protection Agency (EPA) and the National Oceanic and Atmospheric Administration in the US Department of Interior
Hazard modeling	Simulation of a real system or replication of a potential hazard event.
HAZUS-MH	Suite of hazard models developed by FEMA to describe the nature of hazardous conditions for earthquakes, wind, coastal, and flooding hazards, and their economic and social impacts.
Immediately dangerous to life or health (IDLH) level	The IDLH or health (IDLH) level is an exposure limit to hazardous chemicals established to provide guidance to industry and emergency response personnel.
Saffir–Simpson Hurricane Scale	Scale developed as a general guide for use by public safety officials during emergencies to communicate and describe the nature and intensity of hurricanes.
Sea, lake, and overland surges from hurricanes (SLOSH)	A model used by the NWS to surges from hurricanes calculate potential surge heights from hurricanes.
Stability class	A classification system used in dispersion modeling to describe wind speed, atmosphere turbulence, and solar radiation.

ASSESS YOUR UNDERSTANDING

Go to www.wiley.com/go/pine/tech&emergmgmt_2e to evaluate your knowledge of using technology. This website contains MCQ's, self checks, review questions, applying this chapter and you try it.

References

Akbar, M., Aliabadi, S., Patel, R., & Watts, M. (2013). A fully automated and integrated multi-scale forecasting scheme for emergency preparedness. *Environmental Modelling & Software*, *39*, 24–38.

Assaf, H. (2011). Framework for modeling mass disasters. *Natural Hazards Review*, *12*(2), 47–61.

Department of Homeland Security. (2016). *The National Response Framework*. Washington, DC: Department of Homeland Security.

Drager, K. H., Lovas, G. G., Wiklund, J., & Soma, H. (1993). Objectives of modeling evacuation from buildings during accidents: Some path-model scenarios. *Journal of Contingencies and Crisis Management*, *1*(4), 207–214.

Environmental Protection Agency (EPA). (2000). *Toward Integrated Environmental Decision-making* (EPA-SAB-EC-00-011). Washington, DC: Science Advisory Board. http://www.epa.gov/sab/pdf/ecirp011.pdf (accessed May 12, 2017).

Federal Emergency Management Agency (FEMA). (1997). *Hydrologic Hazards: Multi Hazard Identification and Risk Assessment*. Washington, DC: FEMA.

Federal Emergency Management Agency (FEMA). (2003). *HAZUS-MH Riverine Flood Model Technical Manual*. Washington, DC: FEMA.

Goodchild, M. F., Parks, B. O., & Steyaert, L. T. (1993). *Environmental Modeling with GIS*. New York: Oxford University Press.

Greenway, A. R. (1998). *Risk Management Planning Handbook: A Comprehensive Guide to Hazard Assessment, Accidental Release Prevention, and Consequence Analysis*. Rockville, MD: Government Institutes, Inc.

Jelesnianski, C. P., Chen, J., & Shaffer, W. A. (1992). *SLOSH: Sea, Lake and Overland Surges from Hurricanes* (NOAA Technical Report NWS 48). Washington, DC: National Oceanic and Atmospheric Administration, U.S. Department of Commerce.

Kappes, M. S., Gruber, K., Frigerio, S., Bell, R., Keiler, M., & Glade, T. (2012). The MultiRISK platform: The technical concept and application of a regional-scale multihazard exposure analysis tool. *Geomorphology*, *151*, 139–155.

Kaveckis, G., Paulus, G., & Mickey, K. (2012). HAZ-I–a new framework for international applications of the HAZUS-MH flood risk assessment. In *GI_Forum*, Salzburg, Austria, pp. 426–435.

Kirkwood, A. S. (1994). Why do we worry when scientists say there is no risk? *Disaster Prevention and Management*, *3*(2), 15–22.

Leskens, J. G., Brugnach, M., Hoekstra, A. Y., & Schuurmans, W. (2014). Why are decisions in flood disaster management so poorly supported by information from flood models? *Environmental Modelling & Software*, *53*, 53–61.

Mostert, E., & Junier, S. J. (2009). The European flood risk directive: Challenges for research. *Hydrology and Earth System Sciences Discussions*, 6(4), 4961–4988.

Murray-Tuite, P., & Wolshon, B. (2013). Evacuation transportation modeling: An overview of research, development, and practice. *Transportation Research Part C: Emerging Technologies*, 27, 25–45.

National Interagency Fire Center. (2016). National Significant Wildland Fire Potential Outlook—October 2016. Boise, ID: National Interagency Fire Center. Additional Geographic Area assessments may be available at the specific GACC websites. The GACC websites can also be accessed through the NICC webpage at: http://www.nifc.gov/nicc/predictive/outlooks/outlooks.htm (accessed April 24, 2017).

Pine, J. C. (2014). *Hazards Analysis: Reducing the Impact of Disasters*. Boca Raton, FL: Taylor & Francis.

Remo, J., Carlson, M., & Pinter, N. (2012). Hydraulic and flood-loss modeling of levee, floodplain, and river management strategies, Middle Mississippi River, USA. *Natural Hazards Review*, 61(2), 551–575.

Sandia National Laboratories. 2004. *Identification and Analysis of Factors Affecting Emergency Evacuations: Main Report*. Washington, DC: Sandia National Laboratories.

Scawthorn, C., Flores, P., Blais, N., Seligson, H., Tate, E., Chang, S., Mifflin, E., Thomas, W., Murphy, J., Jones, C., & Lawrence, M. (2006). HAZUS-MH flood loss estimation methodology. II. Damage and loss assessment. *Natural Hazards Review*, ASCE. 7(2)(40), 72–81.

Schneider, P., & Schauer, B. (2006). HAZUS, its development and future. *Natural Hazards Review*, Special Issue. Multihazards Loss Estimation and HAZUS. ASCE. 7(2)(40), 40–44.

Stedinger, J. R., & Griffis, V. W. (2008). Flood frequency analysis in the United States: Time to update. *Journal of Hydrologic Engineering*, 13(4), 199–204.

Tomaszewski, B. (2005). Erie County emergency response and planning application performs plume modeling. http://dssresources.com/cases/eriecounty/index.html (accessed May 12, 2017).

Voinov, A., & Gaddis, E. (2008). Lessons for successful participatory watershed modeling: A perspective from modeling practitioners. *Ecological Modelling, 216*, 197–207.

10

OPERATIONAL PROBLEMS AND TECHNOLOGY: MAKING TECHNOLOGY WORK FOR YOU

John J. Kiefer[1] and John C. Pine[2]

[1] Department of Political Science, University of New Orleans, New Orleans, LA, USA
[2] Department of Geography and Planning, Appalachian State University, Boone, NC, USA

Starting Point

Go to www.wiley.com/go/pine/tech&emergmgmt_2e to assess your knowledge of operational problems and technology.
Determine where to concentrate your effort.

What You'll Learn in This Chapter

▲ Barriers to implementing technology in emergency management agencies
▲ The role of the emergency manager in using technology
▲ The pitfalls of technology
▲ How to use technology to overcome organizational boundaries
▲ How to manage technology to ensure the technology contributes to the emergency management environment

After Studying This Chapter, You'll Be Able To

▲ Examine the reasons why emergency management agencies may be slow to implement technology.
▲ Examine ways to adapt to change and help your organization adapt to change.
▲ Compare and contrast the work qualities of humans and machines.
▲ Analyze ways to use technology to overcome organizational boundaries.
▲ Analyze the risks of heavy dependence on technology.

Goals and Outcomes

▲ Design technology around your organization
▲ Assess the contingency approach and how to implement it

▲ Assess strategies to address common technology problems
▲ Select technology to support your organizational needs
▲ Assess the pitfalls of technology and how to overcome them to ensure technology meets your needs

INTRODUCTION

Technology allows us to do things we never before dreamed of. You can send volumes of information around the world within seconds. You can use satellites to take pictures of storms as they move through areas. You can communicate anywhere and anytime. And yet, technology is not the answer to all of our challenges. In fact, along with using technology comes a unique set of challenges. In this chapter, you will examine problems that you may encounter in using technology. Strategies to prevent and minimize the adverse impact of these problems will be presented. Recommendations for enhancing the use of technology will also be provided.

10.1 Barriers in Implementing Technology in Emergency Management

It is difficult to imagine what our lives would be like without the information revolution we have experienced over the past 40 years. It is even more difficult to imagine the state of emergency management without the technological advances of the past three decades. For example, can you imagine working without e-mail? Can you imagine rushing to a disaster without a cell phone? Can you imagine trying to predict the path of a hurricane without access to the Web, the Weather Channel, or satellite images?

Technology is crucial. It provides an important way to link our internal system with our external partners. We have faster and more reliable access to others via phone and wireless Internet connectivity. The technology provides you with broad access to data. We also have the increased ability to collect data. This not only provides improved communication but also gives you additional flexibility. All organizations are heavily dependent on communications. The technology enables even small emergency management operations to function effectively.

You can also use highly specialized technology, such as hazard modeling, Geographic Information Systems (GIS), and remote sensing, that often requires expertise that takes years to develop. We supervise more specialists and become more interdependent with the expertise of others in our systems.

The ease of use of technology is critical. So much of the technology that is being used has come from highly technical research efforts. The technical development staff must package the technology in an easy-to-use manner. It will still, however, require training and support.

With technology, the data quality and availability is essential to any user. Documenting the source of the data and knowing its intended use should be understood by the emergency manager, especially where property and lives are at risk.

As amazing as technology is, it cannot solve all of our problems. In fact, technology brings us its own set of problems. Christopher Reddick (2011) identifies several barriers to implementing technology effectively in emergency management. These include:

▲ Lack of applicable and comprehensive technologies available
▲ Lack of expertise in managing technology
▲ Lack of support from elected officials
▲ Lack of collaboration with other levels of government
▲ Difficulty justifying return on investment
▲ Staff resistance to change
▲ Issues regarding privacy and security
▲ Lack of financial resources
▲ Community resistance
▲ Problems with data quality/quantity
▲ Interoperability in communications systems
▲ Technological obsolescence

Interestingly, when emergency managers were surveyed, they considered economic, political, and social barriers such as financial resources, support from elected officials, collaboration with levels of government, and privacy and security issues, to be greater obstacles to implementing technology than problems with the tools themselves or their ability to use them.

One important technology that has emerged in recent years which transcends many of these barriers is social media. Applications such as Facebook and Twitter are powerful tools for communication that have grown with unprecedented popularity. This technology is free to the public, easy to use, and can contribute to the dissemination of relevant and timely information to the public regarding emergency situations.

To depict the value of the speed at which social media can communicate important information, Jafarzadeh (2011) references an instance in 2008 when an American citizen broke the story of an earthquake in China on his Twitter account an hour before CNN was able to report on it. Recognizing the value of this resource, top officials from the Federal Emergency Management Agency (FEMA) and the Department of Homeland Security have advocated the use of social media in emergency management, a significant show of political support for the technology from the federal government. Despite these advantages, most emergency management agencies have resisted adopting this technology in preparing for and responding to disasters. Jafarzadeh establishes four reasons for this resistance:

▲ Skepticism regarding its usefulness
▲ Resource limitations
▲ Public relations
▲ Legal concerns

Lindell and Perry completed a study in 2001 in which they took data from the Local Emergency Planning Chairs in Illinois, Indiana, and Michigan (Lindell and Perry, 2001). This data indicated that only 59% of the local emergency planning committees (LEPCs) had used technology to calculate vulnerable zones around their community's hazmat facilities. Of those who had calculated them, only 36% used computer models such as Computer Aided Management of Emergency Operations (CAMEO); only a small fraction of the LEPCs used computer-based methods to calculate vulnerable zones (Lindell et al., 2006). One could argue that this is in part because of the extensive training using models requires. However, emergency managers also fail to consistently perform simpler tasks such as posting hazard information to local Web sites (Lindell et al., 2006). Lindell's work further investigates the use of common computer applications such as word processing programs.

FOR EXAMPLE

Budgets and Technology

It can be especially difficult to receive approval for the necessary funds to buy the technology your organization needs. To combat this difficulty, first determine what types of technology your office needs and determine what the priorities are. You will have an easier time receiving approval for one or two technology solutions versus many pieces of equipment, software, or an expensive decision support system. If you do need a technology solution that is very expensive, build support before the proposal comes up for a vote and write a strong proposal as to why it is needed and how much money the solution could potentially save as well as the lives it could save.

Emergency managers most consistently and frequently use word processing applications, e-mail, databases, and spreadsheets. Lindell et al. (2006) refers to these applications as Category 1 applications. Category 2 applications include desktop publishing and statistical analysis. Infrequently used, more complex systems such as GIS, hazard modeling, and CAMEO are Category 3 applications. Lindell found that agencies do not appear to use Category 3 applications unless they have used Category 1 and 2 applications extensively. Clearly, you can anticipate encountering problems and hesitation in applying technology.

10.2 The Role of the Emergency Manager in Using Technology

Kim et al. (2011) establish a framework describing the socio-technical systems that contribute to effective emergency management. The framework centers on the use of technology as a tool in task accomplishment and in the sharing of pertinent information that informs decision making.

McCauley-Bush et al. (2012) identify a series of organizational needs that emergency managers must ensure are met to optimize the use of technology during a disaster. These needs include:

▲ Protocols for interagency communication
▲ Integration linkage of information
▲ Standardization of information
▲ Mobile communication devices
▲ Training programs
▲ Analysis of information fluency during the predisaster phase
▲ Protocols for disseminating information to the public

Meeting these needs is essential to the role of the emergency manager in order for technology to be used effectively in the case of a disaster.

Hurricane Katrina was the most destructive hurricane in our history. Communities from Alabama to Louisiana had extensive damage to residential and business structures as well as highway and rail bridges. The levee breaches in New Orleans had unprecedented catastrophic impacts. After-action reports by response agencies clarified many ways that emergency response efforts could be improved. In fact, these agencies acknowledged the use of technology to simulate a similar disaster. In 2004, federal, state, and local agencies used SLOSH (sea, lake, and overland surges from hurricanes) and other hurricane models to simulate a hurricane in a disaster exercise. The exercise, Hurricane Pam, had sustained winds of 120 mph. It produced up to 20 inches of rain in parts of southeast Louisiana. The storm surge topped levees in New Orleans. More than 1 million people had to evacuate the city in the exercise. The hurricane exercise scenario destroyed 500 000–600 000 buildings. If this scenario sounds familiar, it is because it is close to what happened a year later during the real Hurricane Katrina.

The Hurricane Pam exercise involved an extensive use of technology and planning. However, much more was needed to be prepared for Hurricane Katrina, which hit the Gulf of Mexico coastline in August 2005. Although many plans were developed following the exercise, it did not lead to the type of preparedness required by the devastating impacts from Hurricane Katrina. This is a perfect example of why the success of organizations is complex and depends on many factors.

Effective emergency management relies on a combination of competent, hardworking professionals who can use the technology they need to achieve their goals. Public, private, and nonprofit organizations are not like mechanical or natural biological systems; they are intentionally created by people. The fact that **social organizations** are created by human beings suggests that they can be established for many different objectives; further, they do not follow the same life-cycle pattern of birth, maturity, and death as do biological systems.

Social systems are imperfect systems. The cement that holds them together is essentially psychological rather than biological or physical. They are anchored in the attitudes, perceptions, beliefs, motivations, habits, and expectations of human beings. The key is to appreciate and use technology to keep the system together.

The designers of many technology systems often infer or openly state that there is a best way to solve a problem. The assumption that there is a "one-best way" approach does not recognize the adaptability of technology systems. It does not recognize that an effective solution could be achieved by alternate approaches. In fact, the best approach depends on many factors.

The use of GIS in local governments provides an excellent example of this **"one-best" consideration**. Mapping and GIS continues to grow in use at the local level. How to set up a mapping system depends on many focal factors. No one approach fits all local factors. Developing a comprehensive mapping capability at the local level can be organized in many different ways. One way is to centralize the function in the chief executive's office. It could also be decentralized in many departments. These departments could be planning, public safety, utilities, public works, and emergency management.

Since many local governments have a limited number of staff, designating one unit to serve the local government has proven to be one excellent approach. The best approach depends again on the goals and capabilities of the local government units and their willingness to assume a new role.

As an emergency manager, you know to expect the unexpected. You must be prepared to adapt in emergencies, crises, and disasters. Organizations must have adaptive mechanisms, processes and procedures that keep the system from changing too rapidly or slowly as required and allow the operation to adjust and not get out of balance. It also prevents the system from changing so slowly as to be ineffective in a response.

For example, warning systems can be designed to provide immediate notification of an accidental hazmat release from a facility. Sirens and loudspeakers can be an effective component of an integrated alert system, when combined with education/advertising efforts that inform the members of the population what to do when they hear a siren.

Basic systems such as neighborhood or fire station sirens should not be disregarded as an outdated mode of communication, as they could be the only means of notification that a vulnerable member of the community, such as a homeless person, receives during a disaster (Kiefer et al., 2008).

An adaptive system can also be created to provide backup of critical data.

The data can be backed up to another city or to a critical Web site that can be activated when disaster strikes. An **adaptive mechanism** is created to ensure that the operations center can run when disaster strikes. You need an adaptive mechanism for when normal staffing patterns will not work because of snow, flooding, or sickness that keeps people at home.

10.2.1 Managing an Organization

The view of an organization as a system suggests a very special role for you. You must deal with uncertainties and ambiguities. You must be concerned with adapting the organization to new and changing requirements. Management is a process. The basic function of management is to align not only people, but also the institution itself, including technology, processes, and structure. It attempts to reduce uncertainty while at the same time searching for flexibility.

Comfort points out that a robust information infrastructure is vital for reducing discrepancies among emergency managers. It enables them to access valid and timely information, while at the same time strengthens the capacity of the stakeholders to exchange and search for information (Comfort, 2002).

Organizations face a significant barrier in attempting to bring change to themselves. Reengineering occurs when we introduce new technologies and change the system (Champy, 1996). This barrier is management itself. New technologies require a new configuration and change. The introduction of new technologies provides an opportunity to reassess the emergency management process. You can also assess the role of technology. You must get close to the nature of change so that a full understanding of the implications of the change can be understood. You will need details to understand but you also really need breadth and perspective. You should examine the impact that the technology will have on the current system and how this change can be implemented effectively. These efforts are also known as **support mechanisms**, or efforts initiated by an organization to ensure that the operation functions efficiently and effectively.

Regardless of the organization or the system, there will be failures. Whether you are relying on a host of highly skilled professionals to respond effectively or whether you are using a hazard model, there will be failures. Many experts believe that failures of complex systems are inevitable. Failure happens regardless of the care of operations and the redundancy of safety mechanisms. One may thus assume that the system will fail; planning for alternative means of achieving goals is thus needed. Planning is the key.

FOR EXAMPLE

Adaptive Mechanisms and Staffing

In working with staff members, you have to remember that people are human and not machines. People can easily become ill, not be able to get to work, or have some emergency that prevents them from working their scheduled hours. Because of this, you must have alternative staffing plans, especially when disaster strikes. For the most crucial positions, you will want to cross-train other staff members so you have all the critical job responsibilities covered during a crisis. You will also want to ensure staff members are cross-trained on the software programs and other technology solutions you will need implemented during a crisis.

10.3 Using Technology to Overcome Organizational Boundaries

All organizations have their own "turf." They have boundaries, domains, or regions that define their activities. These boundaries separate communication and interaction between those on the inside and people on the outside. There are many examples of ineffective use of technology for communications between organizations. Technology can be used to bridge these natural barriers. Technology can facilitate transactions necessary for organization functioning.

Technology offers you and others from different groups a way to work together despite jurisdictional boundaries. A regional shelter task force illustrates this concept. The regional shelter task force is composed of local emergency managers who represent different regions of the state. When disaster strikes, the task force is activated. Frequent communication and coordination is facilitated by phone conference calls, electronic mail, and even video conferences.

The task force chair can use technology to communicate beyond individual organizations. This keeps members up-to-date on current needs and polls members on input to problems. The task force uses e-mail as the primary means of communication. It allows all users quick access to information. E-mail is also easier to manage than frequent telephone calls.

The key is that each use of technology is a normal part of operations and not something new brought out in a disaster. Problems with technology can be minimized by looking for ways to bring technology into normal everyday operations.

FOR EXAMPLE

Use of E-mail

E-mail is a great tool. GIS support staff at state and federal agencies across the United States used e-mail to communicate during Hurricane Katrina. The Operations Center in New Orleans was too busy, noisy, and crowded for all these staff to work effectively. Instead, staff worked from many locations, including the campus a few miles away, and sent maps or reports by e-mail to one another and especially to the State Operations Center. E-mail proved to be a fast means of communications. A record of each communication was maintained on computers in the Operations Center and the Louisiana State University (LSU) campus. Fortunately, both the LSU campus and the Operations Center had electrical power and Internet connectivity.

10.4 Pitfalls of Technology

Despite the fact that we can accomplish many goals with the use of technology, technology can cause us problems in emergency management. There are risks associated with any dependence on technology. Understanding how an organization is vulnerable to technology is just as important as what the technology can do for you. You should always design a backup system just in case the technology does not work.

10.4.1 Reliance on Technology

You can take advantage of mobile communication devices to stay in touch such as accessing e-mail remotely. You can also link directly to remote weather and hazard sensors so as to monitor a developing crisis. As you use the technologies, you will become even more dependent on accessing critical information. You are then more vulnerable when the connection to the remote source of information is terminated.

A strategy for alternative access to critical data must be made prior to an emergency. Difficulties in exchanging timely and accurate disaster-relevant information can inhibit coordination. On the other hand, technologies that integrate computers, people, and organizations can be important to ensuring effective response and recovery by allowing emergency managers to communicate across a broad range of distances and organizations (Celik and Corbacioglu, 2010).

10.4.2 Obsolescence

Systems have a life cycle. A **system life cycle** is a time period in which the elements of a system—including software, hardware, or organizational conditions—change, requiring upgrades or operational changes. To help avoid obsolesce within a system life cycle, purchase new computers for critical needs and utilize older ones where they can be used effectively.

Know that as one upgrades computers or software, unexpected problems can be encountered. Test and retest your upgraded systems to ensure that everything works as intended.

10.4.3 Information Overload

Cutter argues that even basic data on the extent and range of hazards has not kept pace with the needs of emergency managers (Cutter et al., 2003). Yet this increasing attention to technology may inadvertently result in information overload. As an illustration, we often use chemical databases to provide detailed information on hazardous substances in a chemical spill. Information from multiple sources may be confusing. The information may be far more detailed than is required. Often the sheer amount of data within an emergency management information system overwhelms the ability of officials to analyze that data (Zagorecki et al., 2013).

10.4.4 Data Integration

Many organizations have been struggling to cope with increasing demands for timely and accurate data. In many cases, the data needed for timely decisions is distributed to multiple units. Maintaining integration between these units is critical in times of crisis. As we prepare for disasters and crisis, we will need to examine what data will be needed. We will also need to know how we can link our operations. The key is to recognize that we are increasing working in a shared and distributed environment. Documentation on the sources of data and data types will be critical. This will ensure that information is used for its intended purpose.

Data sharing and integration between local government units is always an issue. Cooperation between law enforcement and other public safety and social service agencies varies in each community. A critical task for you is to develop a cooperative spirit between these agencies to support emergency management activities.

10.4.5 Real-Time Response Data

You cannot make effective decisions without accurate information. Your information must be current and must reflect the precise situations that are occurring at that moment. Real-time response data enhances the basis for decision making.

Technology allows you access to real-time response data. Lack of access to updated weather data, traffic flow, or modeling applications could inhibit effective evacuation or sheltering decisions.

If the computer fails, you will not be able to get this information. If you experience a loss of power, connectivity, or if the computer system fails, then you will not be able to use the computer to get access to the data. You must plan for alternative methods for obtaining information for these critical functions.

10.4.6 Security

Sensitive data exists on office computers. Limiting access to parts of the network may be required to ensure that the business operation is not compromised and remains secure. The application of technology does come with security risks. Perry and Lindell (2003) argue that accurate knowledge of the threat environment is essential to ensuring security of operations.

FOR EXAMPLE

Real-Time Data

The United States Geologic Survey (USGS) provides information on water levels in streams and rivers through their river gage system. Direct online access to this data is available through the Internet. You can use this data to determine road and bridge closings, warnings to the community, evacuation orders, and routing. Access to this data source is critical to communities that are subject to periodic flooding.

10.5 Managing the Technology

Organizational systems, including emergency management agencies, may be characterized as human or mechanistic-centered operations. For an organization to operate well, it must take into account the strengths of both people and machines (Alter, 1996).

Gopalakrishnan and Okada (2007) highlight several weaknesses in the disaster management environment. These include:

▲ Lack of coordination
▲ Jurisdictional overlap
▲ Duplication of responsibilities among management agencies at different levels
▲ The minimal role played by local entities

They argue there are at least eight institutional design elements they believe can address these weaknesses. These are:

▲ Awareness/Access: GIS, GPS, remote sensing technology, and wireless communications technology can be used to provide decision makers with access to the information they need to become aware of emergency situations so that they may prioritize the distribution of resources according to the most urgent needs.
▲ Autonomy: When technologies such as area-specific disaster simulation models and interorganizational communications networks are applied and established in advance of a disaster, local plans can be disseminated to state and federal agencies. Through the preparedness that they exhibit to regional and national government officials, the products of these technologies can empower local agencies with the authority to make localized decisions in disaster situations without having to gain permission from higher-level authorities.
▲ Affordability: Simple computer technology such as databases and spreadsheets can track compliance to building codes that increase public safety during a disaster and decrease the economic costs of large-scale emergencies. This technology makes it possible to implement and enforce legislation that will save millions of dollars in the aftermath of a disaster. Additionally, on a smaller scale, technology saves time, which has increased monetary value during disasters (many workers are paid time and a half for overtime work required when disaster strikes). Time saved by technology is money saved by agencies and organizations.
▲ Accountability: Technology such as e-mails and even community use of social media provide verifiable records of disaster response actions, considerations, and decision making. Such records contribute to accountability not only through the content they document, but also by time stamping the evidence.
▲ Adaptability: The implementation of an extensive diversity of technologies can help communications networks remain flexible in times of large-scale emergencies. For example, if phone lines go out, cell phones can be used, and if cell phone networks go out, radios can be used. Having several options for the different technologies accessible helps the emergency management system remain adaptable.
▲ Efficiency: Communication technology can help prevent jurisdictional overlap and duplication of responsibilities, which often lead to inefficiencies in disaster management. Additionally, simulation technology can help interorganizational disaster management networks plan ahead in order to avoid inefficiencies, interagency squabbling, and passing the buck, all of which impede efficient emergency management.

▲ Equity: Vulnerable populations are often poor and have limited access to much of the popular technology used to disseminate public information about emergencies. For this reason, it is important not to disregard the value of outdated (and therefore less expensive) technologies such as AM/FM radio communications and news on local (noncable) television stations (Kiefer et al., 2008).

▲ Sustainability: As technology evolves, the intelligence of our technological devices grows at an exponential rate. Each generation of technology applied is improved upon and more closely adapted to our needs. Technology contributes to the sustainability of disaster management environments by providing a more comprehensive understanding of the disaster situation and by helping managers to build the relationships necessary to respond to those situations.

Finally, in order to bring these elements to life, emergency managers must consistently assess the status of the information technology they use. Santos et al. (2011) enumerate a number of technological functions in need of regular evaluation:

▲ Information capture
▲ Information storage
▲ Information dissemination
▲ Information quality
▲ Interorganizational information
▲ Previous information

The performance of your organization's technology is dependent on ensuring that these technological functions are in place. Addressing the elements outlined here will help to give an understanding of the maturity of your organization and will allow you to prioritize what investments are necessary in order to be better prepared for the disaster management environment.

FOR EXAMPLE

Security and Management Controls

Many emergency 911 operations provide an excellent illustration of how to introduce security and management controls. Through technology, 911 operations use caller identification (ID) as a management control. This allows the operators to determine callers are who they claim to be.

Emergency operators computerized mapping systems. They have up-to-date street and road addresses so as to verify the caller's address. They have photographs of the local community for use in GIS. And they have easy-to-use communication systems that provide quick access to response agencies.

Their rapid introduction and adaptation to new technologies using security and management controls together demonstrate that technology systems can be effective. Emergency management can embrace similar new tools to enhance their operations.

SUMMARY

While technology offers you many tools, you must choose and implement technologies that work for you. In this chapter, you examined reasons why emergency managers can be slow in implementing technology. You also examined ways to overcome reluctance to use technology. You assessed the pitfalls of technology and how to avoid them. You examined how technology can be used to overcome organizational boundaries. You also assessed ways to evaluate technology with your office's goals and priorities in mind.

KEY TERMS

Adaptive mechanisms	Processes and procedures in an organization that keep the system from changing too rapidly or slowly, and allow the operation to adjust and not get out of balance.
Social organizations	Social organizations are created by human beings and may be established for many different objectives. They do not follow the same life-cycle pattern of birth, maturity, and death as do biological systems.
Support mechanisms	Efforts initiated by an organization to ensure that the operation functions efficiently and effectively.
System life cycle	A time period in which elements of a system—including software, hardware, or organizational conditions—change, requiring upgrades or operational changes.

ASSESS YOUR UNDERSTANDING

Go to www.wiley.com/go/pine/tech&emergmgmt_2e to evaluate your knowledge of using technology. This website contains MCQ's, self checks, review questions, applying this chapter and you try it.

References

Alter, S. (1996). *Information Systems: A Management Perspective.* Menlo Park, CA: Benjamin/Cummings.

Celik, S., & Corbacioglu, S. (2010). Role of information in collective action in dynamic disaster environments. *Disasters, 34*(1), 137–154.

Champy, J. A. (1996). *Reengineering Management: The Mandate for New Leadership.* New York: HarperCollins.

Comfort, L. K. (2002). Managing intergovernmental responses to terrorism and other extreme events. *Publius: The Journal of Federalism, 32*(4), 29–50.

Cutter, S. L., Boruff, B. J., & Shirley, W. L. (2003). Social vulnerability to environmental hazards. *Social Science Quarterly*, *84*(2), 242–261. Doi:10.1111/1540-6237.8402002.

Gopalakrishnan, C., & Okada, N. (2007). Designing new institutions for implementing integrated disaster risk management: Key elements and future directions. *Disasters*, *31*, 353–372. Doi: 10.1111/j.1467-7717.2007.01013.x

Jafarzadeh, R. S. (2011). Emergency management 2.0: Integrating social media in emergency communications. *Journal of Emergency Management*, *9*(4), 13–16.

Kiefer, J. J., Mancini, J. A., Morrow, B. H., Gladwin, H., & Stewart, T. A. (2008). *Providing Access to Resilience-Enhancing Technologies for Disadvantaged Communities and Vulnerable Populations*. Oak Ridge, TN: Community & Regional Resilience Initiative, Oak Ridge National Laboratory. Retrieved May 1, 2017 from http://www.isce.vt.edu/files/Kiefer,Mancini,%20Morrow,%20Gladwin,%20&%20Stewart,%202008.pdf.

Kim, M., Sharman, R., Cook-Cottone, C. P., Rao, H. R., & Upadhyaya, S. J. (2011). Assessing roles of people, technology and structure in emergency management systems: A public sector perspective. *Behaviour & Information Technology*, *31*(12), 1147–1160. Doi: 10.1080/0144929X.2010.510209.

Lindell, M. K., & Perry, R. W. (2001). Community innovation in hazardous materials management: Progress in implementing SARA Title III in the United States. *Journal of Hazardous Materials*, *88*(2), 169–194.

Lindell, M. K., Prater, C., & Perry, R. W. (2006). *Wiley Pathways Introduction to Emergency Management*. Hoboken, NJ: John Wiley & Sons, Inc.

McCauley-Bush, P., Jeelani, M., Gaines, S., Curling, L., Armbrister, P., Watlington, A., Major, R., Rolle, L., & Sarah, C. (2012, January/February). Assessment of communication needs for emergency management officials in high-consequence. *Journal of Emergency Management*, *10*, 15–25.

Perry, R. W., & Lindell, M. K. (2003). Preparedness for emergency response: Guidelines for the emergency planning process. *Disasters*, *27*(4), 336–350.

Reddick, C. (2011). Information technology and emergency management: Preparedness and planning in US states. *Disasters*, *35*, 45–61.

Santos, S. P., Amado, C. A. F., & Rosado, J. R. (2011). Formative evaluation of electricity distribution utilities using data envelopment analysis. *Journal of the Operational Research Society*, *62*(7), 1298–1319.

Zagorecki, A. T., Johnson, D. E., & Ristvej, J. (2013). Data mining and machine learning in the context of disaster and crisis management. *International Journal of Emergency Management*, *9*(4), 351–365.

11

TRENDS IN TECHNOLOGY: NEW TOOLS FOR CHALLENGES TO EMERGENCY MANAGEMENT

Starting Point

Go to www.wiley.com/go/pine/tech&emergmgmt_2e to assess your knowledge of trends in technology.
Determine where to concentrate your effort.

What You'll Learn in This Chapter

▲ Types of information exchange
▲ Benefits of mapping technology
▲ Sources of emergency management information on the Internet
▲ The need to build organizational collaboration and coordination

After Studying This Chapter; You'll Be Able To

▲ Appraise the use of emergency management technologies.
▲ Understand the value of using visualization technologies.
▲ Examine how information exchange can be used to acquire new knowledge and skills.
▲ Manage new technology in an effective way, ensuring that technology supports personnel effectively.

Goals and Outcomes

▲ Increase your knowledge of emergency management through information exchange
▲ Evaluate how to use visualization, geospatial, and modeling technologies in a disaster
▲ Understand the limits of technology in responding to and managing disasters

Technology and Emergency Management, Second Edition. John C. Pine.
© 2018 John Wiley & Sons, Inc. Published 2018 by John Wiley & Sons, Inc.
Companion website: www.wiley.com/go/pine/tech&emergmgmt_2e

INTRODUCTION

Technology applications are constantly changing. New developments, including communications, information access, training, and modeling, will offer you new tools that may improve your operations. With the new tools, you will be able to communicate more quickly and reliably. Software innovations will continue in communications, modeling, and mapping. You will see more accurate maps, images, and critical infrastructure location data, which will allow for more accurate modeling of both hazards and community vulnerabilities. In this chapter, you will examine ways you can further your knowledge and practice of emergency management through *information exchange*. This will be explored through online information access to digital libraries, Web-based learning, management strategies for information collaborations, and new ways to enhance situational awareness. Finally, you will look at ways to manage the technology so it enhances your workflow rather than becomes a burden.

11.1 Using Technology for Information Exchange

In discussing how to meet national needs for the exchange of information in the coming decade, the focus is shifting from "networks" to "information infrastructure." This means that the emergency management system will depend on networks (Vogt et al., 2011) and information exchange (Lee et al., 2011). It will also involve more than networks. An information infrastructure makes use of communications networks that support other services and access to information. Therefore, you will continue to see innovations. These could be in communicating using wireless technology or running complex models over networks. This will enable to move beyond the simple transfer of data. You can use mapping, modeling, or communicating technology. This will help you solve problems easily and quickly. You will see new applications on the Internet that take advantage of these developments to provide information, research, and education (Inan et al., 2016). The Web provides us with an extensive choice of information services. Simple search capabilities allow the user to find a list of resources relating to any topic. The Internet is also providing innovative examples of information exchange.

Xu et al. (2015) stresses that the growth of the Internet of Things has been complemented by hardware integration and software encapsulation; cloud asset could sense its real-time status, adapt to varied working scenarios, be controlled remotely, and shared among agencies. It enables accurate real-time control of every asset, and thus improves the management efficiency and effectiveness. One of the most important goals of proposing cloud asset is improving the management efficiency of physical assets, and finally facilitating the workflow management in urban flood control.

In their study of cloud computing and urban floods, the observed that there was a difference from the traditional production processes, where the working scenarios in urban flood control are usually varied and unpredictable. As a result, the workflows change frequently, which not only requires assets that flexibly adapt to different workflows, but also expects assets that actively improve the workflow according to these scenarios. Besides, considering the emergency situations in urban flood control, the matching process of workflow with physical assets should also be done in a very short period of time.

11.1.1 Emergency Preparedness Information Exchange

State emergency management agencies in the United States play a key role in information exchange in a disaster. State offices of emergency preparedness provide ongoing information to local disaster agencies, nonprofit agencies, professional organizations, and business enterprises on new approaches and tools that can enhance emergency planning, response, and recovery. Information exchange may also be see on an international level as illustrated by the Disaster Recovery Information Exchange (DRIE), along with its affiliates the Business Continuity Management Information Exchange (BCMIE) and le Réseau d'Échange en Continuité des Opérations (RÉCO-QUÉBEC), which is a nonprofit association of professionals dedicated to the exchange of information on all aspects of business continuity management, from emergency response to the resumption of business as normal.

11.1.2 Television and Internet Information

Newspapers, television organizations, and cable providers give users information. These media allow users to obtain current information instantaneously. Users can monitor extreme weather, emergency incidents, or other regional incidents. Today, many Internet providers give real-time information on developments in a disaster. Many of us look to www.weather.com for current information on local or regional weather conditions. Even local media provide current news stories or updates on disasters worldwide.

11.1.3 Digital Libraries and Publications

The digital environment of the Web is an excellent means of making information available. A **digital library** is a Web-based storage system that enables you to search for books, articles, studies, and videos, similar to the services provided by a conventional library. Borbinha and Delgado (1996) contends that these digital libraries can go well beyond just the preservation and dissemination of knowledge. Digital libraries include depositories of books, research articles, and research papers that are maintained in digital formats and available online. These libraries and depositories are active partners with the potential to stimulate, support, and register the process of creation of that knowledge. Users of the library can view the data/knowledge from different perspectives. Users can raise complex questions that can lead to answers.

The digital library is an "assemblage of digital computing, storage, and communications technologies together with the content and software needed to reproduce, emulate, and extend the services provided by conventional libraries based on paper and other material means of collecting, cataloging, finding, and disseminating information. A full service digital library must accomplish all essential services of the traditional libraries and also exploit the well-known advantages of digital storage, searching and communications" (Gladney et al., 1994).

Borbinha and Delgado (1996) suggests that technology can convert our memory and knowledge to a digital format and store it at an affordable cost. The resulting digital format may be made available to everyone through the Internet, CDs, or by other electronic means. Borbinha wrote, "Computers were first introduced in libraries to help in the management of catalogues ... Finally, the technology brought digital publication. It became easy to write a text, to be stored in a server, and to have it accessible worldwide."

Libraries are also index databases. This allows users the opportunity to find specific information for their use. In addition, the digital library may include photos, maps, or other graphics in a compressed digital format.

FOR EXAMPLE

Digital Information Resources

1. *Natural Hazards Center at the University of Colorado, Boulder*. Universities are one of the largest sources of information and a few like the *University of Colorado in Boulder* have hazard resources available via the Web. The *Natural Hazards Center* at the University of Colorado has a Natural Hazards Center that has a diverse set of resources for any organization interested in emergency management. A few of their resources useful to emergency managers include:

   Natural Hazards Observer: A bimonthly free publication, the *Observer* carries current information on disaster issues.

   Digital Library: Identifying and archiving research publications is one of the main goals of the Center. The staff works toward this goal by editing and publishing many types of books, reports, and bibliographies. These materials are designed to provide information to a wide range of readers. They produce works that appeal to everyone from government officials to emergency managers in private industry. Because they are trying to appeal to this wide audience, the books are edited and produced in nontechnical language. For more information see http://hazlib.colorado.edu/.

2. *The Consortium for International Earth Science Information Network*

   The Center for International Earth Science Information Network (CIESIN) is a center within the Earth Institute at Columbia University. CIESIN works at the intersection of the social, natural, and information sciences, and specializes in online data and information management, spatial data integration and training, and interdisciplinary research related to human interactions in the environment. Extensive datasets are available not only for the United States but worldwide. For more information see: http://www.ciesin.org/.

3. *The Emergency Management Institute within the Federal Emergency Management Agency (FEMA)* has established an online library. This enables you to search for books, articles, studies, and videos at the Learning Resource Center. This collection may be searched at www.lrc.fema.gov.
4. *Emerald Publishing*: Emergency management journals, newsletters, and bulletins are going online. Emerald Publishing manages over 400 journals. These journals include *Environmental Management* and *Health* and *Disaster Prevention and Management*. Users subscribe to a journal and have access to the journal articles in a digital format.

11.2 Distance Learning

It can be argued that one of the most significant forms of information exchange is distance learning. **Distance learning** is an extended learning effort that includes everything from self-paced individual learning to forums or chat rooms that bring together students and instructors. Students and instructors use the Web to allow more timely access to learning and a digital classroom environment. Several groups have initiated innovative extended learning efforts that bring together informed experts. The future may include a new form of classroom that uses the Internet to allow more timely access to learning.

Introductions to topics associated with disasters are available on the Internet. The ease of access to education without leaving home is invaluable to individuals interested in learning and keeping up on the latest news. Tutorials are available from FEMA at the National Emergency Training Center, the National Weather Service, the United States Geological Survey (USGS), universities, and many not-for-profit groups.

Today, many conferences are available on the Internet in real time. Regardless of where you are, you can log on. You can view the presentation and discussion. Or you can tune in later and view a digital recording. Technology also exists that allows you to communicate directly with the speakers.

Although we frequently associate distance learning with obtaining educational degrees, distance learning can also be used for training. Through Web-based technologies, you can take part in a training session with professionals regionally, nationally, and internationally.

FEMA has recognized the need for making training more available to public, private, and nonprofit agencies. More classes are going online and are available at a distance from the Emergency Management Institute in Emmitsburg, Maryland. Some of the classes are available on an independent study basis.

11.2.1 Using Remote Technology

With the help of the Internet, you can also work remotely. You can now use hazard modeling, mapping, and decision support systems on individual computers. Rather than install and run separate programs on a user's computer, you can now go to

centralized Web-based systems. A centralized Web-based system is a Web-based program that runs hazard models, Geographic Information Systems (GIS), and decision support systems on a centralized system rather than on a single-user computer. You can use a centralized Web-based system to understand the depth of the water in a geographic area, find addresses and transportation routes, and determine the dangers associated with a hazardous substance. Access to many of these tools is open to anyone. The tools are easy to use. In the future, you may be able to utilize each of the following types of technology from our wireless phones or other small-computer technologies. It seems impossible now, but consider the types of modeling, mapping, and decision support systems that you use over the Internet. In the near future, you should be able to obtain information for decision support from the field, the classroom, or in your cars or planes. What seems impossible today may be here sooner than you think.

11.2.2 Disaster Situational Maps

Public agencies use Web-based mapping approaches to share information on recent and historic hazard events. You can understand current hazard events through static maps as illustrated by the following examples. Some of the maps show the location of current disasters. Others show maps explaining the potential for hazard events to occur (such as wildfires or earthquakes).

The National Interagency Fire Center provides up-to-date information on current wildfires. Figure 11-1 shows an example of a current fire location in a map format. The use of national mapping programs provides critical information. See www.nifc. gov/firemaps.html for a list of the types of map products that are available for fire hazards. For additional information on fire maps, see http://activefiremaps.fs.fed.us/.

Many federal agencies and universities have applied Web-based mapping technology to show current conditions of hazardous events similar to the large wildfire map in Figure 11-1 shows the status of drought in the United States and provides a nationwide perspective on wildfire conditions on a national scale. This type of information is critical to state and local emergency management staff as well as private landowners and organizations engaged in forest product processing.

Note: Along with the visual map of drought conditions in the United States the Web site also includes a weather outlook. A series of fast-moving Pacific storm systems raced eastward across the lower 48 states this week, bringing light to moderate precipitation to the Northwest, California, and along the southern tier of states. Once the systems reached the Southeast, they tapped moisture from the Gulf of Mexico and produced widespread and numerous heavy showers and thunderstorms, some severe, from southeastern Texas northeastward into the Carolinas. Copious rains fell across much of the Southeast, with more than 4 inches measured from extreme southeastern Texas northeastward into south-central South Carolina. Locally, 7–12 inches of rain was dumped on southern Mississippi northeastward into west-central Georgia. These rains fell on much of the Southeast drought area and provided welcome relief, especially in southern sections. Lighter precipitation (0.5–2 inches) also fell on most of the Northeast and Ohio Valley, including heavy snow (up to 2 feet in Maine) that blanketed parts of northern New England. Unfortunately, little or no precipitation fell on the Nation's midsection, particularly the south-central Plains and lower

Figure 11-1

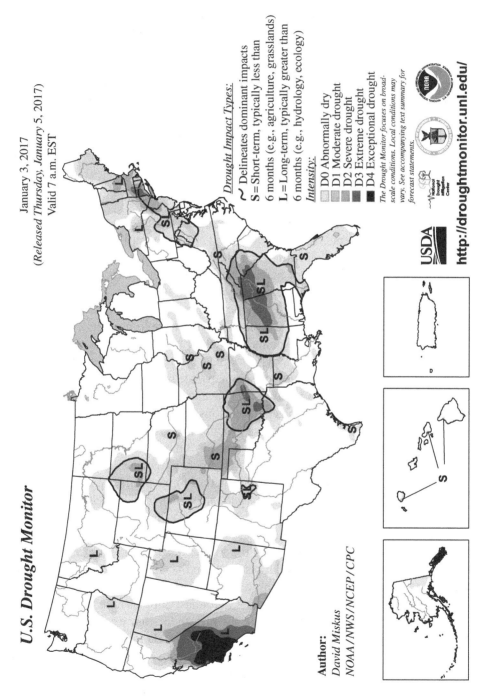

Drought monitoring map of the United States.

Missouri Valley, where above-normal temperatures and lingering dryness dating back to the fall has generated impacts in Oklahoma that were worse than what the data indicated. Weekly temperatures averaged below-normal in the West (anomalies −10 to −15°F in the Interior Northwest and Great Basin) and much above-normal in the eastern half of the Nation (anomalies 10–15°F in the southern Great Plains and along the western half of the Gulf Coast).

11.2.3 Federal Agency Situational Mapping Programs

The National Oceanic and Atmospheric Administration **(NOAA)** has provided maps from the National Hurricane Center to the public for many years that are used by emergency response agencies to understand the development of coastal storms. The image in Figure 11-2 is an example of a hurricane track in 2016 and reflects winds from the storm over time. This type of image is useful to emergency managers to understand the potential impacts of storms in their region. This is also an example of a centralized information source that is simply placed on a public Web site and available to both government officials and the general public. Other hazard images are made available to public officials on restricted Web sites along with training and consultation on the use of the images. Figure 11-3 also reflects

Figure 11-2

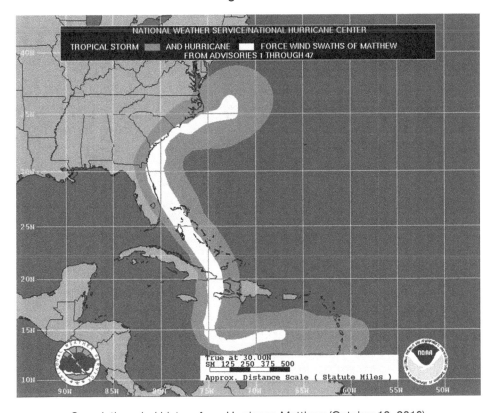

Cumulative wind history from Hurricane Matthew (October 19, 2016).

Figure 11-3

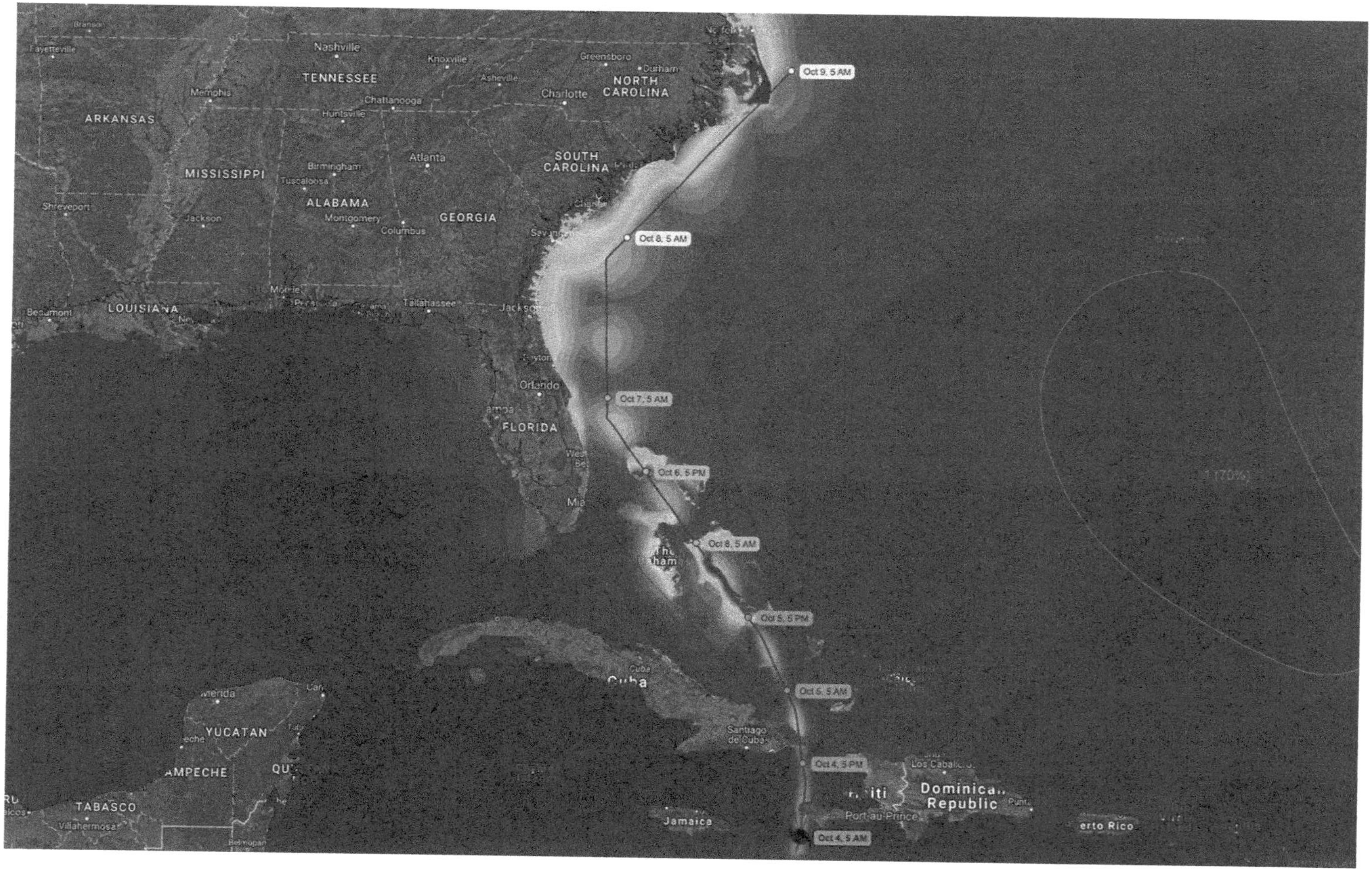

Hurricane storm surge model output (October 4, 2016). Note: ADCIRC projections for storm surge locations and impact from Hurricane Matthew, as seen from the CERA Web site on October 4, 2016.

the impacts of coastal storms and includes additional information that describes predicted flooding in coastal areas.

Federal agency–sponsored modeling of natural hazards has increased in the past 10 years and will likely continue to serve the emergency management community. Modeling efforts described in Chapter 9 of this text notes that modeling of natural and human caused hazards will advance on two fronts. First, more powerful modeling will be available on personal computers and include more dynamic and accurate mapping utilities. At the same time, modeling efforts utilizing super computers and more complex data sources will be developed by federal agencies in collaboration with university research centers. The example provided in Figure 11-3 was supported by the Department of Homeland Security in collaboration with NOAA and their university research partners. The description of the flooding and storm surge impacts from Hurricane Matthew in 2016 was extensively used by Atlantic coastal states and federal agencies. An ongoing collaboration between research entities and public agency users was initiated to ensure that dynamic model output images and data would be used effectively by agency emergency management personnel and public officials.

About the NOAA Image: This graphic shows the geographic area impacted by the storm and how it changes over time. The display is based on the wind radii contained in the set of Forecast/Advisories indicated at the top of the figure. Users are reminded that the Forecast/Advisory wind radii represent the maximum possible extent of a given wind speed within particular quadrants around the tropical cyclone. As a result, not all locations falling within the orange or red swaths will have experienced sustained tropical storm or hurricane force winds, respectively.

FOR EXAMPLE

Support for Hurricane Response and Recovery

Researchers at the Coastal Resilience Center of Excellence (CRC) worked with hurricane forecasters and emergency response officials to track Hurricane Matthew as it made its way through the Caribbean and up Florida to the Carolinas in 2016. Using technology and tools being developed and improved through Center projects, they provided support in the response and recovery process.

The Coastal Emergency Risks Assessment (CERA) group delivers storm surge and wave predictions for impending or active tropical cyclones in the United States. Based on the Advanced Circulation and Storm Surge Model (ADCIRC), the CERA Web application provides an easy-to-use interactive Web interface. Emergency managers, weather forecasters, and GIS specialists retrieve real-time forecasting results to evaluate the impacts of a tropical event or to see the tide, wind-wave, and extra-tropical surge conditions on a daily basis.

Hurricane Matthew has been attributed to more than 1000 deaths in Haiti when it came ashore as a Category 4 storm. Though it slowed as it approached Florida, Georgia, and the Carolinas, the storm has caused more than 30 deaths in the United States, with an initial loss estimate of close to $5 billion.

ADCIRC results are displayed in Figure 11-3: Hurricane Matthew, on the CERA Web site, which was developed and is managed by Louisiana State University, Baton Rouge. This Web site overlays ADCIRC system results on maps of the Atlantic coast and Gulf of Mexico. The development and operation of both the ADCIRC system and the CERA Web site have been partially funded by the Department of Homeland Security.

The results are shared with several groups of professionals, including local emergency management groups, to help local leaders make informed decisions related to road closings, evacuations, and search and rescue. The NOAA, US Coast Guard, US Army Corps of Engineers, and FEMA are among the agencies that factor ADCIRC modeling into their operations.

In the future, emergency managers will have access to national resources such as the CERA Web site, which is supported by federal agencies. Ongoing training is provided to public agency representatives on using the outputs of the ADCIRC hurricane storm model.

11.2.4 Innovative Visualization Efforts

Heard et al. (2014) describe an innovative visualization tool to facilitate collaboration in a disaster response using a shared map of road closures. Standard teleconferencing systems provide a gamut of information-sharing media that include voice and text chat, real-time video, and "shared" slides, applications, and desktops. They observed that information sharing using slides and desktops are usually not collaborative but use just a presentation format, facilitating the dissemination of information, but not interaction or the gathering of knowledge. They describe an alternative that is used in many educational settings which include "presentation with discussion" as one way of to enable collaborations.

Heard's team describes the use of a flexible, collaborative tool for geospatial data called "Big Board" that is based on the gather-and-share paradigm. In a gather-and-share environment, no particular person is the leader of the conference; rather each individual contributes directly to the content of the conference. The Big Board facilitates real-time gather-and-share style collaboration over maps. This approach builds on open source technologies and runs in all modern browsers and standard handheld devices such as smartphones and tablets. A dot on the map indicates a location where road conditions were noted by a human observer. Colors of the dots indicate conditions such as clear, icy, snow, and rain, and mix of rain and snow.

11.2.5 Updating Outputs

The demand for constant updating of information and the need to share expertise in a timely fashion in the crisis management arena means that improvisation work is typical rather than abnormal. Improvisation, then, is a consequence of the demand for real-time, relevant, information (Kawasaki et al., 2012; Ley et al., 2013, 2014).

Wu et al. (2013) observed that there was great value in the collaborative use of visualization tools such as maps. They see that there is a new collaborative system available for teams doing complex geospatial planning tasks. Their process design included a multiview, role-based system that has the potential to improve and extend collaborative tasks in emergency management. The key elements included the following:

▲ Provide both personal (role-specific) and shared (team) maps and support information transfer between them.
▲ Provide tools that allow users to add personal comments and drawings that overlay on maps.
▲ Provide tools for information sorting (e.g., tables) and aggregation (e.g., bar charts and timelines).
▲ Leverage online maps to reduce the burden on technology management and learning.

This Web-based approach offers user-support opportunities to collaborate from diverse devices and platforms. Wu et al. (2013) take a different route, and focus on how Web-based geospatial technological development has changed approaches to disaster response and relief efforts. It demonstrates the growing role of geospatial technologies and shows how such technologies have made possible broader, more focused cooperation in disaster relief support.

A number of studies have outlined the ways in which emerging interactive information technologies such as wiki, Twitter, and blogs have played important roles in disaster response support. Kawasaki et al. (2012) take a different route, and focuses on how Web-based geospatial technological development has changed approaches to disaster response and relief efforts.

These examples remind us that the key is to be aware of our goals and select technology tools and applications that make the best fit. The technology is a means to accomplishing an end. These tools help us to prepare, mitigate, respond, and recover in an efficient and effective manner.

11.3 Managing the Technology

Technology in emergencies has brought many tools that enhance response, recovery, mitigation, and preparedness. You have seen that with the introduction of many of the technology tools. However, when you evaluate whether you should use technology, you have to recognize the limits of technology. The following are some things to keep in mind:

▲ **Person-centered technology**: Refers to a technology system that is designed to fit and adjust to the needs and uses of the individual user. To achieve this, monitor for operator errors or difficulties in using the technology. You will also need to ensure that the application is used to support operations in a productive way.

▲ Scale of application: Keep it simple. Too often users fail to recognize that the technology is overkill when a simpler option is available.

▲ Recognize that the software has limitations and bugs: Monitor for any problems and efforts and solicit feedback from users as to any difficulties they are experiencing.

▲ Data errors: Assessing the quality of the data in an application is critical to ensure that objectives are being met. You want to avoid surprises that undermine the operations.

▲ Dependence on community infrastructure: Emergency management does not operate in a vacuum but in an interdependent manner with the community. Anticipate what your strategies will be for loss of power or the loss of the use of your facilities.

▲ Security: Today's atmosphere on homeland security suggests that we constantly determine how our operations may be vulnerable to security breaches. Dependence on collaboration with many local, regional, state, and national resources opens you up to potential security problems. Monitoring network and site security on an ongoing basis is a must.

▲ Inadequate system performance: Users expect high-performance computers, software, networks, and systems support. Test new technology to ensure that acquisitions enhance your operations. This is critical and avoids costly mistakes.

▲ Liability for system failures: The issue is not a legal one. It centers on ensuring that systems perform at the highest degree. Your goal is to prevent the loss of lives and property. Systems failures that could be prevented work against this goal.

11.3.1 Organizational Coordination and Collaboration Strategies

Curnin and Owen (2013) remind us that collaboration and coordination on a personal scale is critical in the effective use of technology. They found that a reliance on verbal face-to-face communications in crisis situations is key to effective operations. They stressed that there are inherent risks and limitations for stakeholders obtaining information to inform their distributed situation awareness. There is a need to understand why certain cognitive acts are not exploited. The problem-solving activities identified as task execution and sense-making emphasize a dependence on verbal face-to-face communications. Supporting these activities with specialized cognitive actions such as designated disaster management information systems may be beneficial. These cognitive acts are designed to specifically increase the efficient and timely exchange of information.

11.3.2 Technology Life Cycles

Technology has a life cycle. Once it is developed, it evolves over time, gaining operational capabilities; it is reduced in size and is more compatible with other technology. Today very small computers can do mapping, modeling, Internet communication.

They can be highly mobile, durable, and compatible with more powerful computer systems. Today, you can collect data on damaged buildings, bridges, and other structures as a part of damage assessments. You can record the precise location as well as store images of the damaged site. Digital cameras are linked to GPS systems and small computers. You will continue to see new technology that allows us to collect data on current conditions. You will be able to store the data, map the precise location of the area, and record digital images of the event. All of this will be in smaller packages, with seamless linkages. It will also be easier to operate.

It has been argued here and elsewhere (Santos-Reyes and Beard, 2010) that this may not be necessarily the case; technology communication systems should be seen as a component or part of a "wider system"; that is, a "total disaster management system." Moreover, agency communication collaborations may work very well when assessed individually but it is not clear whether it will contribute to accomplish the purpose of the total system; that is, to prevent fatalities.

11.3.3 Engaging Stakeholders

Little et al. (2015) also stress the value of engaging stakeholders as decision support processes are established and used in response operations. They note that engagement strategies increase the likelihood that the "tools" will be included in organizational training activities and thus in response operations. Santos-Reyes and Beard (2012) contend that information communication technology should not be used in "isolation" but it should be seen as "part" of the "whole" system for managing disaster risk.

11.3.4 Information Exchange

As the use of communication technologies increases in disaster response, making sense of all the information and using it effectively is becoming an increasing demand on emergency response agencies. Ludwig et al. (2015) note that citizens are increasingly involved in crisis response efforts. For emergency services, the large amount of citizen-generated content in social media, however, means that finding high-quality information is similar to "finding a needle in a haystack." They see three dynamics that are influencing the increasing amount of data from social networks in disasters. First, computer use is more likely to be group- or team-oriented than previously; that "usefulness" as opposed to usability of information gathered in a disaster is grounded in a range of social and organizational features, that the social media constitute a radically new problem set, and finally that new methods and new concepts may be necessary to understand these complex issues more clearly. They stress that it has also long been known that "information quality" is of paramount importance within emergency services work and that there is a need for efficient and effective information and communication technologies, which enable the assessment of accurate and dynamic information in highly emergent situations.

11.3.5 Dealing with Information Overload

Given the growth of information technologies in emergency management, assessing the value of these technologies is critical. These strategies include different dimensions of information quality clustered into the categories intrinsic data quality (credibility, accuracy, objectivity, reputation), contextual data quality (value-added, relevancy, up-to-datedness, completeness, appropriate amount of data), representational data quality (interpretability, ease of understanding, representational consistency, concise representation), and accessible data quality (accessibility, access security). Despite our understanding of information quality, the contextual weighing of the information as well as the subjective evaluation of quality by the information use is key.

Approaches to understanding this flood of information from citizens is drastically needed and that there will likely be a trade-off in assessing the information from a quality and time perspective to one that is characterized by "satisfice." They suggest that social media will at some point in the future be a critical part of emergency services and integrated into emergency response activities.

As has been noted in earlier chapters of this text, especially by Kiefer in Chapter 10, the key issues in organizational functioning may not be the technology but in organizational dynamics and functioning. Kruke and Olsen (2012) comment on this dynamic in a very perceptive assessment of organizational decision making during relief operations that organizations rely on quality information dissemination between field and headquarters relief organizations. Yet, reporting from the field is often overloaded with misplaced precision, making it difficult for managers at headquarters to grasp the key issues. The manner in which organizations manage information in decision making is increasingly important as the use of technology increases to provide information to response operations. Given the extensive use of communication technology that increases the rate of communication between field and central agencies and the use of social media in disasters, response operations may be flooded with more information than can be managed effectively.

Kruke and Olsen (2012) explain that there is a high turnover rate among international field officers and a lack of inclusion of local staff and partners prevents the development of accumulated knowledge. Further, most relief organizations have a centralized decision-making system which may also be true in the United States and throughout the world. The creation of "collective-meaning structures," based on reliable information at all decision-making levels, opens the way to greater decentralization of decision making in field offices. Thus, what may emerge is greater engagement with interorganizational coordination structures in relief operations. They conclude that more efficient and reliable coordination between organizations relies on improved decision-making systems within each organization. One can conclude that the issue may not be the technology but the human and organizational systems that make use of our growing applications of technology in emergency management.

SUMMARY

New technology tools that can help you do your job more effectively are constantly being developed. You have learned through this chapter that information exchange is now possible, and you discovered the many benefits of information exchange. You can even work with others who live halfway across the world. New technologies such as modeling and mapping also help you be more effective in managing and responding to disasters. As you use the new technology tools, you will want to make sure you can manage the technology. You will want to use only the tools that will be beneficial to you in your goal of saving lives and protecting property.

KEY TERMS

Centralized Web-based systems	A Web-based program that runs hazard models, GIS, and decision support systems on a centralized-based system rather than on a single-user computer.
Digital library	A Web-based storage system that enables users to search for books, articles, studies, and videos similar to the services provided by a conventional library.
Distance learning	Extended learning efforts, including self-paced individual learning, to forums or chat rooms that bring together students and instructors who use the Web to allow more timely access to learning and to a digital classroom environment.
Person-centered technology	A technology system that is designed to fit and adjust to the needs and uses of the individual user.

ASSESS YOUR UNDERSTANDING

Go to www.wiley.com/go/pine/tech&emergmgmt_2e to evaluate your knowledge of using technology. This website contains MCQ's, self checks, review questions, applying this chapter and you try it.

References

Borbinha, J. L. B., & Delgado, J. C. M. (1996). Networked digital libraries. *Microcomputers for Information Management: Global Internetworking for Libraries*, *13*(3–4), 195–216.

Curnin, S., & Owen, C. (2013). A typology to facilitate multi-agency coordination. In *10th ISCRAM Conference*, Baden-Baden, Germany, May 2013, pp. 115–119.

Gladney, H., Fox, E. A., Ahmed, Z., Ashany, R., Belkin, N. J., & Zemankova, M. (1994, June). Digital library: Gross structure and requirements: Report from a March 1994 workshop. In *Proceedings of Digital Libraries*, vol. 94, pp. 101–107.

Heard, J., Thakur, S., Losego, J., & Galluppi, K. (2014). Big board: Teleconferencing over maps for shared situational awareness. *Computer Supported Cooperative Work (CSCW)*, 23(1), 51–74.

Inan, D. I., Beydoun, G., & Opper, S. (2016). Towards knowledge sharing in disaster management: An agent oriented knowledge analysis framework. In *Presented at the Australasian Conference on Information Systems 2015. arXiv preprint arXiv:1606.01355*.

Kawasaki, A., Berman, M. L., & Guan, W. (2012). The growing role of web-based geospatial technology in disaster response and support. *Disasters*, 37(2). doi: 10.1111/j.1467-7717.2012.01302.x.

Kruke, B. I., & Olsen, O. E. (2012). Knowledge creation and reliable decision-making in complex emergencies. *Disasters*, 36(2), 212–232.

Lee, J., Bharosa, N., Yang, J., Janssen, M., & Rao, H. R. (2011). Group value and intention to use—a study of multi-agency disaster management information systems for public safety. *Decision Support Systems*, 50(2), 404–414.

Ley, B., Pipek, V., Siebigteroth, T., & Wiedenhoefer, T. (2013). Retrieving and exchanging of information in inter-organizational crisis management. In *Proceedings of the Information Systems for Crisis Response and Management (ISCRAM'13)*, pp. 812–822.

Ley, B., Ludwig, T., Pipek, V., Randall, D., Reuter, C., & Wiedenhoefer, T. (2014). Information and expertise sharing in inter-organizational crisis management. *Computer Supported Cooperative Work (CSCW)*, 23(4–6), 347–387.

Little, R. G., Loggins, R. A., & Wallace, W. A. (2015). Building the right tool for the job: Value of stakeholder involvement when developing decision-support technologies for emergency management. *Natural Hazards Review*, 16(4), 05015001.

Ludwig, T., Reuter, C., & Pipek, V. (2015). Social haystack: Dynamic quality assessment of citizen-generated content during emergencies. *ACM Transactions on Computer-Human Interaction (TOCHI)*, 22(4), 17.

Santos-Reyes, J., & Beard, A. N. (2012). Information communication technology and a systemic disaster management system model. In N. Bessis (Ed.), *Development of Distributed Systems from Design to Application and Maintenance* (p. 294). Hershey, PA: IGI Global.

Santos-Reyes, J., & Beard, A. N. (2010, June). A systemic approach to managing natural disasters. In E. Asimakopoulou & N. Bessis (Eds.), *Advanced ICTs for Disaster Management and Threat Detection: Collaborative and Distributed Frameworks*. Hershey, PA: IGI Global.

Vogt, M., Hertweck, D., & Hales, K. (2011, January). Strategic ICT alignment in uncertain environments: An empirical study in emergency management organizations. In *System Sciences (HICSS), 2011 44th Hawaii International Conference on* (pp. 1–11). Piscataway, NJ: IEEE.

Wu, A., Convertino, G., Ganoe, C., Carroll, J. M., & Zhang, X. L. (2013). Supporting collaborative sense-making in emergency management through geo-visualization. *International Journal of Human-Computer Studies, 71*(1), 4–23.

Xu, G., Huang, G. Q., & Fang, J. (2015). Cloud asset for urban flood control. *Advanced Engineering Informatics, 29*(3), 355–365.

FIGURE CREDITS

Technology and Emergency Management, Second Edition. John C. Pine.
© 2018 John Wiley & Sons, Inc. Published 2018 by John Wiley & Sons, Inc.
Companion website: www.wiley.com/go/pine/tech&emergmgmt_2e

INDEX